MEGANET

MEGANET

HOW THE GLOBAL COMMUNICATIONS NETWORK WILL CONNECT EVERYONE ON EARTH

WILSON DIZARD JR.

 WestviewPress
A Division of HarperCollins*Publishers*

HE
7631
.D59
1997

Copyright © 1997 by Westview Press, A Division of HarperCollins Publishers, Inc.

Published in 1997 in the United States of America by Westview Press, 5500 Central Avenue, Boulder, Colorado 80301-2877, and in the United Kingdom by Westview Press, 12 Hid's Copse Road Cumnor Hill, Oxford OX2 9JJ

Library of Congress Cataloging-in-Publication Data
Dizard, Wilson P.
  Meganet : how the global communications network will connect everyone on earth / Wilson Dizard, Jr.
    p. cm.
  Includes bibliographical references (p.   ) and index.
  ISBN 0-8133-3017-3
  1. Telecommunication.   2. Telecommunication policy.
3. Information superhighway.   I. Title.
HEY7631.D59   1997
384—dc21   97-13218
                                                                  CIP

The paper used in this publication meets the requirements of the American National Standard for Permanence of Paper for Printed Library Materials Z39.48-1984.

10   9   8   7   6   5   4   3   2   1

For Philip, Wilson,
Alexandra, and Olivia

CONTENTS

PREFACE

Within the next generation, almost everyone on earth will be linked on an electronic network. At the simplest level, this means that we will all be able to make a phone call to anyone any place. Today, only one-half of the planet's population can do this.

Meganet explores this prospect and how it is unfolding. It has taken 125 years, beginning with the invention of the telephone, for a global network to come close to being a reality. The reasons for the delay are complex, as we shall see. But the past two decades have witnessed a convergence of forces—technological, economic, political—that are speeding up the process in extraordinary ways. The number of telephones worldwide has doubled during the past twenty years. The number will double again in the next ten years. And in the decade after that, access to telephones and other communications devices plugged into the network will be commonplace in every inhabited place. It will be a defining moment in human history.

My shorthand word for the network is *Meganet*. It is a cliché, a convenient handle for tagging a set of ideas and events. The driving force in Meganet's new expansion has been a series of technological breakthroughs, particularly in semiconductor chips, communications satellites, and fiber-optic cables. They are the tools that assure that an advanced Meganet can be completed in the next few decades. Moreover, they assure that Meganet will provide service beyond what the telecommunications industry calls POTS—plain old telephone service. The network will be a multimedia resource supplying television, facsimile, radio, data networking, Internet connections, and other services.

None of this will happen smoothly. Technologies do not create networks. They provide options that have to be matched by political and economic decisions. For all the promise offered by Meganet expansion, there are still powerful voices opposed to the changes now taking place. In contrast, there are enthusiasts who see an advanced global Meganet leading us into a sunny new era of world peace and prosperity. In fact, there is a good case to be made for Meganet's disruptive impacts, particularly in upsetting long-standing political, economic, and cultural patterns.

I draw a line—somewhat shaky at points—between Meganet's long-term effects and what is actually happening now. I project a scenario into the early years of the twenty-first century. This leaves the long-term predictions to the futurists, a fraternity that has a consistent record of calling the wrong shots.

Many individuals have helped me in different ways. A special tribute is due to the late Ithiel de Sola Pool of the Massachusetts Institute of Technology, who was a friend and professional colleague of mine for many years. The title of his last book on communications, *The Technologies of Freedom*, summarizes all that this book tries to express. I also thank my colleagues at the Center for Strategic and International Studies and those at Georgetown University. In particular, I want to thank Diana Lady Dougan, chief of the center's international communications studies program, and Peter Krogh, former dean of Georgetown's School of Foreign Service. Both of them gave me the space, time, and other resources to finish this work.

Among others who helped me were Anne Branscomb, Scott Chase, Roger Cochetti, George Codding, Fred Cote, Jan J. van Cuilenberg, Everett Dennis, William Drake, Charles Firestone, Robert Frieden, Gladys Ganley, Linda Garcia, Michael O'Hara Garcia, William Garrison, Henry Geller, Robert Kinzie, Anton Lensen, David Lieve, David Lytel, William McGowan, Tedson Myers, Russell Neuman, Eli Noam, Joseph Pelton, Kenneth Phillips, Michael Potter, Monroe Price, Marek Rusin, Michael Ryan, Rick Schultz, Gregory Staple, Ann Stark, John Vondracek, Ernest Wilson III, and Yvonne Zecca. My sons—John, Stephen, Wilson, and Mark—provided useful comments.

Finally, I extend a special acknowledgment again to my resident editor and thoughtful critic on works in progress, Lynn Wood Dizard.

Wilson Dizard Jr.

BUILDING THE GLOBAL INFORMATION HIGHWAY

It will be the biggest construction job of all time. It is being built now all over the world—in cities and villages, under the oceans and in outer space. The project will be the largest concentration of high technology ever assembled. Its cost, between now and the time it is completed early in the twenty-first century, will be more than $2 trillion.

It is an advanced global communications network, a telecommunications and information grid that will eventually make every place reachable by telephones, computers, facsimile machines, data banks, and all the other paraphernalia of the information age.

It is the Meganetwork. *Meganet.*

This book reports on the progress (and setbacks) in expanding Meganet resources to everyone on earth. Meganet is a project of vast contrasts. At one level, it involves linesmen stringing wire through South American jungles to connect with a village's single phone. At another level, it includes Motorola executives riding herd on Iridium, a $4-billion project to link millions of mobile phones between any two places around the globe. Iridium will use sixty-six communications satellites, orbiting the earth hundreds of miles up in space, to transfer the calls.

Meganet has created its own bumper-sticker vocabulary—information highway, communications revolution, multimedia millennium, computer explosion, global village, and so on. No day passes without pronouncements from self-appointed experts, waxing epochal about the emergence of the new information order. It is an event proclaimed so insistently that, inevitably, a skeptical reaction has set in.

Meganet is a cliché, a shorthand word for tagging a set of ideas and events. Beyond the cliché, however, there is a massive emerging reality—a global network linking a vast array of information resources. Most of it is hidden underground in cables or in microwave circuits that send signals through the air at the speed of light. Taken together, these are the infrastructure of the information age.

Despite its size and geographic reach, Meganet has an elegant congruity. It is a finely meshed electronic web that carries information and ideas—from the profound to the trivial—in the form of electronic impulses across a city or around the globe. It is a work of civilization, comparable to the great cathedrals of the Middle Ages or, in modern times, to the Panama Canal and the Apollo moon missions. The difference is that no other great project in history will be so universally available, affecting the daily lives of everyone on the planet.

Meganet's scope and size can be illustrated by one of its current construction projects. It is FLAG, the acronym for the *f*iber-optic *l*ink *a*round the *g*lobe submarine cable system. FLAG is the longest manmade structure ever built. It stretches 16,400 miles from England to Japan, via the Mediterranean Sea and the Indian and the Pacific Oceans. FLAG's working parts are four glass-fiber wires, each about the thickness of a human hair and armored to protect against fishing gear and inquisitive sharks. The four wires will together provide 120,000 high-speed circuits, capable of carrying 600,000 phone conversations simultaneously. When it is completed in the late 1990s, FLAG will increase international telecommunications capacity between Asia and Europe fivefold. FLAG's capacity will be supplemented by a longer (23,600-mile), more advanced undersea cable, known as SeaMeWe3, linking Europe with several dozen national telecom networks in Asia. The project, announced in 1997, will be operational by the end of the decade.[1]

FLAG and other Meganet construction projects build on the legacy of thousands of smaller networks developed over the past 150 years, beginning with Samuel Morse's forty-mile telegraph line between Washington and Baltimore in 1844. These piecemeal networks, although expanded to global proportions, are still limited resources. Together, they are available to less than half the world's population. Most people on earth have yet to place a simple telephone call, much less use computers or any of the other devices that Americans use regularly to plug into electronic networks.

Meganet holds out the promise of dramatically reducing, within a generation, this global disparity. If this potential is realized, it will be because political, economic, and technological forces now favor the completion of a world network. This convergence of forces is rapidly gaining momentum. Meganet resources doubled between 1980 and 1997, and there is good reason to predict that they will have doubled again within another ten years.

Nevertheless, Meganet expansion is in its early stages. There are great gaps in the current network, both in its physical reach and in the services it provides. Table 1.1 gives a country-by-country rating of information capabilities. The comparisons are indicative rather than definitive. No one has yet figured out how to measure information resources precisely. Table 1.1 shows, however, the stark differences between the information-rich societies at the top of the list and those bogged down at the bottom. Significantly, three countries at the bottom of the list—China, India, and Indonesia—represent more than 40 percent of the world population. Africa, where another 10 percent of the world population lives, is barely represented in the chart.[2]

These information gaps are being closed—but slowly. There is a reasonable prospect that the pace can be quickened. Analysis, a British consultant, estimates that by 2005 developing countries will make up 30 percent of the global telecommunications market, up from 16 percent in the mid-1990s. These estimates are soft but they reflect a significant turnaround in Third World information resources.[3] This growth will take place largely in China, India, and other big Asian economies. Africa and large parts of Latin America will continue to lag behind.

Current Meganet facilities supply telephone service to 2 billion people, heavily concentrated in the industrialized West. If Meganet expansion continues at its present pace, the other 4 billion people can be reached within the next twenty years. One day, the most isolated village will get its first telephone. It will be a defining moment in the information age, a landmark in human history. Everyone on the planet will be plugged into a common communications network.

If Meganet does nothing more than close the telephone gap, it will be an astonishing achievement. Most people will use the expanded network primarily for what the communications industry calls POTS—plain old telephone service. The phone is the ubiquitous symbol of modern life, whether it be a high-tech cellular in a Chicago lawyer's briefcase or a hand-cranked antique in a Chinese village. The way people use phones is a convenient measure of their country's standing in the worldwide information society.

The United States is tops in phone usage, with 1.5 billion phone calls per day—six for every man, woman, and child in the country. Usage in Western Europe and Japan is about half as great. For Asia, Africa, and Latin America, both the number of users and the frequency of calls

TABLE 1.1 The Information Society Index: Measuring Social, Information, and Computer Infrastructures. Composite scores are listed (rankings shown in parentheses).

Country	Social	Information	Computer	Overall Score
United States	487 (2)	2,810 (1)	1,810 (1)	5,107
Sweden	457 (8)	2,116 (2)	1,430 (6)	4,003
Denmark	452 (11)	1,915 (3)	1,475 (5)	3,842
Norway	474 (3)	1,872 (5)	1,409 (7)	3,755
Finland	454 (9)	1,885 (4)	1,383 (8)	3,722
Australia	436 (18)	1,620 (8)	1,648 (3)	3,704
Canada	496 (1)	1,696 (7)	1,302 (9)	3,494
Switzerland	440 (16)	1,331 (14)	1,688 (2)	3,459
New Zealand	474 (4)	1,332 (12)	1,557 (4)	3,363
United Kingdom	419 (20)	1,506 (10)	1,223 (11)	3,148
Netherlands	468 (6)	1,372 (11)	1,259 (10)	3,099
Germany	450 (13)	1,332 (6)	1,188 (12)	2,970
Japan	447 (14)	1,823 (13)	700 (19)	2,970
Hong Kong	454 (10)	1,524 (9)	915 (16)	2,893
Austria	446 (15)	1,263 (15)	931 (15)	2,640
Singapore	233 (45)	1,238 (16)	1,045 (13)	2,516
Belgium	471 (5)	1,094 (19)	910 (17)	2,475
France	431 (19)	1,129 (17)	736 (18)	2,296
Israel	398 (22)	862 (25)	965 (14)	2,225
Italy	375 (25)	1,088 (20)	607 (21)	2,070
Taiwan	458 (7)	1,107 (18)	488 (24)	2,053
Korea	451 (12)	909 (24)	648 (20)	2,008
Ireland	372 (27)	960 (22)	590 (22)	1,922
Spain	403 (21)	918 (23)	551 (23)	1,872
UAE	323 (31)	976 (21)	319 (31)	1,618
Czech Rep.	439 (17)	650 (27)	439 (26)	1,528
Hungary	322 (32)	815 (26)	363 (30)	1,500
Greece	377 (24)	629 (28)	371 (29)	1,377
Portugal	318 (33)	531 (34)	452 (25)	1,301
Argentina	380 (23)	550 (30)	285 (32)	1,215
Chile	352 (29)	446 (38)	383 (28)	1,181
Poland	360 (28)	550 (31)	249 (36)	1,159
Bulgaria	318 (34)	540 (32)	211 (42)	1,069
Venezuela	313 (35)	482 (36)	255 (34)	1,050
South Africa	271 (38)	374 (42)	398 (27)	1,043
Russia	284 (37)	568 (29)	189 (44)	1,041
Malaysia	169 (50)	540 (33)	281 (33)	990
Brazil	244 (43)	463 (37)	254 (35)	961
Costa Rica	374 (26)	338 (45)	240 (38)	952
Panama	298 (36)	402 (40)	218 (41)	918
Mexico	244 (44)	384 (41)	243 (37)	871
Romania	342 (30)	362 (43)	158 (45)	862

(continues)

TABLE 1.1 *(continued)*

Country	Social	Information	Computer	Overall Score
Saudi Arabia	113 (54)	506 (35)	231 (39)	850
Colombia	216 (46)	310 (46)	229 (40)	755
Thailand	181 (48)	348 (44)	196 (43)	725
Ecuador	262 (40)	292 (39)	141 (47)	695
Jordan	249 (42)	301 (47)	145 (49)	695
Turkey	141 (52)	416 (48)	138 (50)	695
Peru	253 (41)	255 (50)	143 (48)	651
Philippines	263 (39)	222 (51)	147 (46)	632
Egypt	179 (49)	270 (49)	137 (51)	586
India	191 (47)	153 (53)	91 (54)	435
Indonesia	122 (53)	145 (54)	120 (52)	387
Pakistan	150 (51)	120 (55)	101 (53)	371
China	91 (55)	160 (52)	84 (55)	335

SOURCES AND METHODOLOGY: Courtesy of World Times Inc. and IDC. The twenty variables in the Information Society Index were drawn from an initial pool of forty potential data points. The list was whittled down by factor and regression analysis to identify the variables that have the most direct connection with countries' access to, and their ability to absorb and utilize, information. Where appropriate, results were then normalized to allow meaningful comparisons between small countries like Israel, Singapore, and Panama and large countries like India, China, and the U.S. (e.g., weighting personal computers shipped to education against the total number of students and teachers in that country). Numerical results were then weighted to bring data into the same order of magnitude so that, for instance, the percentages of fax and radio ownership could be meaningfully compared. In a few cases this was done to better match the index team's view of a factor's significance, a view based on the regression analysis and experience gained tracking information technology developments in the past.

Information infrastructure: *ITU Statistical Yearbook 1994; UNDP Human Development Report 1995/1990; Dorling Kindersley World Reference Atlas/1994; ITU Statistical Yearbook 1995/1994; ITU Statistical Yearbook 1995/1994; Dorling Kindersley World Reference Atlas/1994; ITU Statistical Yearbook 1995/1994.*

Computer infrastructure: *IDC 1995 Worldwide Blackbook/1995; IDC—Individual Country PC Reports/1995; IDC—Individual Country PC Reports/1994; The World Bank Development Report 1995/1994; IDC—Individual Country PC Reports/1994; International Marketing and Data Statistics 1996 and European Marketing and Data Statistics 1996/1992; IDC—Individual Country PC Reports/1994; International Marketing and Data Statistics 1996 and European Marketing and Data Statistics 1996/1994; IDC—In-house research / 1995; www.thelist.com/1996; www.nw.com/1996.*

Social infrastructure: *Dorling Kindersley World Reference Atlas/1994; Dorling Kindersley World Reference Atlas/1994; Freedom House News/1995; Freedom House News/1995; UNDP Human Development Report 1995/1992.*

drop precipitously; even those lucky enough to have a phone find that service is a sometime thing. In Brazil, companies hire boys to listen for a dial tone to let the boss know when he can make a phone call.

Meganet will bridge the global phone gap thanks to a series of technological breakthroughs over the past half century. The process began with a question: Can information be measured? It was first addressed early in this century by two mathematicians, Bertrand Russell and Alfred North Whitehead. They developed the calculus of propositions, or the solving of problems in terms of statements that are either true or false. Around 1940, a young graduate student at MIT, Claude Shannon, demonstrated the practical applications of this calculus for improving the design of electrical circuits. Shannon showed that programming an electronic computer would be a problem not of arithmetic but of logic.

Later, at AT&T's Bell Laboratories, Shannon and fellow researcher Warren Weaver proposed a design for a general communications system.[4] They treated information input as a problem in statistics, permitting precise measurement of the amount of information delivered and the efficiency of the devices that handled it.

They called their unit of measure a *bit*, short for *bi*nary digi*t*. It is the lowest common denominator of information, a unit that resolves uncertainty between two exclusive alternatives—between yes and no, heads and tails, on and off. In choosing, we resolve doubt. By putting many bits together in a computer or communications circuit, symbols that transmit information take shape as words, pictures, or sounds. Whatever symbolic form it takes, the information is transmitted digitally via electrical circuits. To put it another way, the information is coded into a long string of symbolic digits—1 or 0—in patterns that define the information.

Shannon and his colleagues also demonstrated how to measure the capacity of a communications channel in terms of *bits per second* (BPS). The channel capacity for an ordinary telephone wire used for speech purposes is 60,000 BPS; for broadcast television, 90 million BPS; and for a millimeter wave-guide system, 15 billion BPS. This ability to measure capacity made possible the progressive miniaturization of computers from room-sized boxes down to handheld devices.

Bits are the building blocks of the advanced Meganet and other information age resources. Bits are turning the old-fashioned voice telephone network into an all-purpose information machine. Trillions upon trillions of symbolic 1s and 0s move through the advanced Meganet, each a coded part of a message that could be a teenager's phone call, a credit card transaction, a television soap opera, or a weather report from a space station on Mars. Meganet's old equipment is rapidly being replaced to meet this new standard of speed and efficiency. Increasingly, the devices plugged into the network—phones, computers, television sets—are digital. Digitization is turning Meganet into a seamlessly integrated resource, the biggest machine ever built.

The module that powers this system is a direct result of the digital concepts developed by Claude Shannon and other researchers a half-century ago: It is the semiconductor chip, the fingernail-sized common denominator of all present-day electronics. Meganet's rapid expansion in recent years is directly related to the progressive evolution of microprocessors and other chip technologies. Semiconductor buffs have a simple rule to measure the rate of change. They call it Moore's Law, after Gordon Moore, one of the pioneers in a semiconductor industry whose "pioneer days" date only to the 1970s. Moore's Law states that chips get twice as powerful and twice as cheap every eighteen months or so.[5]

This cycle has occurred on schedule since the first devices were developed three decades ago. The first dynamic random access memory (DRAM) chips could store 16,000 bits of information. In the mid-1990s, a single chip could store a quarter-billion bits. By the turn of the century, a billion-bit memory chip will be developed by an international consortium that includes IBM, Motorola, Siemens, and Toshiba.[6]

Chips activate Meganet's big switches, moving increasingly larger amounts of information in all forms through its circuits. In 1996, a consortium of U.S. chipmakers unveiled technology that can pump a trillion bits of data per second over a single, hair-thin optical fiber.[7] Most of the chips currently in use are far less sophisticated. They are proliferating in the machines we use every day. According to research done by Motorola, there were ninety chips in the average car, home, and workspace in 1990. By the turn of the century, this number will have tripled; soon thereafter what now takes a year for microprocessors to compute will take only fifteen minutes. By then, the chip industry will churn out 100,000 on-chip transistors each week for every person on earth. Advances in semiconductor chips and other digital technologies are driving Meganet expansion. Meganet needs have made electronics the world's largest industry in the 1990s, replacing automobiles. Telecommunications networks and the machines plugged into them account for the largest share of the electronics sector's products.

The industry's success in upgrading its digital products is transforming both the technical capacity and the cost of Meganet circuits. Fiber-optic cables are a striking example of this. Fiber wires made of pure glass can trap light waves and carry them long distances with little loss in signal intensity. Their efficiency makes them the technology of

choice for most of Meganet's major terrestrial circuits. The first submarine coaxial cable, put down in the mid-1950s, had a capacity of
eighty-nine circuits and cost $557,000 per circuit. FLAG, the advanced
fiber cable currently being built between Europe and Japan, will have
120,000 circuits at a cost of $1,500 per circuit.[8] As with other trans-
mission technologies, costs are plunging while capacity rises.

Fiber cable and other digital resources allow Meganet to connect
many more people far more efficiently and cheaply than was possible
even a decade ago. As digitization continues to accelerate, the network gains new efficiencies. By reducing all forms of information to
bits, digitization can mix and match wire and wireless resources. This
flexibility makes possible, for instance, easy transfer between wireless
cellular phones and conventional wire-based telephone circuits. This
capability has made wireless telephony the fastest growing sector in
global phone service.

Wireless phones are only one of the technologies contributing to
Meganet expansion. New switches and other digitized machines are
replacing older facilities. This basic conversion to digital is occurring
more swiftly in the United States and other industrialized countries
than elsewhere. Ramshackle phone systems in Asia and Latin America are being digitized more gradually. The biggest single conversion to
digital standards is taking place in China, a country that until recently
had one of the lowest telephone penetration rates in the world. China
plans to have a digitally based phone system that is larger than the
U.S. system by early in the next century.

The transition to an advanced digitized Meganet is not easy. Technology is no longer the problem. The barriers are economic and political. Telecommunications is a notoriously conservative sector. Telecom facilities are still controlled mainly by government bureaucracies
in 180 countries around the world. Most of these agencies operate
telecom systems that serve too few people via too limited services.[9]

The pressure to improve this situation is building. Much of the impetus comes from local businessmen, who are demanding advanced
digital resources in order to compete in the wider global economy as
well as among themselves. Other calls for change come from ordinary
citizens who simply want an ordinary telephone. These pressures are
beginning to get results. Government monopolies are giving way,
slowly, to new arrangements. In one case after another, private-sector
competitors are wedging their way into communications systems.
They are bringing with them much-needed funds for expansion, as well
as critical managerial experience. More than fifty countries around the
world have already begun to dismantle their communications monopolies by turning them, wholly or in part, into private entities.

This retreat from political control of communications systems sets the pace and direction of Meganet's current expansion overseas. Although in many countries there is considerable rear-guard opposition to ending government monopolies, it is retreating before the evidence that privatization results in more efficient, profitable systems—particularly where competition is permitted.

The telling proof of the value of competition has been demonstrated in the United States. As in other countries, U.S. public policy in telecommunications has lagged behind economic and technological realities. However, its strength has been a commitment to private ownership of communications, with limited government controls. The result is a vast continental network, originally built largely by AT&T. In 1934, AT&T was granted a virtual monopoly by the federal government to complete the network based on AT&T's promise that it would supply universal phone service to homes throughout the country. By the 1950s, that promise was largely fulfilled. At that time, more than half of all the telecommunications resources in the world were in the United States.

The "build out" of the U.S. domestic network by AT&T over a thirty-year period was a major achievement. But it became increasingly clear that one company alone could not satisfy the country's fast-changing communications needs in the long run. By the 1980s, the United States was moving rapidly toward an information-based economy, with more than half of its workforce and almost half of its gross domestic product (GDP) devoted to information-based services.[10] The pressure to open up the national network to competition increased.

The result was a series of events that ended the AT&T monopoly and introduced competition. Under pressure from the federal government, AT&T's local telephone operations were transferred to seven regional phone companies in 1984. It was a defining event in speeding up the U.S. transition to information age realities.

Beyond its impact on U.S. developments, the decision to break up AT&T in 1984 set off a series of changes in global communications. As a result, the global Meganet is moving in fits and starts away from monopolistic government control toward a new kind of open, competitive framework. This shift has become the most important factor favoring the completion of an advanced global Meganet by early in the new century.

Other countries are drawing heavily on the U.S. model, adding their own political, economic, and cultural variations. We will take a closer look at these developments later on, but here it is useful to summarize how the United States has taken the lead in organizing and building the Meganet:

- By 1990, the United States had clearly defined itself as an information society. Over half the U.S. workforce is now employed in information-related sectors, which accounted for 76 percent of gross national product in 1995.[11] This shift from a manufacturing economy marks the end of the American industrial age. Many economists estimate that U.S. industrial production will account for less than 10 percent of all economic activity by early in the new century.
- Average U.S. household spending per month for media and communications in 1983 was $81.03. Ten years later it was $146.81.
- By the early 1990s, 40 million Americans were working at home, either in full or part-time occupations. Increasingly, they rely on advanced telecommuting resources.
- The country's 60 million computers—one for every five persons—are now common objects in homes, schools, and workplaces, thereby transforming economic and social habits. In most offices, the boss now has a computer close at hand. One result: The number of secretaries declined from 4.1 million in 1987 to 3.6 million in 1993.
- The United States is the world's information banker. It is the largest producer of electronic databases. In the mid-1990s, its 5,000 major databases doubled the number of those in the rest of the world.[12]
- The first computer-literate generation is entering the workforce. This is only partly because of the current boom in computer training classes, beginning with kindergarten. Another factor is the insatiable appetite of U.S. children (and many adults) for computerized game machines. There are more than 60 million Nintendo-type machines in U.S. homes.

Although these trends had been evident for years, a national consensus on information age issues was slow to develop. An important turning point was Bill Clinton's 1992 presidential campaign, which aimed a spotlight at the issues. It was a shrewd move, targeted at millions of voters whose jobs were being affected by a fast-changing information economy. These "knowledge workers" (to use management guru Peter Drucker's phrase) were a new constituency, hitherto ignored by both Democratic and Republican politicians.

This "information highway" issue had a ring of authenticity about it. Both Clinton and his running mate, Al Gore, gave it strong support. In the 1980s, Senator Gore had sponsored the first substantive legislation to promote national resources for the information highway, including the Internet. He is the first U.S. leader at the White House level to use a computer himself.

Once Clinton took office in 1993, his administration pushed information highway projects. It sponsored pilot projects across the country that demonstrated the value of advanced communications and information resources in education, health care, and other public services. In an administration bedeviled by controversy, these initiatives were popular—and largely bipartisan. One influential supporter was fiery GOP leader Newt Gingrich. In 1995, just after he was elected speaker of the House following the 1994 Republican takeover of Congress, he announced, "We are beginning to invent the American information age." In his enthusiasm for the new age, he even suggested that laptop computers should be an automatically deductible expense on income tax returns.

The favorable public response to the information highway proposal energized the administration, Congress, the corporate sector, and public-interest groups to get down to work on a national legislative agenda for the information age. These efforts involved several years of bruising debate and lobbying in Washington, given the powerful interests involved in restructuring a major economic sector.

The result was the Telecommunications Act of 1996, passed by Congress in February of that year. Its 180 pages lay out the ground rules for Meganet expansion in the United States and, by extension, put an American spin on its global growth. The driving force behind the reform was economics, particularly in defining the roles of the telephone and cable-TV industries, the two major competitors in building the advanced information highway structure. The legislation is, inevitably, a package of compromises designed to satisfy these competing interests. It also represents an uneasy consensus since none of the major industry players had any clear idea of where communications and information technology might lead them in the coming years.

Despite its flaws, the Telecommunications Act of 1996 marks an important milestone in Meganet development. It is the first attempt by any country to reorganize its communications sector on a major scale to meet information age needs. It lowers most of the barriers that have hampered the efficient use of Meganet technology. Previously separate parts of the sector (phone and cable companies, the media, etc.) are now thrown together into one competitive marketplace, offering a full range of services on Meganet's digitized circuits.

Beyond the long-term political and social impacts of the law, the economic competition it released is changing the way Americans deal with each other in workplaces and in their private activities. The impact of telecommunications on the economy was first recognized two decades ago by a research team at the University of Southern California, led by Herbert Dordick. The team forecast the development of a *network economy*, doing business through high-speed circuits that link buyers and sellers in a vastly expanded electronic market.[13] The network economy they predicted began to flourish in the 1980s and has become even stronger in the 1990s.

Consider a familiar application—toll-free phone service (using the familiar 800 exchange). Over 1 million U.S. firms do business via toll-free numbers, involving 100 million transactions a day. The service accounts for 40 percent of the daily traffic on AT&T's vast domestic network. The company estimated that in the mid-1990s toll-free numbers were ringing up more than $100 billion worth of business annually.[14] By 1996, toll-free services had expanded so rapidly that the telephone industry had used up most of the 7.6 million numbers assigned to the service, forcing the Federal Communications Commission (FCC) to authorize a new 888 exchange for toll-free calls.

Consider, too, Americans' continuing love affair with credit cards, a marketing tool completely dependent on electronic networks. Andersen Consulting, a firm that tracks the industry, estimated that the average U.S. consumer held eleven of the plastic cards in the mid-1990s, up from seven in 1989.[15]

By the late 1990s, the financial services industry was shifting a large share of its business to Meganet circuits, primarily to cut costs. A 1995 American Bankers Association survey of banks showed that a single face-to-face transaction with a customer cost $2.93. The cost dropped to $.24 when the customer used an automated telephone response service. In addition to automatic teller machines (ATMs) and other consumer-initiated services, banks are turning to the Internet to deal with customers. Seventy percent of American banks had an Internet presence by 1996, according to a Booz Allen & Hamilton survey.[16]

Electronic networks also dominate transactions among banks. Every day, hundreds of billions of dollars in transactions move through Fednet, the national network managed by the Federal Reserve. Early in the new century, the financial sector will be almost totally automated. Paper currency and checks will steadily give way to various forms of cybercash, money stored as bits and bytes in central computers or on small plastic cards.

Banks and other money centers have been the leaders in moving the U.S. economy to electronic commerce. Other sectors, from automobiles to the fashion industry, are rapidly catching up. The result has been an explosive growth in advanced networks serving an information-intensive economy.

The prime movers in this growth are AT&T and other big communications firms with the financial clout, technical resources, and management experience needed to expand the networks. But they are challenged by agile newcomers who are, collectively, setting the tone and pace of Meganet expansion. A lot of these firms had their origins in an informal fraternity of young computer buffs that formed on the West Coast twenty-five years ago. Many of them were, to use the then-current epithet, hippies. They were bearded, sandaled, highly educated, and disdainful of careers that involved a conventional climb up the corporate ladder.

They were an unlikely bunch to start a global revolution, but that is what they did. They dared to see what they could do by making the new Meganet technologies, then used mainly to serve Big Business, available to ordinary men and women. They brought a variety of talents to the problem and addressed it in different ways. The best known of the group were Bill Gates and his colleagues at Microsoft, whose software breakthroughs made computing available to tens of millions of users. Vinton Cerf, a young engineer, headed another group that invented the software that made the Internet possible. The first commercial personal computer, Apple, was the brainchild of Steven Jobs and partner Stephen Wozniak. Jobs summarized the group's attitude at the time: "We realized that we could build something ourselves that could control billions of dollars of infrastructure in the whole world. . . . We could build a little thing that could control a big thing."[17]

The Internet is a classic example of how these self-styled nerds could transform communications patterns. Cerf and his colleagues built their software around simple technologies—telephone lines and computer modems. Their initial efforts were disdained by the industry's giants. IBM refused to bid on the first Internet-type network, claiming that it would not work.

But the technology was sound, and the Internet expanded from a small electronic gathering place for computer buffs to today's global facility. By the end of the century, the Internet will link more than 100 million users in almost every country in the world using telephone lines and other off-the-shelf technologies. It has become a rough model for Meganet's effort to supply a wider range of advanced services. The big corporations no longer disdain the Internet as a computer buff's toy. IBM and every other major communications and information company are scrambling against one another in the competition to provide Internet resources.

The combined strength of big corporations and agile young challengers has sustained the U.S. lead in Meganet developments. Inevitably, this lead is being challenged abroad as other industrialized countries climb aboard the information highway bandwagon. The European Union (formerly the European Community) has taken strong measures to bring its fifteen nations up to speed in advanced communications and information resources. The Japanese have undertaken similar initiatives, building on their strong research and manufacturing skills in electronics.

To sum up, Meganet is a work in progress. Its future is tied to political and economic decisions being made in more than 180 countries around the world. These decisions will shape and direct a network of networks, connecting everyone on earth for the first time. Beyond its obvious economic benefits to the United States, Meganet can spread the American proposition of an open society, a concept embodied in the First Amendment and played out every day in the rush of facts, ideas, and opinions that flow through the U.S. communications network.

Will our domestic Meganet continue to reflect these values? Will it be the instrument for empowering all Americans with the communications and information resources they need to function in an advanced, postindustrial, global society? There is no guarantee of this. There is instead the possibility that the glitzy new resources promised by Meganet could widen the gap between the information haves and the information have-nots both in U.S. society and in the world at large. Economist Robert Reich, secretary of labor in the first Clinton administration, pointed this out: "No longer are Americans rising or falling together, as if in one large boat. We are, increasingly, in different, smaller boats." The top one-fifth of working Americans takes home more money than the other four-fifths combined. This affluent group is largely made up of professionals who create or otherwise deal with information. In describing them, Reich says that they inhabit a different economy from other Americans: "The new elite is linked by jet, modem, fax, satellite, and fiber-optic cable to the great commercial and recreational centers of the world, but it is not particularly connected to the rest of the nation."[18]

This gap within U.S. society is mirrored by even wider disparities overseas between information haves and have-nots. Twenty percent of the richest countries controls 80 percent of the world's communication resources. Meganet's success will be measured by its ability to close these gaps. The network is a powerful but enigmatic engine of change, the biggest and most complex machine in human history. Its effects are paradoxically universal and parochial, uniting and dividing, constructive and destructive. It will create a new communications culture, overlaid on old ethnic, economic, religious, and national patterns and attitudes. An electronic environment is evolving in which old guideposts are submerged in a stream of bits and bytes exchanging a bewildering variety of messages among billions of individuals.

Meganet's resources—cables, telephones, computers, and the like—are the artifacts of the information age just as plows were during the agricultural age or machine tools during the industrial age. The network is operated by men and women, usually working in small groups, who create information and manage its flow for a largely anonymous audience at the end of a telecommunications circuit. The romanticized vision of Meganet as creating an electronically linked world community is illusory. The system is indifferent to place and distance. It both connects and isolates. As Canadian anthropologist Edward Carpenter once pointed out, the new electronic networks have made free spirits of us all, not in the Sunday school sense of having wings or being good but in the sense of pure spirit, divorced from flesh, capable of instant transportation anywhere.

Meganet is the ultimate electronic mediator, determining more and more how we will deal with one another. It is moving us away from the age-old human experience of communicating directly, face-to-face in a room or village square. It is a prospect that has its dark side. This was recognized a generation ago by Canadian communications guru Marshall McLuhan. He is best known for a catch phrase—*the global village*. The phrase became a cliché, freighted with implications beyond anything McLuhan intended. He was a pragmatic realist who saw the threat as well as the promise of an evolving Meganet. He warned that a universal network could lead to a new tribalism, hindering rather than helping the open exchange of information and the mediation of human differences. In today's world of ethnic and creedal conflicts, his warning seems at least as important as his vision of an inclusive global village.

Communications researcher Gregory Staple has given a name to this new spatial relationship among people. He calls it telegeography: "For most of the world's history, geography has provided something of a cultural buffer between the values of city and countryside and between one religious community and another. Yet in much of the world, the network now threatens to leap-frog this barrier. Telegeography transports every villager's home into the metropolis and settles the atheist next door to the true believer."[19]

It is no longer possible to restrain this force. Bit streams move across borders in electronic packages at the speed of light, largely impervious to censorship and other controls. The recent attempts of politicians to control the network proved inept and, in the long run, impotent. The best-known example of this occurred a decade ago in the futile efforts of Communist leaders in Eastern Europe and the Soviet Union to limit public knowledge of events that were undermining their authority. They were defeated by telephones, fax machines, radio, and satellite television broadcasts. Sooner or later, the same resources will make up the decisive force that overturns totalitarian control in China and elsewhere.

Meganet's circuits are neutral transmitters of information that can disrupt as well as unite. The Internet's World Wide Web provides an example of the network's dark side. Surveys indicate that one of the Web's heaviest uses is as global conveyor of pornography. It far outstrips the distribution capabilities of dirty magazines or X-rated films. The Web can also be used as a forum for political disruption, well beyond the partisan give-and-take that marks normal political discourse. In Peru, for example, an extremist guerrilla group called Shining Path has a Web page to advance its messages of hatred and social disruption.[20] Balanced against this are the World Wide Web's capabilities for linking men and women to vast information and educational resources around the globe.

Meanwhile, U.S. initiatives are setting the pace for Meganet's global expansion—with implications that go well beyond the mechanics of organizing and assembling a network. The most advanced part of the network is in the United States, the largest multicultural society on the planet. It is a reasonably accurate test of the conditions in which the global Meganet will develop. The American version of an information society is not directly transferable abroad. But the lessons are there. The most promising of these is the U.S. lead in setting a goal for universal access to electronic communications. This goal was first established for telephone service sixty years ago, and it has been largely achieved. That goal is now being revised to include the new advanced services that can be delivered over the Meganet.[21]

Meganet's success as a global resource will be measured by the degree to which universal access for everyone is realized in the coming years. This is the network's challenge. In Chapter 2 we turn to the details of its current development and future prospects.

2

THE AMERICAN FACTOR

In his witty novel *Snow Crash*, Neal Stephenson suggests that Americans will soon excel in only two activities: writing software and delivering pizza in less than thirty minutes. His tongue-in-cheek satire touched reality in 1994 when pizza delivery and software converged on the Meganet. The occasion was a decision by Pizza Hut executives to use the Internet to take orders for their products.

It was a calculated step toward protecting the company's dominant position in the pizza-delivery business, with its $10 billion in annual revenues. Market research showed that the Internet's online users, 30 million strong, were good sales target for two reasons: (1) most of them like pizza, and (2) they know how to navigate the Internet.

"What we want to do," said Joe Payne, one of the firm's marketing experts, "is to make it fun to order, and to turn our product into a service." The ordering process is simple. Customers log on to the Internet to reach a centralized computer in Wichita. A list of pizza choices pops up on the screen. The customer makes a selection. Pepperoni, *click*. Anchovies, *click*. Hold the onions, *click*. Instructions go back through the Internet to the store nearest the customer. The order is confirmed, and the pizza is soon on its way. As a result, Wichita becomes the pizza-delivery capital of the nation. Jobs are created, others lost. The mozzarella business gets a lift. Profits rise at Pizza Hut while rivals scramble to match its Internet marketing tactic.

Electronic marketing on Meganet is changing the way America shops. It is no trivial shift: retailing is a $2-trillion enterprise, the largest sector in the economy. The old mom-and-pop stores are disappearing, and Main Street establishments have moved out to the suburban malls. Meanwhile, electronic sales are the fastest growing part of the retail business, from cable TV's shopping channels to Pizza Hut's Internet project.[1]

These changes are part of an evolving Meganet trend: the consumerization of the network as more and more people use it to serve their personal needs and interests, from ordering pizzas to studying nuclear physics on an interactive science network. The trend is evident throughout the industrialized world, but particularly in the United States. Here is where many of the most advanced sections of the global Meganet can be found along with the widest variety of consumer services. Increasingly, the network is determining the ways in which Americans live their daily lives.

The United States is the test bed for Meganet's worldwide growth. It is useful to review how this came about and how it will affect American prospects, at home and abroad, in the new century.

Meganet's American roots go back two centuries, to the First Amendment. A constitutional prohibition against government interference in what people say or write was a revolutionary idea in the 1790s. It still is in most societies. The First Amendment dealt with printed publications, the only public medium available in the eighteenth century. Since then, the amendment's authority has been steadily extended to include new electronic information technologies. A cat's cradle of laws, regulations, and practices has developed to protect First Amendment rights in radio, television, computer networking, and other information transmitters.[2]

The First Amendment's extension to electronic information began with Samuel Morse's telegraph in the 1840s. The success of the telegraph inspired projects for a national information network. One proposal, in 1854, recommended an "information railroad" using rights-of-way for telegraph wires across public lands, as the railroads had done, to create a network from the Atlantic to the Pacific. The wires were to be buried underground, according to the proposal, to protect the network from "storms, wild animals, and Indians."

The language of the 1854 proposal, with its Victorian flourishes, sounds like an overture for the claims of today's information highway enthusiasts:

> The benefits which will follow from the execution of this enterprise cannot be partial or sectional; they must necessarily be of incalculable national importance, and the more influences resulting therefrom will be coextensive with the world of civilization and commerce. . . . In whatever light the subject may be considered, whether in reference to the interests of the government, the prosperity of our merchants and navigators, or the happiness and comfort of the citizens at large, the enterprise is eminently calculated to promote the power, wealth and general prosperity of the country.[3]

The information railroad was never built because its sponsors could not raise the necessary capital. But private telegraph and telephone cable networks soon spanned the continent; they were the forerunners of today's high-speed circuits. Most of the earlier networks were financed and built to serve business and government needs. There was a lag before they carried any significant amount of consumer traffic. Once the consumerization process began, it expanded rapidly. The familiar example is the telephone system, which connects more than 95 percent of all U.S. households. More recently, cable television has become a household item, reaching two-thirds of all U.S. homes. Newer still, consumer data nets, such as CompuServe and America Online, now have more than 15 million subscribers.

The event that set off this network expansion was passage of a law by the U.S. Congress more than sixty years ago. The Communications Act of 1934 was intended to regulate the telephone and radio broadcasting industries. Almost as an afterthought, Congress added a landmark social provision to the bill. In the new law, Congress mandated that all U.S. citizens had the right of access to telephones and radios. This provision for universal service triggered a prolific growth of electronic communications over the next half-century. Telephone service, which earlier had been a limited, elite resource, became commonplace. Radio and, later, television became mass media in the fullest sense of the phrase. Today, there are more than 11,000 radio stations and 1,500 TV outlets across the nation pouring out an eclectic mix of entertainment and news.

The universal-service principle in the 1934 legislation has since been extended beyond telephones and broadcasting. The establishment of this principle was both a cause and an effect of a massive shift in the U.S. economy away from the production of manufactured goods and toward the production and distribution of information. This change was first documented by a Princeton University researcher, Fritz Machlup, in a 1962 work, *The Production and Distribution of Knowledge in the United States*.[4] Machlup identified the number of people involved in producing and processing information in their jobs. He included workers employed in the traditional mass media, as well as those in libraries, advertising agencies, schools, research institutes, and other information-oriented activities. His conclusion was that by the early 1960s more than 30 percent of the U.S. labor force was employed in information work. Moreover, it produced almost half of the gross national product.

Machlup predicted correctly that information production would eventually surpass industrial production as the country's major economic activity. His work was a groundbreaking piece of research, but almost no one paid attention to it at the time. Most experts of the day were of the mind that communications and information were merely "service sectors," not to be compared with the more substantial industrial thrust of the economy.

A few individuals, however, were intrigued by Machlup's findings. One of them was an owlish Harvard professor, Daniel Bell. A former editor of a socialist newspaper in New York, Bell had done an improbable tour as labor editor of *Fortune* magazine before turning to academia. He is best known for coining *postindustrial society* to describe the changes he saw taking place in American life. Bell's seminal 1973 book, *The Coming of Post-Industrial Society*, identified information production and its use as a major agent of change in U.S. society.[5]

He forecasted the explosion of information technologies and the upheaval it would cause. The result, Bell wrote, would be a seismic shift of the economy from industrial production to electronic information–based services. The information sector would be the pivot for innovation, affecting everything from jobs to leisure activities. A new society, based on computers, was being created. Its future leaders would be men and women who understood this change and managed it creatively.

Professor Bell's inventive phrase soon became a trendy part of the language. Pop analysts such as Alvin Toffler and John Naisbitt gave it wide currency. Researchers considered to be more academic have added to and modified the early insights of Machlup and Bell. Sociologist Mark Porat, in a nine-volume study of the information economy, pointed out the distinction between the primary producers of information and the much larger group of information users.[6] At the Berkeley Roundtable on International Economy in California in the 1980s, researchers Stephen Cohen and John Zysman added their own word of caution about drawing premature conclusions regarding the demise of manufacturing. They noted that the choice is not between reducing the traditional manufacturing base in favor of information-dependent services. The two sectors, they pointed out, are inextricably linked:

> If the United States wants to stay on top—or even high up—we just can't shift out of manufacturing into services. . . . Insisting that a shift to services or high technology is "natural" is irresponsible analysis and perverse policy. The competitiveness of the U.S. economy—the ability to maintain high and rising wages—is not likely to be enhanced by abandoning production to others. Instead of ceding production, public policy should actively aim to convert low-production, low-wage, low-skill production processes into high-technology, high-skill, high-wage activities— whether they are included in the manufacturing unit itself or counted largely as service firms.[7]

The smudging of old distinctions between manufacturing and the information-based service industries is part of the story of Meganet's growth in the United States. Industrial production is increasingly dependent on the network's resources. Today, most of the cost of building a Boeing superjet, for example, goes into software, telecommunications, and other electronics-based resources. Aluminum and other "hard goods" are a lesser part of the resources needed to build a modern airplane.

Thus, it is not surprising that information technology is now the fastest-growing sector in the U.S. economy. In 1960, the sector had annual revenues of $15 billion in current dollars. By 1995, its revenues had climbed to $688 billion.[8] This acceleration toward a Meganet-based economy is picking up speed in the late 1990s. A new generation of economists and other experts is defining more clearly the influence this trend is exerting on American life. Working at MIT, economist William Baumol and his colleagues have calculated that more than 70 percent of the U.S. labor force is in information-related work, directly or indirectly. Their comparable estimate for Western Europe is 59 percent; for Japan, 57 percent.[9]

The current debate about the so-called information highway and the role of advanced Meganet resources is overdue. A generation ago, MIT political scientist Ithiel de Sola Pool analyzed the quickening pace of technological breakthroughs in the communications and information fields. He pointed out that forty years separated the introduction of telegraph and telephone technologies. Another thirty years passed before wireless radio was introduced, followed twenty years later by television. In ten years we saw the introduction of computers. Today, the chronological distance between such breakthroughs is often measured in months. The time available for dealing with the economic and political effects of these changes is drastically reduced.[10]

The current information highway debate is setting some useful guidelines for how we deal with the new generation of communications technologies. When the Clinton administration first drew national attention to the subject in the early 1990s, the emphasis was on the effects of these technologies on jobs and international competitiveness, themes that caught the attention of the U.S. business community and broader public. The Clinton proposals also included specific demonstrations of how advanced Meganet resources can affect ordinary citizens in the workplace and in their personal lives.

Some of the most useful of these show-and-tell projects involved schools, libraries, hospitals, and other public institutions across the country. The projects focused on practical uses—how, for example, a rural clinic could be linked electronically with medical specialists at a large regional hospital for diagnostic information. This federal effort was supplemented by hundreds of similar state and local projects. Taken together with other private and public initiatives, these demonstrations made up an impressive inventory of advanced Meganet applications. The esoteric rhetoric of the information age was brought down to local realities in scores of U.S. cities, towns, and rural areas.

The experiments also highlighted the potential role of Meganet technology in strengthening democratic institutions. A team of political scientists from Harvard, NYU, and Brandeis contributed a valuable study of this subject in recent years. The group looked at the emerging "electronic commonwealth" and its role in the new age:

> The electronic commonwealth . . . is not a place of gadgets and gimmicks. It is not—at least not yet—the rallying cry for high-tech politics run amuck. Instead, the electronic commonwealth harks back to the old democratic ideal of congregating people together. The contribution of new communications technologies is not to change or upset that ideal. It is simply to use electronics to practice the lost democratic arts. . . . The congregating or conferencing capacity of the new media can put such a politics into practice if we want it.[11]

This "congregating capacity" is the heart of Meganet's potential contribution to a democratic society. Assuming that the network's resources will be available to everyone, democratic practices can be strengthened at both the personal and institutional levels. But, as past experience with new technologies has shown, universal access to advanced information technologies is not assured in most societies. These innovations have too often been reserved for the elite. In the United States, by contrast, new technologies have usually been dispersed more quickly and widely. This difference has been particularly marked in communications and information resources, from public libraries and telephone services to the current vigorous spread of personal computers (PCs).

But the record in the United States is not perfect. There is a persistent gap between those who get full access to new information resources and those who do not—the information-rich and the information-poor. The gap generally follows the social fault lines created by racial and economic differences. Ninety-five percent of the population has access to telephones, but the achievement is marred by the fact that 10 million people do not. When it comes to the advanced services promised by Meganet, the proportion of have-nots is much greater.

Can the gaps in Meganet resources be closed? It is clear that tension between commercial priorities and social needs exists here as elsewhere. The new consumer information services on the network are designed primarily for individuals accustomed to the advantages of information resources in their personal and professional lives. They are the ones who can afford to pay for them. For the time being at least, the full benefits of an advanced Meganet are not being shared by lower-income Americans.[12]

When communications companies upgrade or add services, they do so in affluent city neighborhoods and suburbs. This exclusivity is evident in the current rollouts of Meganet consumer resources. Charges of redlining have been leveled by public-interest groups such as the Consumer Federation of America against companies pursuing this strategy. (Redlining is a politically charged phrase often used to describe discrimination by banks in lending money to people in lower-income and minority neighborhoods.) In a 1994 petition to the Federal Communications Commission, a coalition of public-interest groups declared: "If substantial segments of the population, particularly those of lower-income or minority status, are denied access to advanced networks, America will be divided into the technologically wealthy and the technologically disadvantaged underclass, and we will all suffer from it." These charges were denied by telephone and cable companies. In a typical response, a US West executive, Jerry Brown, said: "To say that we're going to stay out of areas permanently is dishonest and ridiculous. But we had to start building our network someplace. And it is being built in areas where there are customers we believe will use and buy the service. This is a business."[13]

The issue of universal access will heat up as communications companies continue to expand advanced Meganet facilities in the next few years. The numbers show that as of now Meganet resources are aimed predominately toward satisfying business needs. High-capacity communications and information services are mostly consumed by corporate America, linking headquarters and offices with factories, sales outlets, and other facilities throughout the country.

These industry-oriented, advanced Meganet grids have already created a national "backbone" of high-tech communications, underwritten by firms that need and can pay for the network. U.S. business is now inextricably bound up with these networks. Consider, for instance, Visa, the biggest U.S. credit-card company, which depends entirely on electronic networks to transmit and process more than 6 billion transactions annually, involving 10 million merchants and 20,000 financial institutions here and abroad. The U.S. financial services industry would, in fact, come to a screeching halt if there was a general disruption of Meganet facilities.

Meanwhile, the consumerization of Meganet facilities has picked up speed. The United States is running well ahead of other industrial democracies in marketing competitive, affordable new services to mass audiences. The increasing availability of personal computers is indicative. There are at least twenty-eight PCs for every 100 persons in the

United States. In Japan, the comparable figure is 7.8; in Europe, 9.6. The ratios trail off into insignificance in most of the rest of the world.

Despite the rapid increase in consumer usage, the U.S. telecommunications network has a massive reserve of underutilized capacity. By rough estimate, less than 15 percent of the national network's capacity is used on any given day despite the heavy use of communications facilities by Americans. Americans average six phone calls per day. They also spend more time with TV, radio, and other media (on average, nine hours per day) than with any other activity, including work and sleep.[14]

The marketing strategy for consumer Meganet services centers on persuading customers to use their phones, TV sets, and computers more often. Most of the new information and entertainment services can be delivered over already existing facilities, such as ordinary telephone lines. Cable-TV coaxial-cable circuits are being rapidly upgraded. Fiber-optic circuits crisscross the country with information capacities that are increasing exponentially. In 1996, an advanced fiber-optic system that can deliver a trillion bits of information every second over a single hair-thin wire was unveiled. This is enough capacity to transmit 12 million phone conversations simultaneously.[15]

Are American families ready to pay more for advanced Meganet-based services? Household outlays for communications products have already doubled in the past decade. Billions of dollars are riding on the proposition that consumers want and will be willing to pay for the new services. However, evidence supporting this prospect is ambiguous at best. Surveys show that Americans are generally satisfied with the range of information services they now get. For instance, most respondents say that they watch only a half-dozen cable channels regularly, which is not good news for the proponents of 500-channel services.

The marketing effort to reshuffle U.S. information and entertainment habits will be intense. There will be many corporate winners and even more losers. The trail of Meganet progress will be littered with the bones of entrepreneurs who put their hopes and money on the wrong technology or marketing strategy.

The search is on for what the industry calls the "killer app," the killer application. Killer apps are those innovative new consumer products, designed to be plugged into the Meganet, that turn out to be commercial winners. All kinds of killer-app candidates are in the wings, their makers hoping to repeat such recent marketing successes as videocassette recorders, personal computers, and Nintendo-type game machines. Of these three, game machines have been the supreme killer app of the past decade. More than 60 million of them are installed in U.S. homes. More than any other recent innovation,

Nintendo-type games, with their digital blood–drenched screens, have trained a generation of children to deal with computerization.

As demand for these older products has matured, the electronics industry has been searching for the next consumer blockbuster. The prospects range from wristwatch telephones to slimmed-down PCs designed to cruise the Internet. As we shall see in Chapter 6, this latter prospect—known as network computers—is already sending shock waves through the computer industry.[16]

Predicting killer apps is chancy. There was no rush in the late 1970s to invest in a company called Microsoft, the brainchild of several enterprising college dropouts who saw a potential market for software that would demystify computers for ordinary people. The software they came up with was DOS and, later, Windows, products that put Microsoft on the map and made its chief executive, Bill Gates, the world's number-one corporate billionaire.

A potential winner among the new killer apps is the telecomputer, a fusion of television and PC technologies in a single machine. Telecomputers will supply multimedia services to homes via high-capacity cable or satellite channels. The machines will come in different technical formats. Microsoft is one of a number of companies creating software that will add digital video capabilities to home computers, permitting users to view broadcast and cable television programs. In 1997, Microsoft teamed up with IBM, Sony, NBC, and fifty other companies in a project to develop technology that would enable computers to receive television programs and data services.[17]

Another possibility is to hang telecomputers on the wall. Xerox Corporation has developed a wall-display panel no thicker than a pad of paper that combines high-definition television and multimedia computer functions. Three Japanese electronics manufacturers announced plans in 1995 to produce similar panels for the new generation of telecomputers.

Interactive digital media has been labeled the fastest growing sector of U.S. communications by Veronis, Suhler & Associates, the New York investment house that publishes the most authoritative annual survey of the industry. Its 1995 survey anticipated a yearly compound growth of almost 12 percent in this market in the late 1990s.[18] A 1997 study by Euromonitor, a market research firm, predicted that this growth will be led by telecomputer developments, boosting global consumer sales to more than $146 billion annually by the year 2000.[19]

Other communications firms have identified a new generation of wireless telephones as the next killer app. Known as personal communications services (PCS), the new phones are lighter and cheaper than familiar cellular instruments. They are, in some ways, technologically superior to cellular phones. The industry's willingness to bet on the success of PCS technology was demonstrated in the mid-1990s when the Federal Communications Commission auctioned off the radio frequencies needed to operate the new service. A total of $18 billion was spent by 107 companies at auction just for the privilege of obtaining licenses that will allow them to build personal communications networks. By the end of the decade, PCS operators plan to spend $13 billion constructing their new systems throughout the country.[20] Such investment is an expensive gamble, as it is based on the expectation that many more Americans will pay for the convenience of having a walk-around telephone. The industry's optimism is buoyed by its earlier success in marketing more than 30 million of the larger, more expensive cellular phones. The PCS trade group, the Personal Communications Industry Association, claims that wireless versions will account for one-third of all U.S. phones early in the new century.

Beyond this search for a killer app, a larger Meganet trend is under way. It is the way Americans deal with each other through electronic mediation, staying in touch in new ways. The precedent is the telephone and the second-nature manner in which individuals use the network (over a billion times every day). Plain old telephones will be around for a long time, but computers are creating a new communications pattern. People are using them for *social computing*, a powerful new kind of electronic communication. Social computing is the use of computers and related technologies as mass-communications devices. As Randall Farmer of Electronic Communities in Los Altos, California, pointed out: "Fundamentally, people stop interacting with their computers. They use computers as a device to interact with other people."[21] Social computing supplements and may eventually surpass the role that conventional telephones have played till now.

The trend toward social computing is being hurried along by a new generation of technosavvy young people who have been punching into electronic machines—from TV channel zappers to Nintendo-type games—all their lives. They take for granted the growing ubiquity of computer power in its many forms, including voice, video, and data. The Internet has given a powerful push to social computing, with its interactive ability to connect like-minded groups of people around the globe.

Will social computing foster a new sense of isolation, a fractionalization of relationships? Or will it bring us closer in a new kind of electronically mediated community? Is it just another step upward in consumerization? Or will it also strengthen democratic patterns in a postindustrial society? The idea of an electronic commonwealth holds many uncertainties, including the danger of a society breaking from the tradition of person-to-person relationships as the new electronic devices distance us from one another.

For the present, it is workplaces that are being transformed by social computing. Twenty-five million computers in offices and factories are changing the way most Americans go about their jobs. More significantly, computers and Meganet circuits are eroding the hierarchical structure of U.S. companies, a pattern that has prevailed in the workplace for the past century. Control of information, the traditional prerogative of corporate managers, is slipping out of their hands. As Hellene Runtagh, a former top executive at General Electric Information Services, pointed out: "Communications in a network are absolutely incompatible with a strict, parochial hierarchy. . . . The worst of all worlds is clinging to hierarchical behavior while bringing in network-based communications. You're in for a decade of chaos, frustration and poor financial results." Slowly and often painfully, corporate America is revamping its institutions and practices to cope with Meganet realities. Present-day changes are validating a proposition first put forward by management theorist Peter Drucker fifty years ago. He pointed out that corporations should be seen as social systems and not just as business enterprises. (The case study in his classic 1946 work *Concept of the Corporation* was General Motors.) Drucker suggested that three trends would force a restructuring of corporate culture: (1) the rise of the "knowledge worker" (i.e., someone whose head was more important than his hands); (2) the transition from the assembly line to flexible production; and (3) the inevitable empowering of workers.[22]

What Peter Drucker could not foresee a half-century ago was the pell-mell pace at which the new information-based work environment would develop. At the time, the first working computer (at the University of Pennsylvania) was only two years old. It filled a large room and was powered by 17,000 bulky vacuum tubes that burned out so fast they had to be continually replaced. Computing was very expensive. It was not until computers shifted from vacuum tubes to transistors and semiconductor devices that they became cost-efficient. Between 1960 and 1990, the price of computing power in America shrank, in real terms, by a factor of 6,000—roughly 25–30 percent per year.[23] Prices have dropped even more sharply in the 1990s.

The meaning of "workplace" itself is being redefined by the introduction of advanced Meganet resources. Traditional office routines are going by the boards as more Americans work at home or in satellite work centers, linked to corporate headquarters by telephones and computers. Telecommuting has taken hold after years of hesitation and false starts.

According to Link Resources, a market research firm in New York, 37 million U.S. households—more than one-third of the total—have at least one person doing income-generating work at home. Although many are self-employed, at least 8.4 million of them are telecommuters—corporate individuals who do their jobs full- or part-time where they live—the fastest growing segment of stay-at-home workers.[24]

These arrangements usually suit both the worker and the company. Employees often have personal reasons for wanting to work at home. Corporations encourage the practice as a way to downsize capital investment in office space and to lower operating expenses. Environmental concerns are also a new factor. In California, clean-air regulations permit only seventy-four cars in a company parking lot for every 100 employees, and telecommuting is a way for businesses to conform to the regulation while attracting employees who want flexible work arrangements. A variation on telecommuting is the "hot desk" phenomenon—a single office space used by several workers in succession, alternating between working at home and at the central workplace for a day or a week at a time. Telecommuting and hot desks have become accepted styles of U.S. business activity as companies, large and small, explore the new capabilities of telecommunications and information resources.[25]

These capabilities are changing the design of the U.S. workplace. Traditional corporate structures, with their heavy fixed costs in personnel, real estate, and equipment, begin to look cumbersome and inefficient. New work patterns are emerging, cut to fit Meganet technologies. The ultimate expression in up-to-date workplaces is the "virtual company." The name may reek of management-consultant cyberbabble, but it describes a trend that is catching on in the United States.

Corporate America has not yet agreed on a common definition of a virtual company. It is often a temporary alliance of independent companies, suppliers, customers, and even commercial rivals who share skills and costs in a collective effort to produce specific goods and services. In its purest form, the virtual company has no central office, no hierarchy, no organizational chart. It is more *process* than *place*. The collaboration necessary to produce and distribute the products and services of a virtual company is carried out largely in cyberspace through Meganet resources. The fluidity of the design maximizes flexibility and permits greater control over costs. Once formed, the operating group can exploit specific research, production, and marketing opportunities owned or controlled by the individual participants. When the project is completed, the venture may disband or regroup.

"It's not just a good idea," according to management consultant Gerald Ross of Chane Laboratories International. "It's inevitable." Still, the idea attracts more skeptics than enthusiasts. Andrew Grove, chairman of chip giant Intel, calls it a business buzz phrase that is meaningless. He and others point out that despite the talk of how technology will facilitate the virtual company, there are some old-fashioned obstacles to overcome. Not the least of these is the need for major changes in antitrust policy and intellectual property laws.[26]

Virtual companies may be the ultimate form of electronic commerce—business done through computer-driven machines over Meganet circuits. The hallmark of this new form is flexibility. Researchers at Xerox's Palo Alto Research Laboratories put the emphasis on what they call "ubiquitous computing." They want to get rid of present-day desktop computers and replace them with many smaller computers that operate unobtrusively in the background of a workplace, sensing and serving their users' needs.[27] Other research groups are experimenting with a different approach. Rather than follow the Xerox strategy of cramming computers into every possible nook and cranny of the workplace, these researchers propose using personalized computer assistants or "agents" as electronic valets and secretaries.

As they evolve, virtual businesses will test a variety of approaches. But the result will be a very different kind of environment from the one that nurtured traditional companies and other institutions. Its technological basis will be open-system computerization, replacing the many separate computer networks developed over the past forty years. The problem with separate networks is that they cannot, to use the computer buff's phrase, interoperate among one another. Information and software in open-system computing can run on any hardware platform regardless of location, size, or brand. This interchangeability is critical to making Meganet a totally integrated grid. By the mid-1990s, more than half of U.S. medium- and large-sized organizations had already adopted open-system computing as their operating standard.

One thing is certain: More than corporate efficiency and bottom-line profits is riding on Meganet technologies. Changing business patterns are part of larger changes as to where people work, what they do, and how they do it. In the past, such adjustments took place over long periods of time. Now it is happening in a rush.

Another departure from past experience is that job disruptions are no longer limited to lower-income groups, those who may not have the skills to deal with newer technologies. In the past, middle-class workers did not usually feel their economic security threatened by technological advances. This is less true these days. There is an increasingly large segment of U.S. workers who are falling into what economist

Robert Reich calls the anxious middle. Many middle-income jobholders are justifiably uneasy about their own standing and fear for their children's futures. Their uneasiness is tied to rapid technical changes in the workplace and the personal adjustments they require.

Reich's anxious middle covers a broad spectrum of workers, but divisions within the class remain. Handicaps in education and training are not leveled but exacerbated. Two-thirds of computer users have college degrees, one-third are high-school graduates, and about 10 percent are school dropouts. The result is not only a gap in skills but also in income and expectations. With each advance in communications and information technologies jobs are won and lost. Workers are transferred to different locations, not necessarily as a move up the economic ladder but simply as a response to new technological imperatives. Others find their skills and their jobs declared obsolete.

Job anxieties fuel the ambivalence many workers feel in dealing with new, Meganet-based technologies. A 1995 Gallup poll found that about half of white-collar workers surveyed admitted they were cyberphobic, resistant to trying new technologies. Their unease had less to do with computers and other machines themselves than with questions about how these devices might intrude into their personal lives by eroding their privacy and by isolating them from their fellow workers.[28]

Technology races ahead of our understanding of its human effects. Slowly, a new consensus for dealing with this blind spot is beginning to form, at least in recognizing the emotional and social impacts of advanced technologies in the workplace.

The need to consider these human factors was underscored in a pioneering study, *In the Age of the Smart Machine,* by Shoshana Zuboff of the Harvard Business School. She studied workplaces to document the ways in which information technology is transforming the nature of work in the United States. Her conclusions criticized the tendency of many managers to look at new technologies primarily in cost-cutting terms rather than as an opportunity to strengthen the skills and commitment of their workforce. The result of management's shortsighted approach, she concluded, has been to widen the gap between managers and workers, eroding the benefits that automation can bring to the production process as well as to the lives of the men and women involved.[29]

The task of integrating the new technologies into the warp and woof of American life is beginning to be addressed. At the national level, this effort has been boosted by the Clinton administration's information highway initiative. It focused on issues and actions in Meganet-related areas that had been given only scattered attention before.[30] Significantly, corporate America weighed in on the side of the administration's information highway plans. The initiative benefited from the leadership of Vice President Al Gore, a knowledgeable as well as practical advocate of the positive role of advanced technology in postindustrial America.

Michael Prowse of London's *Financial Times* noted:

> It matters that Mr. Al Gore cares passionately about technology. One of the peculiarities of modern politics is that most politicians spend most of their time on issues that have little or no bearing on the future prosperity of nations. Diplomacy, for example, continues to outrank economics and finance, which in turn outrank science and technology. Yet we live in the age of the microchip, not the age of Metternich. . . . One reason for being confident about America's long-term future is the attention it is now paying to technology.[31]

This new focus on Meganet-related issues is critical in the global competition for political and economic advantage in the twenty-first century. When the cold war gridlock ended, geoeconomics began to displace geopolitics in the national strategies of the big industrialized countries. Geoeconomics (a phrase coined by Edward Luttwak of the Washington-based Center for Strategic and International Studies [CSIS]) is a hard-fought game. "There are no nice guys on the battlefield of economics," Luttwak has warned.[32]

Luttwak and others are part of an academic cottage industry studying current developments in geoeconomics, particularly how it will influence America's future. They track the growth of Meganet resources with a view toward assessing the relative strength of information age resources in the strategic balance among nations. Experts in global strategy now accept the fact that the old measures of national strength—land mass, natural resources, military strength, and industrial capacity—are no longer adequate or even primary reservoirs of power.[33]

Meganet has revived but in a different form, an old analytical model for measuring comparative national strengths. Known as the country life cycle, it is based on the theory that countries go through a series of developmental phases in the following order: emerging, industrializing, maturing, and declining. The model attempts to identify each country's relative position in the world at each stage of the cycle. In its original form, the life-cycle model was flawed, particularly in its assumptions as to which resources give countries their comparative advantage at each stage. The model assumed that relative power could be measured effectively in terms of material resources such as tons of steel and barrels of oil. It failed to recognize that the world was moving beyond industrialization into an era where Meganet-based communications and information resources were becoming critical measures of national strength.

Today's strategists are revising life-cycle models to take these new resources into account. As economist Cornelia Small noted: "To move to the postindustrial cycle, the country must permit old wealth based on industrial technology to be destroyed, while accepting a new source of wealth creation based on information technology. The ability to jump from the old curve to the new curve requires a country to be flexible enough to reinvent itself. As this happens, there will be a change in the way the economy works, in the political power base, in society, in the concept of what we think a country is."[34]

In this new environment, the old assumptions as to economic advantage are increasingly irrelevant. Nations are facing depowerment of their sovereignty in ways never before experienced. Their ability to control their economies is being undermined by information age realities. Power is being transferred from governments to commercial institutions. The balance of power is tipping toward global corporations that have the mobility, technical expertise, and management skills to exploit the new, Meganet-based resources.

Nowhere is this more evident than in the flow of money across national borders. Every working day, Meganet circuits carry more than $1 trillion in transactions in the form of digital bits among banks and other financial institutions around the globe. Governments once had a monopoly on setting the values of their currency. This function has now been taken over by traders in the high-tech, cacophonous money bazaars of New York, London, and Tokyo. As a result, governments are losing control of their own currencies. Their occasional attempts to get the upper hand by intervening in the market with a few billion dollars have little effect against the daily $1-trillion torrent of private transactions. As British financial analyst Philip Coggan pointed out, "They might as well attempt to repeal the laws of gravity."

The strategic implications of these changes for the United States are formidable. Almost 20 percent of U.S. production, in both goods and services, now depends on overseas sales. This ratio has doubled in the past twenty years. Increasingly, U.S. overseas trade is shifting from manufactured products to services such as financial transactions, data networking, and tourism. In 1995, to take a recent example, the U.S. had a trade surplus in services of $63.1 billion, offsetting a merchandising trade deficit of $174.5 billion.[35]

At the same time, America's share in world markets has decreased sharply in recent decades as foreign economies have boomed. International competition in the electronics sector is particularly intense. Michael Dertouzos, head of MIT's computer science lab, pointed out that in the 1960s the United States produced more than 90 percent of the world's consumer electronics. This has dropped in recent years to 5 percent, due largely to competition from Japan, Korea, and other East Asian countries.

Despite hand-wringing over the alleged loss of U.S. competitiveness in world markets, gloom and doom are hardly justified. The United States is now in first place in most surveys of global competitiveness, after several years of trailing behind Japan. Increasingly, the best prospects for U.S. trade advantage lie in Meganet-related advanced technologies—what London's *Economist* calls the "ultratech sector." And ultratech competition is where the future measurements of relative national strength are being decided. The United States is still the greatest single source of technological innovation. But technology can no longer be kept secret. Once upon a time Chinese emperors could behead any subject who revealed the empire's technical secrets to foreigners. But most ultratechnology research is now international in character. Advanced research projects are scattered across the globe in many different countries. Moreover, Meganet facilities provide the electronic sieve through which vast amounts of high-tech information move digitally through global networks. Silicon Valley innovations show up in research labs and factories from Osaka to Munich almost simultaneously, often in improved versions.

The U.S. lead in science and technology is challenged in the new race for economic advantage. This is particularly true in Meganet-related sectors, where the trade stakes are very high. The telecommunications industry's global revenues in the mid-1990s totaled about $1 trillion, according to estimates by Salomon Brothers, the New York banking house. The United States accounted for about 30 percent of these revenues, even though it has only about 5 percent of the world's population.[36]

America's democratic partners in Western Europe and Japan are closing in on this lead in building the global Meganet. The Europeans have directly targeted advanced telecommunications and information as critical resources in their national economies. These sectors have been given particularly strong support by the European Union, the fifteen-nation consortium that has been promoting the region's economic integration for the past forty years. These efforts were once hobbled by the monopoly controls that European PTT (posts, telegraph, and telephone services) organizations held over the region's communications. In the mid-1980s, however, the European Union (then the European Community) launched a successful effort to break up those monopolies. Private competition was encouraged. Now, the region's communications industries have been toughened by competition to the point where they are directly challenging the U.S. lead in Meganet goods and services. In 1994, spurred in part by the Clinton administration's information highway initiatives, the European Union approved a comprehensive program named Europe and the Global Information Society to further strengthen regional technological and economic resources in the new global competition.[37]

The Japanese have long recognized the importance of information and communications to promoting national development and expanding global exports. As early as 1972, a white paper entitled *The Plan for an Information Economy* was issued by the Ministry of International Trade and Industry (MITI), the government's lead agency in strategic economic planning.[38] In recent years, the Japanese have reinforced their commitment to this goal. A 1994 government statement of information age objectives emphasized the importance of "high-performance infocommunications" in Japanese national strategy as the country moves into the twenty-first century.

The newest players in this global scramble for position in the Meganet environment are countries who would have been counted out a decade ago: the emerging economies of East Asia and Latin America. In telecommunications, as in other ultratech areas, the Western democracies still dominate. In the new century, this dominance will be challenged by a group of emerging economic giants— China, India, Brazil, and Mexico, among others. After decades of experimenting with socialistic managed economies, these countries are opting for market-friendly economic reforms and opening their borders to foreign investment.

Economic reforms by Asian and Latin American countries have often been hesitant and stumbling. But the overall trend is clear. It is reflected in World Bank estimates of GDP growth—a useful measure of where an economy is headed. Real GDP growth among the industrial democracies is projected by World Bank at 2.7 percent annually through the end of the 1990s; the comparable figure for Asian and Latin American countries is almost double. Although these latter economies are growing from a much lower base than those of the West, they represent the biggest shift in global economic strength in more than a century.

There are variations in the economic expansions taking place in Asia and Latin America. One constant, however, is a new attention to telecommunications and information resources. For years, economists and others have been documenting the stunting effects of poor communications facilities on national development. Most Asian and Latin American nations still lack modern telephone systems—but this is changing. Every major Asian and Latin American country—and many of the smaller ones—are upgrading their telecommunications structures to global Meganet standards. A precipitating event was Mexico's 1989 decision to turn over the government's telephone monopoly,

Telmex, to private control and to invite competition from Mexican and foreign companies. In the first five years of private operation Telmex doubled its telephone facilities.

Other Latin American countries have since moved toward at least a partial privatization of their telecommunications monopolies and have experienced similar expansion. The price tag for these changes is high. The Organization of American States estimates that its member countries—in order to merely maintain current telephone line per-capita levels—will require $100 billion in new investment by the end of this century.

Meganet growth in Asia and Latin America has important political and economic consequences for the United States. Of all the developed nations, the United States has the largest pool of financial resources and technological expertise to support newly privatized telecommunications sectors in Latin America and Asia. U.S. strategic interests stand to benefit as improved communications contribute to long-term political and social stability within these economies.

The United States is only one voice in this global dialogue on communications resources—but it is a powerful voice. Much of its authority will come from the example it sets in creating a democratic information environment at home. This calls for the kind of national consensus that is difficult to achieve in a society of so many competing interests. For all our attachment to efficiency and planning, we are not moving in an orderly fashion into the information age. We are backing into it with, at best, an over-the-shoulder view of things to come. And there are few junctures along the way that permit us to stop and get our critical bearings in the new Meganet environment.

An assessment made some years ago by a Harvard University study group remains true in today's more complex information environment:

> Decisions of vital importance—national, international, corporate and personal—are being fought out in dimly lit areas under rules that are not clear even to the lawyers, engineers, economists and bureaucrats who devised them. Rosters and score cards are rare. Some of the players are unnumbered; others wear the wrong numbers. . . . There are many kinds of information technology, but it is becoming clear that there is really only one information system, no matter how disconnected the parts may seem. Information is a basic resource, fully as important as materials or energy. While materials and energy have not lacked for public scrutiny and policy attention, information resources have developed willy-nilly, their potency overshadowed by their technical details, their pervasiveness so complete they are taken for granted, like the clean air we breathe.[39]

In summary, U.S. strategic interests at all levels are involved in Meganet's global expansion. In its role as a Meganet leader, the United

States faces two challenges. The first is to shape its domestic Meganet to meet the needs of an advanced postindustrial democracy. The second is to involve itself in Meganet's overseas expansion in ways that strengthen the prospects for an open global society. This is the broad significance of Meganet, and in Chapter 3 we turn to the details of its current development and future prospects.

3

THE MASTER
BUILDERS:
THE AMERICANS

Meganet is a jigsaw puzzle with thousands of pieces. At a distance, it appears as a single unit, linking phones, computers, and other devices around the world. At closer range, it takes on a different look. It is a patchwork of networks—big and small, local and global, primitive and high-tech—that fit together because they share compatible technologies.

Meganet is the creation of many organizations, from massive corporations like AT&T to a small rural telephone co-op in Bolivia stringing wires on makeshift poles across the Andean plains. Identifying the network's builders and managers was easier a dozen years ago than it is now. At that time, builders and managers were overwhelmingly the government agencies that controlled domestic telecom networks in most countries. (The United States, with its private telephone systems, was the major exception.) The same agencies also owned most of the international circuits, the forerunners of today's global Meganet.

Most of these monopolistic institutions still exist, but their operations are being reshaped by technology, economics, and politics. Government control of telecommunications is a fading relic of the late industrial age. The traditional rationale for the existence of phone monopolies was that centralized control was necessary to assure technical and management efficiency. Technology has turned this argument on its head. Thanks to new digital technologies, communications resources are immensely flexible these days. They can be mixed and matched in so many ways that monopoly control over large networks is no longer possible.

The old monopolies are in forced retreat. They are being challenged by private competitors that are able to outstrip them in technical efficiency, range of services, and profitability. The newcomers have the fiscal resources and management skills needed to complete the global network. They are the new Meganet master builders, each coping with the complexities of the largest construction project of all time.

In this chapter, we look at America's master builders. In Chapter 4, we survey the changing telecommunications sector in the rest of the world.

There are several reasons for beginning with the Americans. First, the business of creating an advanced competitive Meganet structure is furthest advanced in the United States. Secondly, the U.S. effort is setting the pace and direction of Meganet growth around the world.

Corporate competition, American-style, is pushing global Meganet development. The trend is documented in a recent survey of the growth of private telecom enterprises worldwide. The survey, conducted by Salomon Brothers, the New York investment house, shows that in 1983 there were fewer than ten publicly traded phone companies with a market capitalization of $100 million or less. Most of them were American. By the early 1990s, there were about sixty such phone companies in all parts of the world. The survey estimates that there will be close to 100 publicly traded telephone companies worldwide with a combined market capitalization approaching $1 trillion by the turn of the century. In most cases, they will either replace telecom services previously supplied by government-owned monopolies or be competitive with them.[1]

This has led to a wild scramble for position as new players challenge the old government monopolies. In this new scramble, three kinds of organizations are in competition:

- Traditional government-controlled PTT organizations, which still operate the telecom systems in most of the world's 180 countries. The exceptions are in the advanced industrial democracies, all of which have moved toward competitive telecom structures. The holdouts are in the emerging economies of Asia, Africa, and Latin America, but they are losing ground. A defining event was the 1989 privatization of Telmex, Mexico's government monopoly, that opened the way for competitive services as well as for minority investment by French and U.S. companies. This action created a domino effect whereby privatization moved throughout Latin America.
- The old-line private telecommunications companies that are restructuring to deal with a more competitive environment. In

the United States, these include AT&T, MCI, Sprint, and the regional Bell telephone companies such as US West.

- Agile new entrants, attracted to Meganet's promise of expanded business opportunities and greater profits. Many of them have no previous experience in telecommunications. Their strength is in management skills, money, and a willingness to go after niches in the market, particularly risky new services that many of the older telecom organizations avoid.

The multiplicity of new players around the world was foreshadowed by events in the United States twenty years ago. At that time, U.S. telecommunications was characterized by three letters and an ampersand—AT&T. There were, in fact, hundreds of U.S. phone systems, most of them small rural cooperatives and other local networks. But they were all dependent on AT&T's national network, including the company's twenty-two local Bell companies.

AT&T's dominance was guaranteed by federal legislation—the Communications Act of 1934, which gave the company a practical monopoly in the national network in exchange for a commitment to provide universal telephone service. AT&T fulfilled its commitment. It was *the* telephone company, with a cautious image that earned it the sobriquet "Ma Bell." The company was closely regulated by the FCC and, eventually, all fifty state public utility commissions. Despite its undoubted accomplishment in supplying mass phone service, AT&T was inhibited by government regulations—and by its own conservatism—from adequately exploiting new technologies. Ironically, many of these technologies—from transistors to communications satellites—were developed in its own Bell Laboratories.

The result was to slow down the introduction of advanced technologies that could provide new, more efficient services. Beginning in the 1960s, potential competitors pressed the federal government to modify AT&T's monopoly position. In response, the U.S. Department of Justice started antitrust proceedings against AT&T designed to prove that the AT&T monopoly harmed telecommunications expansion.[2]

Meanwhile, the FCC took steps to reverse its decades-long policy of protecting AT&T's market dominance. The change was led by an activist FCC chairman, Richard Wiley, a Washington lawyer. He and his colleagues proceeded to take actions that eroded AT&T's control of the market. Their decisions allowed new companies to compete in long-distance services, equipment manufacturing, and other areas where AT&T was dominant.

These FCC actions were limited in scope, but they opened the door for an advanced Meganet in the United States. By the early 1980s, it was quite clear that this transition would not take place as long as one company continued to dominate the field. The turning point took place in 1982 with a decision by AT&T to give up its rear-guard resistance to the new competition. It negotiated an end to the Department of Justice antitrust case, agreeing to divest itself of its local Bell phone companies. It was a signal event in U.S. business history—the largest company in the country giving up 60 percent of its operations. The local Bell companies were restructured as seven regional operating firms. In return for divesting itself of the local Bell companies, AT&T was allowed to enter manufacturing and service areas previously denied to it.[3]

The divestiture agreement went into effect in 1984, setting off an unprecedented decade of communications growth. New services were introduced and the cost of communicating was generally lowered in the new competitive environment. An icon of the new order was wisecracking actress Candice Bergen, who in television commercials told viewers that they could get a better phone deal from Sprint.

Telecommunications became the darling of Wall Street investors. The industry's gross annual revenues, in goods and services, approached $1 trillion by the mid-1990s. Average yearly growth was 10–15 percent, with little slackening during economic downturns. Nevertheless, an additional $100 billion in capital funds will be needed to finance domestic Meganet facilities between now and the end of this century.[4]

Meanwhile, venerable firms like Western Union, ITT, and RCA Global Communications have disappeared from the telecommunications scene because they could not compete effectively. The question that intrigued the industry was whether AT&T would be able to keep up. Not only had it given up its profitable local phone companies but it lost 40 percent of its long-distance traffic to MCI, Sprint, and other competitors. It was, moreover, a business whose primary experience was in POTS at a time when the industry's operations (and therefore its profits) were switching to computer-based multimedia services.[5]

The prophets of AT&T's doom were wrong. The company stumbled in the years immediately after its 1984 breakup as it adjusted to new competitive realities. But it roared back in the 1990s, reasserting its role as the corporate leader in U.S. communications. AT&T demonstrated its resilience in 1995 when it decided to give up centralized management of its far-flung operations. It split into three companies, separating its manufacturing (Lucent Technologies), telecommunications (AT&T), and information-networking operations (Global Information Solutions).

AT&T's 1995 decision showed a realistic accommodation of new Meganet realities. POTS is still the core business of the national network. But voice telephony is gradually being displaced on the network by a new generation of multimedia services, operational methods, and corporate competitors. In a digital era when all kinds of services can be sent down a single high-capacity line in a variety of ways by many competitors, the U.S. telecommunications sector is in a state of splendid disarray. A dozen years after the AT&T telephone monopoly was dissolved, the sector is an intricate pattern of old and new providers, each vying for a piece of the $1-trillion annual market.[6]

We will soon look at this mix of old companies and new entrants in this competition, but first it is useful to identify them by service sectors:

- *Plain old telephone service (POTS).* This is still the single biggest sector in the telecommunications industry. The companies that provide POTS are known as "common carriers," regulated providers of telephone and other services to anyone who pays their bill at the end of the month. The definition of common carrier is being expanded well beyond AT&T and the other old-line phone companies these days as new competitors enter the field.

- *Cable television.* Cable-TV companies now provide high-capacity coaxial cable service to more than 60 percent of U.S. homes. These cables pass by another 30 percent of homes that do not subscribe to the industry's services. With some technical adjustments, these cables can be used to provide telephone service and a range of other interactive information and entertainment services.[7] This challenge to the old-line common carriers is already under way as cable companies gear up to match phone companies' capabilities.

- *Cellular phone services.* Wireless telephony has been available for decades in the form of clunky police and taxi radios. It took a new technology—cellular phones—to make it available efficiently on a mass basis in the 1980s. In an effort to promote competition, the FCC decided to issue cellular licenses in each market to two companies—the local phone company and a competitor. Although the phone companies dominate the cellular market, they have had to fight for their share of a business that had more than 30 million subscribers by 1997.

- *Personal Communications Services (PCS).* A larger challenge to the phone companies will come from PCS, a recent arrival on the market. Like cellular, PCS involves handheld mobile phones. It promises not only to be less expensive than cellular but also capable of providing a built-in paging option. In 1995 and 1996, more than 100 potential PCS providers anted up $18 billion in an FCC auction for regional licenses to supply the service throughout the country. Although old-line telephone companies were represented among the winning licensees, they face strong competition from new entrants. PCS is expected to attract tens of millions of subscribers in the next few years.[8]

- *Satellite services.* Communications satellites have been used by telephone companies as carriers for long-distance traffic since the 1970s. In the mid-1990s, however, satellite companies have taken on a new role as competitors to the phone and cable-TV industries. Direct-broadcasting satellite networks are supplying a wide range of information and entertainment products to household consumers. Three U.S. direct-broadcasting networks shared 4 million viewers in 1997, fewer than three years after they began full-scale networking. The market is expected to grow to 15 million subscribers early in the twenty-first century.[9] By taking a strong lead early, the three satellite networks are in a strong position to compete against telephone and cable companies in the fast-growing multimedia services market.

- *Oil and electric utility companies.* The most unlikely new competitors to traditional phone companies are public utilities. As it turns out, they possess a resource that makes them important players in the new communications mix: thousands of miles of rights-of-way for their pipes and electric transmission lines, which can also be used to accommodate telephone and other communications circuits. The utility companies have been using these rights-of-way for their own telecommunications networks, but they were prohibited from selling telecommunications services to outside customers until recently. These restrictions were lifted by Congress in 1996, opening up a potentially profitable new line of business for the utilities that they have begun to exploit.[10]

- *The bypassers.* Federal deregulation of the telephone business has given rise to a new kind of competition known as competitive-access providers (CAPs). More informally known as bypassers, CAPs lease circuits wholesale from the big telephone companies and resell them to businesses at rates as much as 15 percent lower than conventional phone charges. In the late 1990s, CAPs were a $1-billion business, a tiny slice of the total telephone pie but a looming threat to the old-line carriers. As phone companies move into new Meganet services, they will have to consider what may be lying in wait for them in terms of bypass competition.[11]

- *The Internet.* For its first two decades, the Internet was a limited network used by computer buffs. This changed radically in the early 1990s with the introduction of World Wide Web software that made Internet resources more easily available to tens of millions of consumers. All of the major U.S. phone companies have joined other access providers in offering dial-up Internet services to their customers. AT&T established itself as a major competitor in this field in February 1996 when it announced that Internet service would be available at reduced rates to its 80 million residential and 10 million business customers.[12] In the larger sense, additional Internet services are being phased in: the network is acquiring video, audio, and graphics capabilities to add to the print data that already exists. Potentially, the Internet can supply computers with an expanded range of Meganet communications services, including telephone calls.[13] These new Internet capabilities are still largely untested. However, most telecommunications analysts believe that they will claim their place in the market as a distinct challenge to phone companies and communications providers. In 1996, fewer that 20,000 people were regular users of Internet phone services, according to International Data Corp., a Massachusetts consulting firm.[14] But dozens of innovative companies are developing software programs for Internet phone calls. Formats to make such calls easier have already been built into many PC software products, including Microsoft's Windows 95. In 1996, AT&T began marketing a computer-telephone service using this standard in what was a preemptive move to establish a foothold in the Internet voice market.[15]

In summary, the old-line telephone companies face formidable competition from thousands of new enterprises. To complicate matters, the phone companies are competing among themselves for business. For decades, federal and state regulators carefully controlled the services each phone company could offer. Different services were regulated separately. However, the distinctions among these services are becoming more and more blurred as digital technologies erase the separation among delivery of voice, data, and video by allowing all three to flow over a common circuit.

Once the common circuit became technologically possible, old rules no longer made economic or technical sense. In particular, digital technologies eroded the regulatory separation of local and long-distance phone services. AT&T, MCI, and the other long-distance companies wanted to compete in the $90-billion local market. For their part, the regional Bell companies, formerly owned by AT&T, wanted to get into the $70-billion long-distance business. At the same time, the cable-TV industry saw an opening to compete with both AT&T and the regional Bells for telephone customers.[16]

By the early 1990s, pressure mounted for a major change in the way that the U.S. telecommunications sector was regulated. The result, after years of intense lobbying of Congress by the industry's competing groups, was the Telecommunications Act of 1996 (see Chapter 5 for a closer look at this legislation and its implications). As finally drawn up, the law dismantles most of the barriers that had prevented telephone, cable-TV, and other communications companies from competing with one another in most services. The law's result, over the ensuing decade, will be a massive transformation of U.S. communications, with a major impact on the development of the global Meganet. Thus, it is useful to take a closer look at how this is affecting the major U.S. players.[17]

Any such survey begins with AT&T. The company is the Comeback Kid of late-twentieth-century U.S. business. In 1984, it had more than half of its assets stripped away by the government breakup decree, a loss that would have fatally weakened any other company. But AT&T reinvented itself, to the point of maintaining its leading position in the industry. In its consumer ads, AT&T still likes to portray itself as a warm-and-fuzzy telephone company. The reality is that it has shed its old Ma Bell image to become an aggressive, innovative, and sometimes arrogant competitor. In the sober world of FCC regulation, only AT&T has had the distinction of being labeled a "dominant carrier" in U.S. telecommunications. The company was so big that even after breaking itself up into three parts in 1995 it has to be handled as a special case in government regulatory matters.

AT&T's telecommunications assets are indeed formidable. They include the world's largest communications network, a powerful brand name, a huge customer base (95 million) and strong financial resources ($11 billion operating cash flow in 1994). The company is the major player in building Meganet, both at home and abroad. More so than any of the other big operators, the reorganized parts of AT&T are involved in every aspect of Meganet's activities. It is network builder, communications carrier, equipment supplier, management consultant, and financial source.

This success story began uncertainly in the early years after the 1984 breakup. AT&T's position at that time looked shaky. Coming out of the cocoonlike protection of its monopoly, it found itself in the unaccustomed glare of competition—and it blinked. Most of its employees, from top executives on down, had always regarded the firm as a service organization that was somewhat above the competitive fray. They took a Ma Bell–knows-best attitude toward their captive cus-

tomers. The 1984 breakup was a corporate cold shower. Reorganization plans were announced. Employees were put through "sheep dip"
retraining courses, to cleanse them for the new competitive era. It was
not enough: The old imperial attitudes were hard to cure. It took almost ten years and a series of painful restructurings to turn the company around. As Robert Allen, the AT&T chairman largely responsible for the changes, noted: "At AT&T, we once viewed competition in
the U.S. telecommunications industry as heresy. Now it is our cate-
chism."[18]

Reborn, the firm rose again as an innovative and very profitable operation. As one industry expert has observed, "AT&T is still the big
elephant, but it has learned to tap dance." By the mid-1990s, ten years
after AT&T had lost half its business, the price of its stock had
quadrupled and company profits had doubled as AT&T matched, and
often outmatched, the competition in its core long-distance services
with improved facilities and aggressive marketing.

The company also learned how to take big, expensive risks. At the
time it was broken up in 1984, AT&T was saddled with a vast inventory of older equipment—a serious disadvantage in competing against
MCI and the other competitors with newer facilities. AT&T junked a
large part of the old equipment at a cost of $5 billion, then proceeded
to upgrade its entire network. Despite these bold moves, the company
lost about 40 percent of its long-distance customers to competitors.

Meanwhile, AT&T looked around for new businesses. It came up
with a mixed bag of success and failure. A clear success was its entry
into the fast-growing mobile communications sector. In 1993, it acquired McCaw Cellular Communications for $12.6 billion, the second
biggest takeover in U.S. business history up to that time.[19] AT&T was
also successful when it set up its own version of a bank credit card,
which became the second largest of its kind in the country, surpassed
only by the Citicorp card. It also maintained a strong lead in producing
telephones and other telecommunications equipment. These are markets where the AT&T logo reminded customers of the company's long
history of equipment reliability. The company also became a major
supplier of cash-dispensing ATMs, cornering one-third of the world
market.

AT&T's core business was still its long-distance phone operations.
Before the company's 1995 split into three separate units, long-distance service accounted for 65 percent of the firm's revenues and 85
percent of its profits. Although it lost 40 percent of its long-distance
market in the years after the 1984 breakup, it fought back with an intense marketing campaign. In 1994, it managed to add more than 1
million customers, its first annual net gain since the breakup.[20]

Its long-distance operations gave AT&T a solid base from which to launch new telephone initiatives, both at home and abroad. In 1997, it moved back into the U.S. market for local phone service, a sector dominated by the regional phone companies that had been part of AT&T's regional Bell system. Known as the Baby Bells, the regional companies are neither small nor helpless; each is a $10 billion–plus operation. The 1984 divestiture agreement prohibited AT&T from ever acquiring any former Bell assets, a corporate move that would have been the fastest route for reentry into the local markets it had given up.[21]

AT&T decided to compete directly against its former Bell companies. The prize was a $90-billion local market, and AT&T had a century of experience in serving it. Moreover, by the 1990s, AT&T was paying out more than $13 billion per year in access charges to local phone companies for the right to connect its long-distance traffic to their networks. This heavy expense would be reduced if AT&T could take over part of the local market.

In addition to its longtime expertise in local phone service, the company had two important competitive advantages. One was its recently acquired McCaw cellular network, now marketed under the AT&T logo in more than 100 cities. The other was the twenty-one licenses it acquired in 1996 to build local PCS mobile networks throughout the country. In 1997, the company introduced an advanced mobile phone service, AT&T Digital PCS, in forty major metropolitan areas with a potential customer base of 70 million homes and businesses. Both its cellular and PCS assets could be used to connect directly into the AT&T national network.

AT&T's prospects for providing local phone services dramatically improved as a result of the 1996 congressional overhaul of telecom industry regulations. The new law removed most of the barriers that had prohibited local and long-distance companies from competing in another's market. The result is a marketing battle for customers that will engage the U.S. phone industry well into the twenty-first century.[22] In February 1997, less than one year after the legislation was passed, AT&T began offering local phone services, competing against Baby Bells.[23]

AT&T also made moves to bolster plans to become a full-service communications provider at both the local and national levels. In January 1996, it acquired a minority stake in DirecTV, one of the three U.S. direct-broadcasting satellite companies. Part of its strategy was to explore the possibility of using satellites to beam long-distance traffic directly into homes, bypassing local phone companies' circuits. As Mark Langner, an analyst with TeleChoice Inc., pointed out: "AT&T doesn't have one local strategy. It has five or six local strategies, any one of which could be put in place, depending on how things develop."[24]

Like most other U.S. phone companies, AT&T was slow to realize the Internet's potential impact on its operations. It made amends in February 1996 with a spectacular entry into the Internet market, offering its 80 million long-distance customers low-cost access. Within a few months after announcing its WorldNet service, the company received more than 500,000 requests for the enabling software.[25] The response was so strong that it made AT&T an instant leader among Internet providers. Its entry into the Internet business sent shock waves through the online-access industry, affecting such companies as Microsoft, CompuServe, and America Online, all of whom had lucrative, growing Internet-access services. Meanwhile, AT&T's telephone competitors, including the regional Bell companies, speeded up their plans to offer similar Internet-access services.[26]

This pell-mell expansion added to AT&T's stature as an innovative and profitable leader in U.S. telecommunications. But it also raised doubts as to the company's grand vision of combining a vast range of activities in a coordinated operation that spanned the globe. Despite its overall successes, the company had made some expensive mistakes. One of these was its 1991 decision to buy NCR, an old-line computer firm. The project was bedeviled by technical and management problems, resulting in losses of more than $2 billion by the time AT&T decided to unload it in 1995.[27]

Was it time for AT&T to change its corporate culture once again, as it had after the 1984 breakup? The answer came without warning in September 1995 with the announcement that AT&T would split itself into three separate firms. It was a sharp change of direction for a business that had chased the idea of product-and-service convergence more aggressively than any other in history. The decision was prompted largely by regulatory and technological changes in the U.S. communications sector. AT&T's managers came to the view that in an era of more intense competition the advantages lay with smaller, more focused operations.

The three-way split was a rejection of the prevailing corporate gospel of synergy, which declared that related goods and services could be produced and marketed more profitably under a single management. It is a flawed doctrine, according to Eli Noam of Columbia University's business school: "Computing and telecommunications are closely related technologically, but that doesn't mean you have to do it under one roof. AT&T has learned that lesson the hard way."[28]

In the new arrangement, AT&T ($49 billion in 1994 revenues) would focus on long-distance and wireless communications. Lucent

Technologies ($20 billion) would produce and sell telephones and other hardware equipment. Global Information Solutions ($8 billion) would develop and market complex information systems to business firms. The realignment was accompanied by sizable cutbacks in the firm's workforce, with 40,000 jobs—13 percent of the total—scheduled for elimination by the end of the decade.[29] The new realignment also affected AT&T's balance sheet. Its stock fell 24 percent in the months after the split. A year later, when the company announced lower profit expectations, its stock dropped almost 10 percent in a single day, wiping out $9 billion in market value.[30]

These developments underlined the problems the three spin-offs faced in a new and uncertain business environment in U.S. telecommunications.[31] The 1996 telecommunications legislation has lowered most of the sector's barriers to competition at all levels. There will be many contestants in this free-for-all for customers, led by the telephone companies. And as noted earlier, they will be challenged by cable-TV operators, broadcast satellite networks, and even electric utility companies. Looming over all of them is the Internet, the rogue technology that no one company or sector controls. The Internet has already captured the public imagination as a forerunner to the kind of easy-to-use information utility consumers want and that the industry could deliver in the new competitive environment.

This competition is energizing the U.S. domestic communications sector, which already is the largest in the world and growing fast. Increasingly, however, the sector is looking at market opportunities abroad as the advanced Meganet expands around the globe. A 1995 report by Lehman Brothers, the New York investment house, underlines this trend. It notes that international long-distance use is expanding at a rate of 15 percent annually.[32] For the present, Western Europe and other developed areas are the most lucrative targets for U.S. communications companies. However, the largely untapped markets of Asia, Africa, and Latin America are becoming more attractive.

Among U.S. companies, AT&T has taken the lead in expanding into global markets. The company has always had a strong international presence as the major provider of U.S. long-distance calls to overseas phone systems. The company's circuits carry twice as much overseas traffic, measured in minutes, as the next two largest international phone systems (British and German) combined.[33] AT&T's interest in foreign markets goes back to the early part of the century when it founded NEC, now Japan's largest communications and computer firm, as a subsidiary of its Western Electric manufacturing arm. The company's ability to operate worldwide was reaffirmed during World

War II when it was largely responsible for building a global military network for the U.S. Army Signal Corps. This wartime project laid the basis for U.S. communications leadership overseas in the postwar decades, overtaking the British and French.

After World War II, however, AT&T retreated from the international arena (except for its long-distance telephone operations). Government regulatory strictures discouraged AT&T operations that did not fit its primary job of supplying domestic telephone-network services. These restrictions were largely lifted in the 1984 breakup agreement, allowing the company to enter new businesses at home and abroad. A small international division grew into a major element in the firm's reorganization plans. Company executives announced that overseas operations would account for half the company's revenues by the end of this century.

The prediction was overoptimistic. In the mid-1990s, AT&T's overseas business (including long-distance operations) accounted for about 25 percent of its revenues. Although this was below earlier expectations, it is an impressive growth record nonetheless. Industry observers expect that international operations will account for 40 percent of the business done by the three companies that emerged from the 1995 AT&T split.[34] According to Robert Morris, a telecommunications expert at Goldman Sachs, the New York investment house, "The AT&T brand could be to the world-wide communications business what Coke is to the beverage business."

In the first years after the 1984 breakup, AT&T's overseas ventures did not go smoothly. Joint manufacturing agreements with two major European firms, Phillips and Olivetti, fell apart. The Olivetti deal, in which the Italian company agreed to build AT&T-brand small computers, ended after a reported loss of $3 billion for AT&T. Following a series of painful reorganizations, AT&T's international division became more surefooted.

The result was a global operation that touched every facet of Meganet expansion. The company moved a large part of its equipment-production activities abroad. By 1990, all of its telephone-instrument production had been transferred to Mexico and East Asia. It became, for instance, the largest exporter of electronic products from Taiwan. AT&T also stepped up its operations as a major builder of international networks. It has a fleet of seven cable-laying ships, sophisticated vessels that are in constant movement on all the world's oceans. One of the company's most ambitious projects is a fiber-optic cable that will encircle Africa like a necklace. The $2-billion project will connect with thirty-two coastal countries and, by extension, other markets inland. Its completion will vastly improve communications on a continent that has heretofore been largely marginalized during the expansion of Meganet resources.

AT&T's primary goal is to lead the market for integrated communications services, a strategy known in the industry as "one-stop shopping." Its purpose is to offer a full range of services under a single trademark. The idea is to convince customers of the advantages of having a single point of contact for all their communications needs, including one bill at the end of the month. This marketing strategy has also been adopted by the other major U.S. telecommunications companies—MCI, Sprint, GTE, and the regional Bell phone companies. The strategy was given special impetus by the removal of most barriers to competition thanks to the 1996 telecommunications law. The law, in effect, validated the concept of one-stop shopping by allowing companies to compete with one another in marketing a wide range of services.

The big companies can expect competition for one-stop customers from smaller, independent firms who hope to take one-stop business away from the major carriers. They are known in the industry as competitive local exchange carriers (CLECs). One of the most successful CLECs is McLeod, Inc., a company little known outside its Upper Midwest operational area. McLeod operates in 100 local markets as a full-service, vertically integrated provider, offering a range of services to business and household customers. Its competitive advantages, according to one Wall Street analysis, are "cutting-edge systems capability, a long track record of superior customer service, and, frankly, a huge 'home court advantage' over the big companies."[35]

Another set of strong competitors in the one-stop market are companies that have focused on providing specialized telecom services to business firms. In most cases, they have leased lines from AT&T and other phone companies. More recently, they have relied more heavily on their own facilities.

A spectacular example is MSF WorldCom, a network created in 1996. It is the result of a $14.4-billion merger that combined the resources of two smaller business services firms, WorldCom and MSF Communications, into an integrated national network. "They've positioned themselves as a business-to-business powerhouse," according to Christine Hecket, an industry consultant in New Jersey. In 1997, MSF Worldcom was the only global carrier that offered the business community a complete one-stop menu of advanced voice, data, and Internet services, using its own local and international facilities.

Amid such formidable competition, AT&T remains the company to beat in the race to develop one-stop services in the United States.

These services are also an increasingly important force in the overseas operations of AT&T and its competitors. Their strategies are based on the strong demand for global integrated communications services, particularly among multinational corporations. By rough estimate, the big multinationals spend at least $10 billion per year on international communications services. They have not been well served by conventional practices, which usually require them to deal with dozens of communications providers in many countries to get the global services they want. By working with a one-stop telecom supplier, corporate customers avoid many of the headaches involved in negotiating and managing their own arrangements for overseas telecom connections.[36]

Although one-stop arrangements are still a small part of the global communications pattern, their appeal to big international companies already makes them a lucrative business. Current revenues are, however, insignificant compared to those that are to be gained from the eventual expansion of customized one-stop facilities to smaller organizations and individuals, once advanced Meganet facilities become more widely available. The current, limited one-stop arrangements are, in fact, only a test of what will be a conventional service for ordinary users worldwide in the future. One-stop shopping is the Big Idea behind much of the current push for global Meganet expansion.

No single company can develop one-stop resources on a global scale on its own. The evolving advanced Meganet is still primarily a collection of individual national networks. Telecommunications regulations in almost all countries abroad limit foreign companies from setting up one-stop operations. In order to enter this market, they have to form alliances with local telecommunications companies, whether private or government-controlled. A number of U.S. companies are vying to line up favorable arrangements with local operators abroad to form one-stop networks. AT&T's main domestic rivals, MCI and Sprint, have developed partnerships with the leading West European carriers (MCI with British Telecom and Sprint with France Telecom and Deutsche Telekom).

AT&T has had more difficulty in attracting one-stop partners. Its initial project, WorldPartners, began in the early 1990s as a $450-million joint venture with KDD, Japan's international phone company, and Singapore Telecom, the most aggressive and successful Asian communications group outside of Japan. In its early years, WorldPartners had limited success, primarily because its service, known as WorldSource, did not offer the full range of advanced capabilities needed by many large international companies.

WorldPartners had another problem: It lacked a strong base in Europe, the largest telecom market outside of the United States. AT&T

needed a link with a European partner rich enough to help finance the hundreds of millions of dollars needed to build advanced WorldSource facilities throughout the continent. It approached Deutsche Telekom and France Telecom, Europe's biggest telephone groups. Both companies had good reason to be interested in an AT&T connection. Although they were making healthy profits from their voice telephony monopolies, they knew that their protected markets would be open to full competition in early 1988 as a result of free trade decisions taken by the European Union.

This meant competition from foreign rivals, the most formidable of which was AT&T. Although an alliance with AT&T would have given the Germans and French an easier entry into the lucrative U.S. market, they decided against the move. Instead, they invested $4.2 billion for a 20 percent stake in Sprint, the number-three U.S. telephone company. British Telecom bought a similar stake in MCI, thus improving its own access to the U.S. market. These moves, in turn, gave both Sprint and MCI a foothold in the growing European market, including opportunities to promote one-stop ventures.

Rebuffed by the two biggest European operators, AT&T continued its search for European partners. In 1993, the company reached an agreement with Unisource, a consortium of the Dutch, Swedish, Swiss, and Spanish phone organizations. The Unisource partners joined the AT&T-sponsored WorldPartners arrangement with a 20 percent stake, giving them access to a global one-stop network. But they hedged on taking on AT&T as a full participant in their own consortium. At home and abroad, AT&T was still too formidable to be regarded as just another partner. However, in May 1996, Unisource and AT&T did merge most of their European operations, thereby further strengthening their one-stop alliance.[37]

AT&T has been less successful in developing similar one-stop arrangements in other parts of the world. It has had to fall back on investments and operating agreements in individual countries. In a typical deal, it bought a 49 percent share in a private Mexican venture, Grupo Industrial Alpha, which began offering long-distance services in 1997. AT&T also has a one-third stake in Unitel, a Canadian long-distance company. It is teamed with Germany's Deutsche Telekom in a joint venture with the new national phone company in Ukraine. By 1997, AT&T had concluded agreements to market its World Partners services in a dozen other countries in Asia and Latin America.

The company's biggest overseas target is China. The stakes are huge. Although China is among the bottom-ranked countries in per capita communications resources, it could be the biggest single market for telecommunications and information products in the twenty-first century. As William Warwick, chairman of AT&T China, recently pointed out: "The choices for U.S. companies are stark. Either we establish a major presence in the China market or we forget about being a global player, forget even about being able to defend our home market."[38]

With fewer than three telephones per hundred Chinese, a huge telecom vacuum is waiting to be filled in a country that is already the world's third largest economy. China's potential for telecommunications growth presents the single biggest challenge for Meganet's master builders. Chinese government officials want to add 15–20 million phone lines annually for the rest of the decade. This is the rough equivalent of building a new Baby Bell every year or so. If the Chinese come anywhere near striking distance of their goals, they will have added more new phone lines between now and early next century than currently exist in the United States—still less than 20 percent telephone penetration of China's domestic market.

The Chinese need a lot of outside help to reach this goal, which explains why AT&T and the other large phone companies have lined up to do business with them. The companies learned quickly that Chinese authorities are tough negotiators, particularly concerned about preventing foreign control of their domestic network. The Chinese are mainly interested in POTS, especially in locations where it will help the country's economic expansion. They are conspicuously uninterested in such Western frills as movies on demand or interactive video computer games.

AT&T has done well in the competition for China's telecom business. Beginning in the early 1990s, it has negotiated a series of contracts for modernizing the national telecom system. These include deals to supply individual Chinese enterprises with a wide range of telecom goods and services.

In summary, AT&T is already an impressive global Meganet player—little more than a decade after winning the legal right to join the competition. At the time of the 1984 breakup, the company had only sixty employees outside the United States. Ten years later, its overseas employees had increased to 50,000. This decade was, moreover, a period in which AT&T faced strong competition for international business from other U.S. firms.

The strongest of these competitors is MCI, which has become the classic case study of American onward-and-upward corporate innovation. MCI's founder, William McGowan, was a tough-talking Irishman from upstate New York. He and a partner went into the telephone business in 1969 with a single microwave line along the interstate highway between St. Louis and Chicago. It was a small but defining event in Meganet's history. McGowan's microwave line was the first significant breach of the AT&T long-distance monopoly allowed by the FCC. McGowan gloried in David-and-Goliath stories of how little MCI took on the AT&T giant. One of his favorite aphorisms, according to company lore, was "the meek shall inherit the earth, but they won't do anything for your market share." Now, some thirty years later, MCI has more than 1 million miles of fiber-optic cable installed across the country.

The company is legendary for watching its costs. A 1995 survey by the Economic Strategy Institute found that annual revenues per MCI employee were $383,000 per year. The comparable figure for its two main competitors, Sprint and AT&T, were $216,000 and $213,000 respectively. As employees enter the firm's Washington, D.C., headquarters each day, they are confronted with a chart listing MCI's stock price from the previous day and a notice that today's price will be up to them.

In the 1980s, MCI consolidated its position as the second largest domestic long-distance company by corralling 20 percent of the traffic, cutting deeply into AT&T's business. MCI pursued aggressive marketing strategies, including a "Friends and Family" promotion that offered reduced rates to household consumers who wanted to set up their own personalized network. Five million customers—most of them defectors from AT&T—signed up for the service in its first few months of operations.

MCI's focus on long-distance services served it well during its first twenty years. By the 1990s, however, the company came under pressure to adjust to new technologies, changing markets, and revised government regulations. More specifically, it needed to expand beyond the $70-billion long-distance business into the $500-billion potential market for new digitized products. It decided to apply a full-court press to AT&T as well as to the cable-TV and satellite industries, all of whom were moving into advanced services. The 1996 congressional legislation reducing barriers to market entry opened the way to greater competition in long-distance telephone services. At the time, MCI earned 90 percent of its revenues from these services. This part of its business was also threatened by local phone companies' plans to capture as much as 15 percent of the long-distance market.

Faced with these problems, MCI made a sudden corporate turnaround, led by Bert Roberts, who took over the company helm after Bill McGowan's death in 1992. Roberts set a goal of realizing 50 percent of the company's revenues from new ventures by the end of the decade. "We want to get as many hooks into each of MCI's customers as we can," he declared.[39] The firm laid out plans to spend $10 billion in the late 1990s to upgrade its operations, largely in partnerships with other communications and information services companies. If its strategy is successful, it will give MCI strong resources in such areas as videophones, digital cellular phones, teleconferencing, and direct broadcasting from satellites.

In one of his first moves, Roberts challenged the local phone companies with MCI Metro, a $2-billion project to build fiber-optic loops in two dozen major U.S. cities. The service bypasses the local companies, connecting business firms directly to the MCI long-distance network. Among other advantages for MCI, the service eliminates many of the access fees paid to local Bell companies to connect MCI traffic to their networks. These fees had been taking a hefty $.45 out of every $1 of MCI's revenues. MCI also moved belatedly into cellular phone operations, buying Nextel Communications, a major wireless firm, in 1994. By 1997, it was operating in thirty major cellular markets, covering one-quarter of the U.S. population. It added a new marketing touch by offering its cellular customers frequent-flyer points on participating airlines. The company also announced plans to market advanced personal communications services in more than sixty major metropolitan markets by the end of 1998.[40]

In 1995, MCI formed a spectacular alliance with media mogul Rupert Murdoch to develop a direct-broadcasting satellite network. The following year, the company made a successful $625-million bid for an FCC license to operate the last available broadcast-satellite slot with full coverage of the continental United States. Murdoch will use some of its 150-channel capacity for his News Corp. entertainment programs. MCI is more interested in the satellite's use for nonvideo services such as the fast-growing data transmission market. The satellite can download material to any point in the country as much as 100 times faster than an advanced phone circuit, and at lower costs. MCI and News Corp. said they would invest more than $1 billion to build the system, which they hoped to have operational in 1998.[41] By 1997, however, MCI had cut back its commitment to the Murdoch satellite project, preferring to focus on other telecom services.

Like other phone companies, MCI was slow in recognizing the Internet challenge. It hurried to make up for lost time in 1996 by allying itself with Microsoft, the world's largest software firm, to market a version of the Microsoft Network (MSN), which will make Internet access available to MCI's 20 million customers.

MCI strategic plans also have a global reach. "International expansion is critical to our ability to continue to gain domestic market share," according to MCI chief Bert Roberts. The company moved into international services in the 1970s through deals with European phone companies that agreed to accept MCI transatlantic traffic. At the time, MCI was dependent on circuits leased from AT&T and other international carriers. This dependence was reduced somewhat in the late 1980s when it acquired its own transatlantic cable facilities in partnership with a British firm, Mercury Communications.

MCI now has long-distance phone connections with carriers in more than 100 countries. Its global capabilities were strengthened when British Telecom, one of the major European carriers, bought a 20 percent share of MCI for $4.3 billion. The two firms moved quickly to integrate their resources for international services, creating Concert, billed as "the first global network."

In November 1996, their alliance was sealed in a $21-billion merger agreement that created Concert Global Communications. It will be the world's third largest telecommunications organization after AT&T and Japan's Nippon Telephone and Telegraph. Although MCI and British Telecom will continue to sell services under their own names in their own countries, they will merge their international activities as a single global supercarrier. This will include a major focus on expanding their advanced Internet facility (Internet Plus), which by 1997 had increased Internet transmission capacity by one-third around the globe.

AT&T's other big domestic competitor besides MCI is Sprint, the third largest long-distance carrier. Sprint has had an undeserved image as the little kid competing against the bigger boys. It is, in fact, a multibillion company with 40,000 employees. Moreover, it was the first U.S. phone company to offer local, long-distance, and cellular services—a three-way combination that its two bigger rivals have been struggling for years to put together. Sprint's experience in coordinating the three types of service gives it a special advantage in offering one-stop shopping to its U.S. customers.

Sprint is the result of the series of amalgamations of old-line phone companies that occurred in the mid-1980s. After several corporate missteps, Sprint recovered its management and technical poise to become a formidable competitor in the domestic market. It was helped by an inspired advertising campaign that included TV commercials featuring slow-motion views of a pin dropping to demonstrate the clarity of Sprint's fiber-optic circuits. The company also showed its management savvy when it challenged its two bigger rivals for a share in the risky new business of consumer multimedia services. In 1994, it joined three U.S. cable companies in a partnership to supply local, long-distance, and mobile telephony, as well as multimedia entertainment and information service. Its partners—Tele-Communications Inc. (TCI), Comcast, and Cox Communications—are respectively the first, fourth, and sixth biggest cable operators in the country. With a 40 percent stake in the alliance, Sprint will be able to provide long-distance phone service over its partners' local cable networks.[42]

Sprint is a latecomer to international markets. The firm has less than 10 percent of U.S.-originated telephone traffic to overseas points. Its initial experience with other services abroad was Sprintnet, a global data network that uses leased lines to reach customers in more than 100 countries. In 1991, Sprint expanded this service to include virtual private networking (VPN), which gives corporations and other large organizations the equivalent of their own internal proprietary networks at a much lower cost than if they operated their own facilities. MCI and other carriers have since followed Sprint in offering similar networks. VPN arrangements are an example of how technologies are being implemented in ways that challenge PTT monopolies overseas. Because they are closed systems, they can carry voice traffic whether or not the local PTT holds a monopoly on voice telephony over the public network.

Sprint increased its global resources substantially in 1994 by selling 20 percent of its operations for $4.2 billion to two European telecommunications powers, Deutsche Telekom and France Telecom. This alliance strengthened all three companies by making them serious challengers in the emerging market for one-stop international telecommunications services. The link with Sprint benefits its French and German partners by assuring better marketing access, through Sprint, to U.S. multinational firms. Sprint in turn won entry into the two largest European markets, as well as a sizable kitty to finance expansion of its domestic and international facilities. In 1994, the company made its first deep inroad into the burgeoning Latin American telecom market when it formed a strategic alliance with Telmex, the privatized Mexican carrier.

The flurry of international deals made by AT&T, MCI, Sprint, and others will contribute to Meganet expansion in the coming years. These powerful alliances have the advanced technical expertise, management skills, and funding needed to build and operate full-scale global networks.

Their current marketing strategies focus on serving big international corporate customers. In itself, this is a substantial market. Not only do these companies spend billions of dollars annually for global telecom services, they are usually at the mercy of overseas phone companies. Most foreign carriers are still monopolies that charge high rates because their customers generally have no choice. A 1994 British study found that for a big user such as an international bank these inflated prices can raise telecom costs to almost 30 percent of turnover charges—nearly double the proportion in the United States. International charges are now dropping as competition among telecom carriers increases.

Big global carriers like AT&T and MCI will be around for a long time, if only because they have the economic weight and technical resources to match Meganet needs. Their current dominance may be temporary, however, as it is overtaken by new forces early in the twenty-first century. The signs of this change are already evident. The old giants have no guarantee that they can continue to divide up world markets among themselves, as they did in the past. They were, in effect, a cartel in all but the legal sense. Slowly but steadily, they are now forced to cede market share to new challengers who are determined get a share of the fast-growing, volatile telecommunications sector.

The new competition is global, but its power center is American. The latest entrants into the field are the Baby Bells, the regional phone networks. Having broken out of the local phone company mold in the past decade, they now are free to provide a full range of voice, video, and data services.

In particular, the Telecommunications Act of 1996 gave the regional Bells a green light to expand beyond local phone services. The initial result was a flurry of buyouts and alliances. In 1996, Bell Atlantic linked up with Nynex in a $23-billion deal that merged their operations from Virginia north to Maine. California's Pacific Telesis made a similar $17-billion arrangement with SBC Communications, the regional Bell company in Texas and the Southwest.[43]

Deals like these gave the Baby Bells strong new marketing clout. They have embarked on a variety of initiatives designed to expand their business activities beyond local phone service. A key goal is to challenge AT&T, MCI, and Sprint in the lucrative long-distance market. Their ability to succeed will have important effects on the shape and direction of Meganet developments at home and abroad into the next century.[44] In 1997, Ameritech became the first regional Bell to request FCC permission to operate a long-distance service.

The Baby Bells have also been looking overseas for new business. What they saw were telecommunications markets expanding faster and more profitably than their own regulated local phone operations. Moreover, the Bells showed up at the right time. Telecommunications opportunities were opening up abroad as government-owned phone organizations started down the path toward privatization and a competitive future. Newly dismantled government monopolies were suddenly confronted with such unaccustomed demands as operating cost-efficient networks and responding to customer needs for new services.

The Baby Bells had the technical and management skills they needed to make this turnaround.

Beginning in the late 1980s, the Bells spread out overseas, looking for telecom partners. Between 1990 and 1992, they arranged more than forty international partnership deals. This pace has slowed down somewhat, but cross-border alliances, mergers, and buyouts by the regional U.S. phone companies are now part of the worldwide Meganet pattern. In their decision to go global in the 1980s, the Baby Bells removed any lingering expectations that they might settle into a niche as local telephone companies. They were helped by a provision in the federal government regulations governing their activities during the post-AT&T breakup transition. It permitted them to use as much as 10 percent of their profits for activities outside their local phone businesses. Although foreign operations were unfamiliar territory for them, the seven Bell companies sought out business opportunities on all continents. Bell Atlantic alone had put more than $2.5 billion into equity investments outside the United States by the mid-1990s.[45]

In their initial enthusiasm, some of the Bells rushed into foreign projects that were badly planned and executed. Their skill in supplying good phone service in a Wichita or Walla Walla did not always transfer smoothly to the more exotic political, economic, and cultural complexities of an Indonesia or Argentina. Nevertheless, the lure of new business and greater profits kept them interested. The result is that the Bells' involvement abroad now encompasses all phases of the telecom business—investment, construction, management, and ownership.

Following some earlier missteps, the regional Bell companies have become more adept at identifying and exploiting overseas business opportunities. The best-known venture was in Mexico, where Southwestern Bell (now SBC Communications) became a major investor in Telmex, the national phone company. (The other foreign investor is France Telecom.) The investment was part of Telmex's transition from a government agency to a private corporation, one of the first and most successful of the privatizations undertaken by telecom monopolies in Latin America. The new Telmex has benefited hugely from the management and technical resources of its two foreign partners. Its revitalized operations put it in a strong position to compete when the Mexican telecom market was opened to full competition in late 1996.

Another active global player was Nynex, the regional carrier in the Northeast, which merged with Bell Atlantic in 1996. Nynex's overseas ventures included projects in Japan, Thailand, Indonesia, Gibraltar, and Greece. It and other Bell companies collectively became the largest block of owners of cable-TV companies in Great Britain. Nynex also became the managing sponsor of FLAG, the world's longest undersea fiber-optic cable and which links Great Britain with Japan via the Mediterranean Sea and the Indian Ocean.

Bell South, the southeastern phone company, has concentrated on cellular phone ventures in its overseas investments. Its cellular investments in Latin America, Europe, and Asia make it the largest global cellular operator based in the United States. Bell South took the lead among the Bell companies in applying its domestic experience with cellular to develop the technology to serve as an important alternate phone system in developing countries. As John Clendenin, Bell South's chairman, pointed out: "Cellular in many of these countries has been a Godsend. The telephone system in Caracas was so bad you couldn't get a call through even if you were president. Cellular came in and bypassed the local system, and performed marvelously as a substitute for local phone service."[46]

Ameritech, the midwestern regional Bell, and Bell Atlantic each have a 25 percent stake in Telecom New Zealand, the first national system abroad to completely privatize its operations with minimal government oversight. Asian markets generally have a strong appeal for the Bells because of their dynamic economies and large unmet telecommunications needs. But these markets are still risky. China and India, with their enormous populations, are particularly seductive markets, despite their economic unpredictability.

The Indian market could, for instance, absorb $100 billion in new equipment and services in the next decade—a prospect that has attracted the Baby Bells and every other large phone company in the world. Among the Bell companies, US West went into India early. In 1993, it entered into a joint project with local investors to build a regional telecom network in South India. Work on the $350-million project has languished, along with similar joint ventures by local and foreign investors, largely because of the snail-like pace of government decision making in India.

In summary, the regional Bell companies are increasingly active in global Meganet development. So far, it has been a good business for them. Furthermore, by challenging AT&T and other longtime global operators, they have helped spur competitiveness abroad—a prerequisite for encouraging expansion of advanced Meganet resources in the coming years.

The Baby Bells and other long-distance competitors are facing competition from a new source: American builders and operators of communications satellite networks. Except for MCI, none of the companies building these networks are traditional phone companies. They are coming into the market because of recent breakthroughs in satellite technology that offer new opportunities for delivering advanced services competitively. These breakthroughs are making U.S. satellite companies a significant factor in the U.S. telecommunications mix, even more so in the global Meganet.

U.S. firms benefit from the long lead the United States has had in satellite technology and applications since the 1960s. U.S. industry has supplied most of the technology and equipment for the International Telecommunications Satellite Organization (Intelsat), the global communications satellite network, during the past thirty years. From the beginning of the satellite era, communications satellites have played a useful, if minor role in U.S. domestic communications. This role dates from the early 1970s, when the FCC adopted its "open skies" satellite regulations. In effect, the FCC ruled that any company could build and operate a satellite network if it had the technical capability and the money. In the decade that followed, AT&T and the Communications Satellite Corporation (Comsat) emerged as the foremost providers of satellite telephone and data services.

Other satellite enterprises found smaller but still profitable niches for specialized services. In the 1980s, however, the demand for voice and data services via satellite fell off as transcontinental fiber-optic networks captured most of this traffic. Until recently, U.S. domestic satellites were used primarily to deliver video signals to television and cable-TV operators.

This market experienced a new surge of activity in the mid-1990s with the sudden growth of direct-broadcasting satellite entertainment programming.[47] Three U.S. DBS companies, each offering more than 100 channels, signed up more than 5 million subscribers by 1997. Direct broadcasting by satellite has also caught on overseas, particularly in Asia and Latin America. Rupert Murdoch's News Corp. operates the Star DBS network, headquartered in Hong Kong, which transmits a mix of regional and Western programming to more than thirty countries from the western Pacific to the Mediterranean.

Two U.S. groups participate in international consortia that are sponsoring broadcast satellite operations in Latin America. Murdoch's News Corp. and Tele-Communications Inc., the largest cable operator in the United States, are teamed up with a major Brazilian media group, Organizacoes Globo, and Grupo Televisa of Mexico, in operating DirecTV. Their competitor is Galaxy Latin America, whose majority shareholder is Hughes Electronics, a division of General Motors. Minority shares are held by Brazilian, Venezuelan, and Mexican media companies. News Corp. and TCI hope to sign up several million subscribers by the end of the decade.[48]

Renewed interest in satellites has been stimulated by another technology: mobile communications. Mobile satellite service is, in effect, a space-based version of a cellular telephone network. Its "birds" differ from conventional satellites, which operate like switchboards in a wired telephone system, transmitting between fixed points on earth. Mobile satellites can receive voice, video, and data messages from users anywhere within its ground "footprint" (which can cover the entire United States) and transmit them to any other point in the footprint.

Mobile satellite services are relatively new, emerging only since 1990. They were introduced in the United States first, but they have since expanded into wider regional and international areas. As a result, mobile network projects are now a significant element in the growth of the global Meganet.

Mobile satellite technology has been around in various forms for thirty years. Its range was limited, however, and the earth stations that transmitted and received signals were bulky and cost as much as $25,000 apiece. Commercial exploitation of mobile satellite services awaited technical advances both in ground equipment and in space components. Breakthroughs in both areas occurred in the 1980s. Advances in microelectronics made it possible to cram an earth station, capable of sending and receiving signals, into a handheld instrument smaller than a conventional telephone. These instruments are the descendants of the familiar cellular phones, which operate between ground stations. The second breakthrough was improvements to the satellites themselves. Most of the conventional early satellites were geostationary, floating through space 22,300 miles above the equator. At that height, they moved at the same speed as the earth's rotation, thus appearing to be stationary. Mobile communications operate best at lower orbits, from 1,000 miles up to about 6,000 miles in space. By the early 1990s, two types of mobile satellites had emerged—low earth orbiting (LEO) and medium earth orbiting (MEO). LEOs orbit the earth at about 1,200 miles and need more satellites to cover the portions of the earth they serve; LEOs generally provide higher transmission quality. MEOs orbit at about 6,000 miles and require fewer satellites, but they have technological drawbacks.

There are at least a half-dozen telecom enterprises betting up to $10 billion that there is a market for the global mobile services that these satellites can provide.[49] They hope to parallel the success of earthbound cellular mobile networks, which had signed up more than 50 million customers worldwide by mid-decade. The new satellite entrepreneurs claim they can help double this number in the next decade. This prospect has created the telecom equivalent of the Klondike gold rush. "People can smell the money," said Michael French, editor of *Satellite Week*, an industry journal. The mobile satellite field has been dominated by the Americans from the start. The first network, built by American Mobile Satellite Corp. (AMSC), was authorized by the FCC in the late 1980s and went into service in 1996. It provides voice, data, fax, and two-way video communications in the United States and Canada. AMSC hopes to take advantage of its early start to dominate the North American mobile communications market, the largest in the world.

Other mobile satellite entrants are looking at a wider geographical market. At least a half-dozen major projects for providing global mobile satellite services are already under way. The leading contender is Iridium, sponsored by Motorola, which will offer worldwide voice, data, fax, and paging services beginning in 1998. The Iridium network consists of sixty-six satellites passing over both poles. The satellites are programmed in an intricate orbital pattern that allows them to cover the entire surface of the earth, relaying voice and other messages sent up from a user's handset, which is similar in appearance to a conventional cellular phone. The message is transmitted among Iridium satellites until it reaches one that can pass the message on to the earth station nearest the call destination for onward transmission to a conventional or cellular telephone network. The entire operation takes place in milliseconds.

Iridium has an impressive head start on its competitors, having placed its first satellites into orbit in early 1997. The fact that it is sponsored by Motorola is no small advantage. Motorola is the world's leading producer of mobile communications equipment, having gotten its start by producing the first, primitive car radios in the 1930s. The company also has a strong international presence. Half of its business is overseas. Iridium's technology is a product of Motorola's world-class research labs. Moreover, the company has the financial resources to provide the initial funding for a project that will eventually cost almost $4 billion.

Motorola expects to retain only a 15 percent stake in Iridium once the network is in operation, with the rest held by a group of major international investors, including firms from Japan, China, India, Korea, Italy, and Saudi Arabia. By early 1997, Iridium had raised $1.9 billion in equity and was well on its way to raising the rest it needs to begin global operations in 1998.

Iridium faces strong competition in the global mobile satellite market. AMSC's North American network will have a three-year head start in that crucial market. At least three other U.S.-sponsored networks will compete globally with Iridium. Globalstar, developed by Loral, a defense electronics firm, and Qualcomm are both pioneers in mobile and data communications technologies. Another competitor is

Odyssey, sponsored by aerospace manufacturer TRW in a joint venture with Teleglobe, a Canadian telecommunications operator. Each of these systems use some variation of basic mobile satellite technologies to reach their intended clients. Odyssey, for instance, does not plan to cover all parts of the earth. Its dozen satellites will serve mainly business customers concentrated in heavily populated geographic areas.

An especially formidable mobile satellite competitor is the newest entrant, Teledesic, which proposes to deploy a mobile communications space network with an astonishing 840 satellites. Thanks to its sponsors, the $9 billion project cannot be dismissed as a Star Trek fantasy: They include, among others, Bill Gates, the head of Microsoft, and Craig McCaw, the most successful of the early U.S. cellular phone entrepreneurs. Gates and McCaw each entered the venture in 1994 with a 30.8 percent equity stake.

Teledesic proposes to offer a greater range of services than Iridium and its other competitors. Its menu will include videoconferencing, interactive multimedia, and advanced data transmission, as well as voice telephony.[50] Teledesic's managers plan to have their network operational by 2002. This means launching all 840 satellites in two years, more than the rest of the world's satellite launches combined.

Most of the half-dozen serious competitors in the mobile satellite sweepstakes will probably drop out of the race eventually. Despite rosy predictions issued by each of the current contenders, there is no immediate, large-scale market for all the facilities they propose. According to telecom consultant Hershel Shosteck, the industry was in a "hysteria-driven speculative bubble. . . . The only question is when and how it will burst." Despite such skeptics, there will likely be one, perhaps two, satellite-based mobile networks operating profitably before the turn of the century.

Iridium and the other mobile satellite operators are the latest addition to the mix of U.S. master builders of the new high-capacity Meganet. Their success in creating an advanced communications system at home has energized Meganet development in the rest of the world. They have been quicker than their overseas competitors to recognize that their domestic and international operations are parts of an integrated global resource. One example is the 1997 decision by PanAmSat, a Connecticut-based satellite operator, to provide high-speed access to U.S. Internet services on its global network.[51]

U.S. firms may have given substantial reality to the Meganet idea, but they can only be a small part of its full implementation. A generation ago, most of the world's telecommunications resources were in the United States, including half the world's telephones. In the past twenty years, this ratio has been declining. This trend is bound to accelerate as Meganet expands in both geographic reach and range of services across the globe. Nevertheless, American master builders will continue to be a significant force in building the global Meganet. The U.S. domestic network is the largest demonstration of an advanced communications system, one that attempts to provide full access to a wide range of information resources. This goal is still imperfectly fulfilled, but its feasibility is being tested on a grand scale in the United States. Bringing it closer to full reality may be the most valuable contribution Americans can make to the global Meganet and to human society.

Meanwhile, the network's global evolution depends largely on actions taken in more than 180 other countries that will be linked to its advanced facilities. Thus, it is useful to look at how the telecom sectors in those countries are preparing for this prospect.

4

THE MASTER BUILDERS: THE INTERNATIONAL PLAYERS

When the advanced global Meganet is completed early in the twenty-first century, it will be a network of networks. Its linkage will be, at it is to some degree today, the digital technologies that will allow its separate parts—local, national, and global—to operate as a single unit. Beyond this commonality, the network mirrors the political, economic, and cultural diversity of almost 200 countries and territories around the globe.

The entire enterprise has a catch-as-catch-can aspect. There is no master plan or central organization that oversees Meganet's construction or manages its operations. The U.S. telecom companies described in Chapter 3 have an important but subordinate part in the process. The larger role will be played by telecom groups in countries other than the United States.

Overseas, Meganet's builders are the government agencies that have controlled local electronic communications for more than a century, beginning with the telegraph. Known as PTTs (for *p*osts, *t*elegraph, and *t*elephone services), their justification is a carefully nurtured political axiom that telecommunications services are a government responsibility, not a market commodity, something that until recently was never questioned in most countries.

Technology, economics, and politics are now combining to undermine this axiom. The PTT monopolies are based on two premises, neither of which work in the new communications environment. One is that control over communications is a sovereign right, a concept that is a throwback to a simpler age of kings and clerics who enforced their authority over books and other information sources. This is an anachronism. Information moves increasingly over high-speed digital channels whose content cannot be monitored and controlled.

The second justification for government control was that only a centralized telecom authority could ensure technical integrity and management efficiency. Any alternative, the argument went, would be chaotic. This claim has been overtaken in the new age of flexible networking by a wide variety of transnational information services that crisscross many networks, using common technical standards.[1]

America's experience in breaking up AT&T, its modified version of a PTT, exposed the fallacy of the efficiency argument. A monopoly may have been needed to build the early U.S. phone network, given the limited technology of the time. But by the late 1960s AT&T's dominance became a barrier to the introduction of advanced technologies and services. New telecom challengers, eager to exploit these resources, argued for opening up the entire telecom structure to competition. Ultimately, they won, thanks to a series of federal government decisions that eroded various parts of the AT&T monopoly and culminated in the 1984 divestiture of AT&T's local phone companies (the Baby Bells).

This latter event resonated throughout the world, for the same forces that led to the restructuring of the U.S. communications system are now at work in other countries. PTT monopolies are crumbling abroad, despite rear-guard resistance. The PTTs have not, however, marched quietly into oblivion. Their persistence reflects, in part, a deep-seated fear of change. As late as 1991, a British chancellor of the exchequer could declare in a House of Commons speech that mobile phones were one of the greatest scourges of modern life.

His attitude masked a general attitude among politicians that the common citizenry should be thankful for telecommunications services, however inadequate, that a beneficent government bestowed on them. There was also a pragmatic edge to this defense of the old ways. The PTTs were cash cows, filling government coffers and usually subsidizing postal services and other money-losing operations. The PTTs were the largest employers in some countries, with workforces eager to protect civil service benefits. Aside from citizens' normal grumbling about bad phone service, telecom issues inspire no great populist passion of the kind that sends protesters marching into the streets.

Nevertheless, the pressure for change has mounted abroad. It came first from local business communities, increasingly aware of the economic penalties that poor telecom services wrought in competitive global markets. A more parochial argument for reform played on fears that U.S. and Japanese superiority in telecom and information goods and services would overwhelm local economies. This fear was particularly strong in Western Europe, where U.S. and Japanese companies were establishing strong footholds in electronics production and marketing.

The loudest alarm bell was sounded by the French. An early critic was Parisian journalist Jean Jacques Serban-Schreiber, who in the 1960s wrote about *le défi américain*—the American challenge—to the French economy and culture. IBM was the enemy, he declared. The theme was taken up by others. A government study by two civil servants, Alain Minc and Simon Nora, stressed the need to protect French interests in the new U.S.-dominated communications era.[2] In the late 1970s, the influential Paris newspaper *Le Monde* documented, in a special report entitled "The Global Information War: IBM Is Watching You," the dangers involved in U.S. technological infiltration.

The French were the most articulate promoters of the Americans-are-coming theme. Their call to arms was picked up by other Europeans. They saw that the Americans and the Japanese were better prepared to operate in the regional free trade economy championed by the twelve-nation European Community. Local investments by U.S. and Japanese firms challenged the Europeans in their own backyard, particularly in the high-tech communications and information sectors. A European Community survey in the 1970s of West European electronics industries warned of the extent of this foreign invasion. It pointed out that European companies accounted for only 15 percent of global trade in telecommunications goods and services.[3] The survey concluded with a bottom-line indictment of European regional communications, fragmented at the time into twelve separate telecom systems, and the similarly divided industrial base.

The Europeans' initial reaction was to circle the wagons to protect their communications sectors. They raised trade barriers and increased subsidies favoring their national industries. Inevitably, these defenses failed. The first to recognize the need for a more positive approach were the British. A Conservative government, led by a no-nonsense prime minister, Margaret Thatcher, decided in the early 1980s to open up the telecom sector to competition. Her policy was clearly influenced by the U.S. decision to break up AT&T. Foreign companies were actively encouraged to move into the British electronics sector, directly or through partnerships with domestic firms. The Thatcher government also decided to end the century-old national PTT monopoly.

This monopoly was run by the British Post Office, a reliable hand at delivering the mail but considerably less adept in dealing with rapid changes in telecommunications. The British phone system could not meet the country's economic and social needs. Telephone penetration had fallen well below that of other industrialized countries. In 1981, Post Office telecom operations were transferred to a privatized entity, British Telecom. It was the first move toward a competitive telecom market by any industrialized country outside the United States—but it was only a half-step. A second company, Mercury Communications, was given limited rights to compete against British Telecom. The result was a duopoly—a far cry from the vigorous competition set in motion by the breakup of AT&T in the United States.

Mercury had an important advantage. It was owned by Cable & Wireless (C&W), an old-line telecom carrier with more than a century of experience in serving Britain's imperial outposts in Asia, Africa, and Latin America. In the postcolonial era, C&W continued to thrive as a supplier of telecom services in these regions. It also became the fifth largest supplier of telephone services in the United States.

Under the tutelage of Cable & Wireless, Mercury became a feisty competitor to British Telecom. By the early 1990s, it had captured 10 percent of domestic phone business, mainly in the business community, and almost 20 percent of British Telecom's former overseas traffic. Meanwhile, both British Telecom and Mercury soon faced unprecedented competition from a new direction—U.S. communications companies. Attracted by the more open environment, U.S. firms, led by the regional Bells, moved into the British market. By 1995, the regional Bells were the dominant owners of British cable systems. A year later, the British government licensed AT&T to offer long-distance and international telephone services throughout the country.

Confronted with new competition, British Telecom dropped its monopoly mentality and bureaucratic practices. In addition to competing vigorously against Mercury and AT&T, it took on a group of newer British companies that were offering wireless telephone and other advanced services. In 1996, British Telecom began providing British households Internet access, expanding on its earlier Internet services for businesses and schools. The company projected that its Internet revenues would reach $3 billion by the end of the decade.[4]

British Telecom has also been newly active in international markets. It bought a 20 percent stake in MCI in 1994 (see Chapter 3), which gave it special access to the U.S. market. It consolidated its position as a major global player in November 1996 with a proposal for a full merger with MCI costing $21 billion. When the merger becomes fully operational, the new firm, Concert Global Communications, will have annual revenues of more than $40 billion, serving almost 50 million customers in seventy countries.

British Telecom has also adopted a strategy of alliances and investments in Western Europe as part of a multibillion-dollar gamble to become Europe's dominant telecommunications company early in the new century. Its business partnerships include operations in Germany, France, Italy, Spain, the Netherlands, and Sweden.[5] Britain's 1991 decision to privatize its phone system was watched closely by its partners in the European Community. The decision received close attention, particularly at European Community headquarters in Brussels. There was a good reason for this: The European Community's grand plan for a regional economic union was stalling in the mid-1980s. European Community officials recognized that telecom reform was one of the actions needed to break the gridlock.[6] An advanced regional economy could not be sustained when its communications resources were divided among twelve national systems, all of them government monopolies (except in Britain).

The European Community's first step was to issue a comprehensive proposal, known as the Green Paper, on the need for regional telecom reform. The Green Paper focused on two major goals: first, to develop an efficient regional network to support EC economic integration; second, to strengthen Europe's communications and services industries to compete regionally and in global markets.[7] The Green Paper's reform proposals were advanced by another 1987 EC initiative, the Single Europe Act. This legislation was a blueprint for speeding up the economic integration of Western Europe. (The plan's shorthand name, EC-92, reflected a completion goal of December 1992.)

European telecommunications was a prime consideration in the EC-92 revitalization effort. Telecom reform was not, however, a popular issue among most EC governments, primarily because it would require a radical restructuring of their cozy, profitable phone monopolies. Nevertheless, they grudgingly accepted the fact that organizing their national systems into an effective regional network was crucial to EC-92 goals. The point was made in a survey of data networking in the region, sponsored by Eusidic, a private association of information services suppliers. The survey showed that almost 25 percent of Eusidic members' international calls on public data networks were not completed, mainly due to PTT inefficiencies.[8] The Eusidic survey exposed the disadvantages of tolerating telecom capabilities that trailed behind those of Europe's trade competitors, notably the Americans and Japanese. The point was made forcefully by a French industry minister, Alain Madelin: "Europe has no choice but to become a third pole of equivalent weight to the U.S. and Japan. Or else, poor in raw materials, politically divided, technologically dependent, it will in fact become nothing more than a subcontractor for the other two."[9]

The PTT traditionalists fought a rear-guard action to delay telecom reforms. They were initially successful in protecting their core business—ordinary telephone services—by having it declared off-limits in the reform process. This restriction put 95 percent of their operations beyond the reach of reformers at the EC's Brussels headquarters. Nevertheless, a coalition of EC bureaucrats and European business leaders pressed for changes. New EC laws and regulations mandated the reorganization of the PTTs and the phased introduction of private-sector competition in data networking and other value-added services (i.e., everything but ordinary phone service). These were limited gains but they were effective in breaking down monopoly barriers throughout the region. In the end, competition in conventional voice telephone service was added to the list of EC telecom reforms. January 1998 was established as the target date for ending this last vestige of PTT monopoly control in most of the fifteen member countries of the now renamed European Union.

Meanwhile, EU members have been experiencing a rapid expansion of wireless services, including cellular phones. It is the fastest-growing sector in European communications, with an annual growth rate of 60 percent. By the mid-1990s, sales of wireless instruments began outpacing those of conventional wired phones.[10] A 1995 survey by Goldman Sachs, the New York investment house, projected a total enterprise value of more than $100 billion for the European mobile communications industry, making it larger than the entire regional telecommunications sector of a few years earlier.[11] The wireless sector in Europe has seen an unprecedented flurry of mergers and acquisitions in recent years, with more than 100 deals (worth more than $4 billion) consummated since 1992.[12]

The old PTTs will be a powerful factor in Europe's newly competitive telecom environment. They still control most of the network structure. New telecom companies will have to rely heavily on the former PTTs to supply the circuits they need to deliver telephone and other competitive services to customers.

But this dependence may not last. In 1994, the EU issued regulations that would allow other telecom service providers to set up their own networks. The general assumption at the time was that it would be years before private networks could offer significant competition to networks controlled by the newly deregulated PTTs. However, competition has cropped up from an unexpected source—Europe's railroads. In 1995, Hermes Europe Railtel, a consortium of eleven railroads, announced plans for a $1.2-billion trans-European advanced network along the rights-of-way of its owners. The consortium will be a "carriers' carrier," selling telecom capacity to phone companies and corporations.[13]

Another group of challengers to the former PTTs are the so-called resellers. These are firms that lease lines wholesale from traditional carriers and then market them to customers at discount rates. By 1997, four U.S. companies (IDB Worldcom, International Discount Telecommunications, Esprit, and Viatel) were active in this business. Their success in signing up customers put pressure on the high tariffs charged by the former PTTs throughout Western Europe.

In balance, the EU reform initiatives have been successful. By 1997, they had reduced most of the communications barriers that had held back Western Europe's transition to an integrated regional economy. A newly competitive telecom industry has emerged as one of the strongest sectors in the European economy. In the mid-1990s, telecommunications generated more profits than any other sector, according to the Paris-based Organization for Economic Cooperation and Development.[14]

These changes also strengthened Europe's role in building the global Meganet. The EU set its goal in this area in a key document adopted in June 1994, *Europe and the Global Information Society*.[15] The report laid out a series of recommendations aimed at challenging the U.S. and Japanese leads in the global communications and information sectors. "A race is on at the global level," declared Martin Bangemann, the EU official who was the leading author of the report. "Those countries which adapt themselves most quickly will set technological standards for those who follow."[16]

Despite this warning, West European efforts to develop advanced communications and information resources have lagged. A 1997 study sponsored by the EU's Council of Ministers called for urgent actions to close what it called a disturbing competitiveness gap with the United States and Japan. "Europe's progress in closing the gap is slow or even non-existent," the report said. The main reason for this, it noted, was a fragmented information and communications sector with differing legal, technical, and commercial standards in each of the EU's fifteen nations.[17]

The report emphasized the importance of private-sector involvement in building Europe's advanced telecom systems. It marked a long ideological jump from the monopolistic attitudes and actions that had governed the region's telecommunications only a decade before. The European Union followed up on the June 1994 recommendations by allocating $175 billion for upgrading the region's telecommunications infrastructure by the end of the 1990s. The Union also authorized the European Telecommunications Office, located in Copenhagen, which would speed up the paperwork involved in authorizing private companies to operate across European Union borders.

Despite the inroads made by new private enterprises, the former PTTs still control most of the region's telecom resources. However, their primacy will be under heavy competitive pressure by the end of the decade. This has already stimulated a boom in European communications. Arthur D. Little Inc., a U.S.-based market research firm, predicts that telecom and telecom-related sectors will overtake automobiles as the leading regional industry within a decade. Revenues for the telecom sector are projected at $516 billion, as opposed to $390 billion for autos. The revamped PTTs will have the largest share of this market, but they will be challenged increasingly by scrappy newcomers, particularly after the transition to full competition in 1998.

This transition to a competitive environment takes different forms in each of the European Union's fifteen member countries, reflecting their political, economic, and cultural differences. As we have seen, Britain began earlier and traveled further than the others in creating a Meganet-based information society. Britain has, in many ways, set the pace for its European Union partners.

The bellwether countries during the next few years will be Germany and France. Both moved cautiously to meet European Union mandates to restructure their telecom monopolies, the two largest in Europe. The French PTT was a classic example of national *dirigisme*, the policy of government control over the pace and direction of a centralized economy. The policy worked reasonably well in the first years after World War II when the French economy was being rebuilt. By the 1980s, however, *dirigisme* had become a serious handicap.

The French PTT, along with other large, government-owned sectors, was part of the problem. In response to increasing public disaffection with the inadequacies of the telephone system, the government undertook a massive upgrading of the network in the 1970s. The result was to give France the leading digital network in Europe, with facilities well ahead of any other country. Among the network's innovations was an electronic consumer information service, a simple version of today's America Online and CompuServe services. Known as Minitel, the service allows French households to tap into a wide range of information resources through a small computer monitor attached to the telephone. Minitel monitors have been installed in more than 6 million homes, offering access to more than 24,000 local and national information services provided by more than 10,000 companies. These range from weather reports and train schedules to horoscopes and personal messages.[18]

During the upgrade, the French government kept tight control over the system throughout the 1980s. Eventually the pressure for reform had its effect. Much of the pressure came from the French business community, frustrated over the slow introduction of the advanced telecom services they needed. Pressure also came from Brussels, where EC bureaucrats were pushing for an end to PTTs.

The French government slowly retreated. In 1989, the PTT ministry was reorganized to conform with an EC mandate to separate regulatory functions from operational functions. The operational part of the old PTT was transferred to a privatized corporation, France Telecom. Although all of the assets of France Telecom continued to be owned by the government, the change did mark the first in a series of hesitant steps toward more competition. Government control over France Telecom was modified again in the mid-1990s, when outside organizations were allowed to own a limited share of its equity capital. In 1996, legislation was passed that completed the organization's conversion from a government agency into a partially privatized joint stock company. France Telecom made its first major offering of public shares in April 1997. However, the government continued to hold a majority stake in the new operation.

France Telecom's annual revenues of more than $30 billion in the mid-1990s, along with control of more than 90 percent of the domestic market, attracted strong investor interest. Moreover, the company entered into promising international telecom ventures, including its 1994 alliance with U.S.-based Sprint and Germany's Deutsche Telekom.

In January 1996, the French government announced a comprehensive proposal to meet the EU's 1998 competition deadline. The plan assigned a continuing strong role for France Telecom.[19] By June 1996, the French parliament passed legislation that deregulated French telecommunications well beyond the requirements laid down by the EU. French private firms, meanwhile, were preparing for the new competitive era. A construction company, Bouygues, and a water company, Compagnie Generale des Eaux (CGE), began competing with France Telecom in the cellular phone sector. In 1994, CGE strengthened its cellular operations within France by taking in U.S.-based Southwestern Bell as a minority investor. In turn, CGE took a 10 percent stake in Southwestern Bell's mobile phone franchises in the Washington, D.C., and Baltimore areas. In 1996, another U.S.-based firm, MSF Communications (now MSF Worldcom), became the first company to get a license in France to create a full-service telecom network independent of France Telecom. Although the license limited its operations to serving business customers, MSF Communications moved quickly ahead to build a sixteen-mile fiber-optic network in the center of Paris, running its circuits through the city sewers.[20]

The French government has also given serious consideration to the creation of a national *autoroute d'information*, or information superhighway. The plan, authored by Gérard Théry, a former France Telecom managing director, proposed a fiber-optic network linking every household and business establishment by 2015 at a cost of about $30 billion. This bold plan was generally welcomed, but critics questioned its apparent intent to rely on France Telecom rather than private-sector businesses to carry it out.[21]

Germany, with the largest telecom network in Europe, also prepared for the EU's 1998 competition deadline. In the postwar years, the national PTT, Deutsche Bundespost, was an outsized power, with $31 billion in annual revenues in 1991. It employed the largest labor force in the country. It was, moreover, protected by a constitutional provision that called for a complex legislative process to change its structure. There has been more than a little rigidity in the way the Germans have dealt with the mandate to introduce competition.

Partisan politics came into play. The governing Christian Democratic Party generally favored reforming Deutsche Bundespost. It did not, however, have the necessary parliamentary votes to override the constitutional strictures. The minority Socialists, beholden to the telecom unions, were opposed to any radical changes. Under pressure to conform to the mandate to deregulate, the government eventually pushed through legislation in 1994 that started the privatization process. Deutsche Bundespost's telecom and postal operations were separated. A private corporation, Deutsche Telekom, was created to replace the state monopoly.

The final step in opening up German telecommunications was taken in July 1996. The parliament passed a comprehensive law that removed almost all restrictions to full competition. The law provided that any enterprise could get a license to operate a communications facility. An independent regulatory agency, similar to the FCC in the United States, was authorized to monitor the transition to a competitive industry. "Market-dominating enterprises" (i.e., Deutsche Telekom) were subject to a special code of conduct in this transition.[22] Germany's privatization timetable was complicated by a traumatic political event—the 1989 collapse of the communist regime in East Germany. West Germany faced the harsh imperative of integrating its own vibrant economy with a bankrupt one. A major problem was the dilapidated state of East Germany's telecom structure. Replacing it ultimately cost more than $40 billion. Ironically, the eastern portion of Germany's network is now more technically advanced than the western, since much of it is entirely new.

Integrating the two systems made Deutsche Telekom the third largest network in the world, behind AT&T and Japan's Nippon Telephone and Telegraph (NTT). However, the integration effort left

Deutsche Telekom with a huge debt, a factor that hastened the privatization process because of the need for new funding. The 1996 sale of equity shares in the privatized Deutsche Telekom amounted to more than $9 billion. It was the biggest financial offering of its kind ever traded in Germany. This huge stock deal opened the free market era in the German telecom sector with a flourish. Although the sector will not be fully competitive until 1998, private firms surged into those limited areas where competition was already allowed under EU rules. The newcomers have ranged from giant corporate conglomerates to small firms looking for a niche in a market that could mushroom into the country's largest economic sector early in the twenty-first century.

By 1997, more than a half-dozen private companies had entered the race to supply voice and data services to corporate customers in Germany. They include the Thyssen steel conglomerate, which hoped to be the country's number-two telecom operator by the end of the decade. By 1995, Thyssen had already lined up partners (including Bell Atlantic) to build a digital cellular phone network to compete with Deutsche Telekom. At the same time, British Telecom allied itself with Viag, one of Germany's top-ten industrial groups, to offer voice and data services to national and international companies. These moves assure that Deutsche Telekom will face heavy competition in the race to build Germany's part of Meganet.

The greatest challenge to Deutsche Telekom in the postliberalization era may come from DBKom a consortium formed in 1996. Its major investors are Mannesmann, a large industrial group, and Deutschebahn, the German railroad system. The group also has international partners, including Unisource, an alliance that includes AT&T and several West European telecom operators. DBKom's major asset is a 24,000-mile communications network running alongside Deutschebahn's tracks. This network, originally built for the railroad's internal communications, will be expanded to serve corporations and the general public.[23]

As it prepared for stiff competition on the domestic front, Deutsche Telekom expanded its international operations. Its first outside venture took place in 1994 when it joined France Telecom in buying a 20 percent stake in U.S.-based Sprint. Since then it has invested in telecommunications ventures in China, Russia, Ukraine, Malaysia, Switzerland, Austria, and the Netherlands. Most of these investments have been made by its DeTeMobil mobile telephone subsidiary, which by 1997 had become the world's third largest mobile network operator.[24]

Meanwhile, PTTs in other West European countries have been adapting to the liberalization rules issuing from EU headquarters in Brussels. Italy's perennially chaotic telecom system was operated by five state-controlled companies before it was integrated into a single Telecom Italia in 1994. The new company is the sixth largest telecom enterprise in the world. In 1996, the Italian government took the first steps toward privatizing its telecommunications operations by proposing a $16-billion sell-off.[25] Like its counterparts elsewhere in Europe, the newly privatized Italian company will face stiff competition in the post-1998 competitive environment. A leading challenger is Olivetti, the Italian computer group. In March 1996, Olivetti announced plans for a long-distance network as an international joint venture that includes Bell Atlantic.[26]

Unable to compete directly with the big telecom powers, former PTTs in smaller European countries are forming alliances among themselves. Tele Danmark, the Danish operator, linked up with Ameritech and Singapore Telecom in 1996 to buy a one-half interest in Belgium's national telecom group. At the same time, the Irish phone company, Telecom Eireann, took on Dutch and Swedish telecom groups as strategic partners.[27]

The Dutch added a special flourish by privatizing their telecom and postal systems at the same time. Both systems are moneymakers for the Dutch, who have been innovators in setting up public demonstrations of information age resources. One project, dubbed Digital City, gives Amsterdam residents access to a wide range of interactive database services on home computers and at public information kiosks. The services are similar to those offered by CompuServe and America Online—but with a significant difference. Digital City is, in effect, a public utility, with access provided for the price of a telephone call.

The most surprising example of European telecom reform and renewal occurred in Spain. Its PTT, Telefonica de Espana, faced extinction when competition was introduced. Its service was poor, and millions of households were on waiting lists for telephones. Nevertheless, Telefonica responded energetically to the EC-92 call for telecom modernization. It installed advanced network equipment and added 1 million telephone lines per year in the early 1990s. Waiting lists for telephones virtually disappeared.

Telefonica's operational reputation had been so poor that it had asked the European Union in Brussels for a five-year extension beyond the Union's 1998 deadline for opening all its services to competition. The company reversed itself in 1994, announcing that it would follow the Union's fast-track timetable. By 1998, open competition is expected in a full range of telecom services. A consortium of Spanish and foreign investors (including U.S.-based Airtouch, a Pacific Telesis affiliate) was granted a license in 1994 to develop a second cellular network, competing against Telefonica. Meanwhile, the government sold its remaining shares in Telefonica in February 1997, completing the company's privatization.

Telefonica's vigorous domestic reforms are making a difference internationally. Its overseas affiliate, Telefonica Internacional, is a partner in telecom operations in Argentina, Chile, Venezuela, Colombia, Uruguay, and Puerto Rico, as well as in ventures in Portugal and Romania. Regarding the company's Latin American investments, Candido Velazquez, chairman of the international group, pointed out, "We decided it was time to share not only language and culture, but also business."[28] In fact, Telefonica has outmaneuvered a succession of U.S. and European companies seeking entry into the fast-growing Latin American market. It is the leading force in the region's telecommunications, serving more than 110 million customers—almost double its domestic base in Spain.[29]

In summary, Western Europe has made substantial progress toward bringing its telecom structure up to advanced Meganet standards. It still has a ways to go. Despite recent reforms, West European telecommunications is still a collection of fragmented national networks. Although privatized, these local giants have generally been reluctant to move out beyond their national frontiers. Their market dominance has held back private operators from competing to build the cross-border facilities that would give Western Europe the strong regional telecom links it needs. As a result, the region still lacks the strong synergy of continental-sized networks and competitive markets—the combination that drives the U.S. telecommunications sector. The European transition to a mix of former monopolies and new competitors may have to be closely regulated at the regional level if the combination is to work. A European Union group has proposed a European version of the FCC to do this. Whether or not Western Europe's still fragile political unity will support this kind of regional regulation remains to be seen. The difficulties are summed up in a small but telling instance of regulatory gridlock among European Union members: the effort to get agreement on a single standard for ordinary household wall plugs. There are still a half-dozen plug standards in the region despite twenty years of negotiations.[30] Europe's overall effectiveness in the global Meganet will depend on how well it can settle problems like this.

On the other side of the globe, the Japanese are building Meganet resources in their own way. Japan was among the first countries to recognize the importance of making the transition from an industrialized society to an information-based, postindustrial model. The subject was first articulated in the late 1960s in a White Paper issued by the Ministry of International Trade and Industry.[31] MITI is the government agency that guided Japan's successful emergence as a global economic power after World War II. Its White Paper argued that Japan's future lay in exploiting information and communications resources. The document was twenty years ahead of its time in identifying the importance of advanced Meganet resources to economic development.[32]

The MITI document served as a general blueprint for Japanese industrial policy in the electronics sector. Part of the policy was to encourage pilot projects throughout the country, demonstrating advanced telecommunications and information uses. The first showcase demonstrations took place in the late 1970s near Osaka, where hundreds of households were wired with fiber-optic cables transmitting a range of interactive multimedia services. The government also sponsored "science cities," huge research parks where billions of yen were invested in R&D of advanced communications and information technologies.

Not all these initiatives were successful. One innovative effort, known as the Fifth Generation Project, aimed to give Japan a leading role in computers. The field had been dominated by IBM, whose research labs were the seedbeds for the first four generations of computer technology. Announced by MITI with great fanfare in 1982, the goal of the Fifth Generation Project was to make a quantum leap ahead of IBM, using techniques that would approximate human-style reasoning to solve problems.[33]

A less publicized objective was to jump-start the Japanese computer industry, making it more competitive in world markets. Japan's computer companies were conspicuous abroad by their absence. At the time the Fifth Generation Project was announced, the big three Japanese computer makers, Fujitsu, NEC, and Hitachi, held three-quarters of the domestic market among them but less than 5 percent of markets in the rest of the world.

The Fifth Generation Project sent shock waves throughout the U.S. electronics industry. U.S. entrepreneurs feared that that the Japanese were about to do to Silicon Valley what they had done to Detroit. Fifth Generation, the argument went, was another example of how MITI and other government agencies collaborated with Japan's big conglomerates to challenge U.S. technical and manufacturing strength in critical markets.

These fears were decidedly premature. Despite the massive amounts of money and other resources poured into Fifth Generation, it soon bogged down. The effort resulted in important research advances but not nearly enough to make the generational leap it had originally promised. The project was closed down in 1992.

Meanwhile, Japan's other Meganet-related projects moved ahead. These included MITI's long-term proposal to build a high-speed telecom network as the central facility for a Japanese information society. The project centered around Nippon Telephone and Telegraph, the government-owned telecommunications monopoly. NTT was, and is, a formidable power, with a capitalization ($135 billion in 1996) that made it the largest quoted company in the world until it was displaced by General Electric in 1996.[34] Prompted in part by the U.S. decision to break up AT&T, the Japanese government privatized NTT in 1985 but kept two-thirds of its stock in government hands.

NTT also kept much of its traditional control over the basic national network. Competition was opened only in long-distance networks and in specialized value-added services such as data networking. By 1996, there were almost 3,000 carriers competing against NTT, most of them smaller local operators.[35] The new entrants proved to be agile in sparring with NTT's bureaucracy-bound operations. Three private long-distance companies captured 30 percent of the national traffic in a few years. They also pushed down the price of phone calls, helped by the fact that many Japanese phones are fitted with a microprocessor chip that automatically routes calls via the cheapest long-distance firm.

Despite these inroads, NTT still dominates Japanese telecommunications. Several attempts by the government to break up the company in the early 1990s were defeated.[36] The company uses its formidable political and economic clout to protect its dominant position. This has had the effect of slowing down the pace of Japanese advances in adapting to new information age resources. For instance, the proportion of mobile phone users, where NTT had 60 percent of the market, has been among the lowest of any industrialized country. NTT's plans for installing a national fiber-optic network is scheduled to be completed in 2015, well after comparable U.S. and European projects.[37] In an attempt to improve NTT's performance, the government approved a plan in 1997 to reorganize the company, splitting it into three separate phone networks. The assets of the three new entities are owned by a restructured NTT holding company. Meanwhile, the Japanese government has taken a new look at the country's information age prospects. A 1994 MITI report urged that the Japanese information highway infrastructure be completed by 2010, five years earlier than planned by NTT.[38] The Ministry of Posts and Telecommunications (MPT) also pressed for faster action, implicitly confirming the need to catch up with the Americans.

In a report that echoed MITI's arguments, the MPT's Telecommunications Council called for a "shift of perspective in which the goods- and energy-oriented 20th century gives way to the information- and knowledge-oriented 21st century based on an infocommunications infrastructure. . . . High-performance infocommunications is the most important type of infrastructure Japan can acquire as it works to solve its problems and build the intellectually creative society of the 21st century."[39]

Japan's plan for an infocommunications society has some curious aspects. One is an apparent reluctance by its citizens to use some of the electronic resources for which its industries are justly famous. In the mid-1990s, only about 6 percent of Japanese homes subscribed to cable TV, compared with more than 60 percent in the United States.[40] Internet use in Japan is rising, but it is far below that of other industrialized countries.[41] As a group, Japanese executives can be viewed as being behind the curve, so to speak, technologically (a 1995 joint U.S.-Japan survey of their computer usage found that 8 percent of Japanese executives considered computers essential to their work; for U.S. executives, the figure was 64 percent).[42]

The rush to improve high-performance infocommunications was, in part, a reaction to the economic shocks Japan suffered in the early 1990s. The yen fell from its commanding perch among the world's currencies, reflecting a decline in Japan's extraordinary economic strength. The "export miracle" faltered, forcing a domestic review of Japan's place in a changing global economy. Information society concepts advanced by MITI and others took on practical meaning as leading-edge trade issues. Japan, in effect, acknowledged that it trailed the United States in critical information highway technologies, including multimedia software and advanced microprocessing.[43] Even when Japan became rattled by economic setbacks, none of the global competition questioned that it would rebound, particularly in the markets created by information age demands. Japan is rebounding, but in its own way. Unlike their counterparts in the United States and Europe, Japanese telecommunications companies have been generally reluctant to negotiate alliances with potential overseas partners, either for developing their domestic network or for moving into foreign telecom ventures.

NTT, in particular, has few foreign involvements. Until recently, it limited its overseas activities to providing consultant services for Japanese companies building telecom networks in other countries. NTT ventured into a foreign market for the first time in 1993. It was a small step, involving the purchase of 1.2 percent of Nextel, a New York–based digital wireless operator, for $74 million. In 1995, it formed a partnership with Britain's C&W to promote mobile phone operations outside the Japanese market.[44] NTT has also linked up with three U.S. software firms—Microsoft, Silicon Graphics, and General Magic—as part of its plans to expand beyond traditional telecom network operations. In 1997, NTT shifted its cautious strategy on international operations when it announced that it would expand its overseas market presence by leasing lines from foreign carriers. This strategy set NTT apart from other major carriers such as AT&T and British Telecom, all of whom were relying on alliances and mergers to expand their global presence.[45]

Meanwhile, the traditionally closed Japanese telecom market is facing outside competition. U.S. firms sought entry, with painfully slow success, for more than twenty years. The Japanese government set up regulatory and technical roadblocks, pressured by the domestic electronics industry's fear of losing its grip on the home market. The result was a series of sharp confrontations in U.S.-Japan trade relations. The situation was aggravated by a heavy electronics trade imbalance between the two countries that favored Japan.

Japan's resistance to competition in its domestic electronics markets began to give way somewhat in the early 1990s. Motorola, the world's largest mobile communications firm, got permission to sell its products to a Japanese cellular company. In another instance, two U.S. firms, Airtouch, a cellular telephone operator, and GTE, were allowed in as minority partners (at 4.5 percent each) in Digital TU-KA Chugoku Co., a Hiroshima-based cellular network.

The Japanese cable-TV sector, long restricted by government regulations, will likely see significant expansion as the result of a 1995 decision by Time Warner, the U.S. media giant, to form a joint venture with two Japanese companies. The venture intends to spend $400 million to develop major cable-TV systems. A more flamboyant foreign investment deal was struck in 1996 when media magnate Rupert Murdoch teamed up with a Japanese partner to take a 21 percent stake in Asahi TV, a major television network. It was an unprecedented breakthrough for one of Japan's most tightly regulated industries.[46]

Japan, Western Europe, and America: these are the information age powers in Meganet development. However, a group of so-called second-tier countries is also contributing substantially to Meganet progress.

Canada and Australia, at opposite ends of the Pacific Ocean, have strong Meganet capabilities. The Canadian telecom network is the equal of its U.S. counterpart in quality and breadth of services. Although it is dominated by Stentor, a powerhouse group of nine provincial phone companies, the overall market is increasingly competitive. Competition was introduced in the long-distance market in 1992. The government took another long step toward a liberalized market in August 1996 when it announced plans for open competition among telephone and cable-TV companies. The move was especially significant since Canada has one of the world's highest cable-TV penetration rates (about 80 percent of households).[47] U.S. companies, including AT&T, MCI, and Sprint, are major players in Canadian telecommunications. Canada is, in fact, the largest single market for U.S. telecom companies: "If you are going to expand globally, you have to be there," according to John Cahill, a Sprint executive.[48]

Korea, Taiwan, China, and Singapore are developing advanced Meganet resources at a rapid clip. Singapore has transformed itself into a high-tech center, an "information island" in both a geographical and figurative sense. It is the most advanced producer of information goods and services, on a per capita basis, in the East Asian region. These Asian countries are exceptions.[49]

Most of the other 150 countries in Asia, Africa, and Latin America are only beginning the transition to modern communications systems. Africa is the most marginalized region of the world in terms of telecom resources. It probably has suffered a net decrease in per capita telecom resources in recent years, when measured against the region's explosive population growth. The Middle East contains a patchwork of networks, ranging from Saudi Arabia's sophisticated system, linking cities and desert tents, to the ragged facilities available in countries outside those that are oil-rich. Nations that emerged from the breakup of the former Soviet Union and the newly independent countries of Eastern Europe are all struggling with neglected communications needs, a legacy of the communist era.

In Latin America, several countries are emerging as candidates for fast-track Meganet development. Mexico is well on its way to completing an advanced network as the result of privatizing Telmex, its national PTT, in the late 1980s. More recently, Mexico's government has opened most telecommunications services to full competition.

The innovator in Latin American telecom is Chile. It was the first country in the region to privatize its domestic system. In addition to upgrading local communications, the main private company, ENTEL, has moved into the international field, with alliances and investments throughout the Western Hemisphere. A more than symbolic turning point in the history of Latin American communications took place in 1994, when ENTEL became majority owner of a Miami-based company, AmericaTel, which provides satellite-based services throughout the hemisphere. After a century, in which *Yanqui* telecom colonization of the region was the norm, a Latin American enterprise had turned the tables.

In Chapter 8 we take a closer look at telecom developments in these emerging economies. Collectively, they represent the largest market for Meganet expansion in the coming decade.

A special group of Meganet builders is the international satellite organizations. The leader is Intelsat, the oldest and largest of the satellite networkers. For three decades, it has been the single most important force in validating the idea of a universal global network. Intelsat gave political and economic reality to the Meganet idea. Newer technologies have since been added to the Meganet mix. None of them, however, can match the satellites' capability of supplying communications services between any two places in the world.

Intelsat links hundreds of national and regional ground networks into a world system. Its technological resources are unmatched. In 1965, its first satellite had 240 circuits and operated only in the North Atlantic region. Thirty years later, there are more than twenty-five Intelsat satellites providing services to users in more than 180 countries and territories on all continents, including Antarctica. The network carries more than half of all international phone traffic and virtually all transoceanic television broadcasts. It also supplies the domestic services for more than thirty developing countries.

Each of the satellites in the current generation of Intelsat "birds" has a capacity of 112,500 digital phone circuits and three video channels. The early Intelsat satellites provided only limited services to huge earth stations, using 100-foot dishes that cost tens of millions of dollars. The current generation, the Intelsat 8 series, can deliver services to inexpensive earth terminals that are as small as a pie plate.

Intelsat's relative strength as the leading global network is currently being challenged as new technologies threaten its economic base. Fiber-optic cables were still a laboratory experiment in the 1960s when Intelsat was created. These high-capacity cables now cover the globe in networks that compete directly with satellites, particularly on international routes. This competition is strongest in the North Atlantic and North Pacific regions, where Intelsat has traditionally earned more than 80 percent of its revenues.

Another challenge to Intelsat's competitive position is changes in its global traffic patterns. Thirty years ago, almost two-thirds of Intelsat traffic began or terminated in one country—the United States. This pattern has changed markedly: U.S. traffic now accounts for less than 25 percent of the total. The regions with the most rapid telecom growth are Asia, Africa, and Latin America. Because telecom traffic in these regions is expanding from a much smaller base, it provides less than 20 percent of Intelsat's revenues. The remainder has been redistributed among the northern industrialized countries.

Intelsat's future will also be affected by the current shift away from monopolies to private competition in many countries. Intelsat is a cartel, owned and controlled by more than 140 government-regulated

PTTs. The exception is the United States, whose Intelsat shares are owned by Comsat, created by Congress in 1962 to represent U.S. interests at Intelsat.[50]

This institutional arrangement has been eroding throughout the 1990s. Intelsat is still a cartel of its member governments, but it has increasingly been challenged by a new competitive mix of private satellite networks. A U.S. satellite firm, PanAmSat, a decade ago became the first organization to breach Intelsat's hold on global satellite services. Since then, many other private competitors to Intelsat have emerged. Satellite-based mobile phone operators such as Iridium and Globalstar are potentially formidable threats to Intelsat's strong position in transoceanic phone traffic.[51]

These changes have transformed the satellite business in recent years. Twenty years ago, Intelsat commanded the field. It now accounts for less than one-fifth of the $5 billion in communications satellite annual revenues, according to Euroconsult, publishers of *World Space Markets Survey*.[52] Most of the rest of the market is divided among private-sector systems or regional and national networks controlled by individual governments. A 1996 survey by *Via Satellite*, an industry trade journal, identified 157 communications satellites in orbit worldwide, with eighty-three more on order (less than thirty of them were Intelsat satellites).[53] Out of necessity, Intelsat is evolving from a protected cartel to a marketplace competitor. It has expanded its services to include a wide range of business-oriented innovations such as private-line network, high-speed data transmission, and video-conferencing. Besides diversifying its services, Intelsat has become more price-competitive, responding to competition from a dozen private satellite operators in the Atlantic and Pacific regions—its two most important revenue sources.

At the same time, Intelsat's major technological rival, submarine fiber-optic cable networks, has been expanding. In two years, from 1993 to 1995, the capacity of international fiber-optic circuits tripled. Bruce Crockett, a Comsat executive, pointed out that these new cables had enough *unused* capacity in the mid-1990s to absorb all of Comsat's services to Europe, the Mediterranean, the Middle East, East Asia, and the Pacific Islands.[54]

Restructuring an organization as big and complex as Intelsat is a difficult job. Nevertheless, with twenty-one satellites in orbit and thirteen more to be launched before the end of the decade, Intelsat is a formidable presence. A fully privatized, unregulated Intelsat could probably drive most of its competitors out of business.

This is unlikely to happen. First, the commercial satellite lobby is powerful worldwide. It is not about to allow any Intelsat reorganization plan that threatens the economic interests of its members. Second, some of Intelsat's functions will be hard to privatize. Under the terms of the international treaty that created it, the organization is committed to providing services to all parts of the globe.

This has meant, in effect, that revenues from heavy traffic among prosperous countries—particularly in the North Atlantic—subsidize "thin route" communications in Asia, Africa, and Latin America. Intelsat supplies services to these poorer regions in a way that no private system could afford to do. Cutting back or withdrawing these services would be a serious blow to global Meganet expansion.[55]

Intelsat will probably be restructured as a hybrid private-public organization before the end of the decade. It will be regulated in ways that create safeguards against its domination of the market. Its mandate to provide universal service will also be modified to spread the risks involved in supplying unprofitable services to developing countries. A plan incorporating these ideas was submitted by the U.S. government in 1995. However it is reorganized, Intelsat will continue to play a strong role in the worldwide Meganet.[56]

These changes are part of the many adjustments needed to create the advanced Meganet. Its intercontinental links (satellites and fiber-optic cables) already give the system worldwide reach, connecting 180 or more national networks. Meganet will be a reality when these global and local resources converge in a network providing services to everyone—even in the most remote places on earth.

MEGANET TRADE: THE HARDWARE BUILDERS

Meganet is a structure made up of billions of components, from ten-ton satellites to ten-ounce telephones. Most of these parts are products of the electronics industry, which replaced automobiles as the world's leading industrial sector in the 1990s.

The global network's needs are driving this expansion. In the mid-1990s, global trade in information and telecommunications equipment rose faster than in any other manufacturing sector.[1] Electronics is such a sprawling business that there are no reliable figures on its overall production. Most economists agree that its output exceeds $1 trillion in value annually. These products are triggering massive changes in other industries that rely on Meganet resources in their own production and marketing activities.

The new upsurge in electronics is also changing old trade patterns. The sector's production resources are still largely concentrated in the industrialized nations of the North Atlantic region. But this pattern is shifting. In the mid-1990s, the eighteen countries that make up the Asia Pacific Economic Cooperation Forum included the fastest-growing economies on earth. The World Trade Organization estimates gross domestic production in East Asian countries, averaged annually, will grow at a rate of 7.6 percent in the years up to 2003, compared with 2.7 percent in the industrialized West. Telecommunications and information resources play an especially important role in these newly expanding Asian economies.[2] A similar pattern is emerging in Latin America, where the Organization of American States has estimated that more than $70 billion will be needed by the end of the decade just to maintain current telephone line per capita levels.[3]

These developments are changing a sector that was until recently a staid, conservative business. Only a handful of countries, led by the United States, have a significant manufacturing capability for telecommunications and information services equipment. Until the 1980s, the sector was dominated by two companies—AT&T in communications and IBM in computers. Each firm had the technological edge in its respective field. Other companies had to adapt to their standards. AT&T's manufacturing arm, Western Electric, produced half the world's telecommunications products. IBM's lead position in the computer industry was so strong that it was known as Snow White in an industry characterized as Snow White and the Seven Dwarfs.

Both AT&T and IBM are still major players in the electronics trade. But electronics is no longer dominated by a few corporate giants. It is an intensely competitive industry that is in splendid disarray. Traditional boundaries are blurred as AT&T, IBM, and their rivals adjust to the technological, economic, and political changes brought about by Meganet expansion.

One part of the electronics sector plays a special role in this development. It is the semiconductor industry, which did not exist thirty years ago. Today it is a global enterprise, with more than $150 billion in annual sales. Its products—microchips—are the building blocks of Meganet. The global network would be much smaller today without the technical breakthroughs made by small teams of engineers in Texas and California, beginning in the 1950s.

These engineers—Willis Adcock, Jack Kilby, and Robert Noyce, among others—are largely unknown, but their collective achievement matches those of Morse, Bell, Marconi, and other electronic pioneers.[4] Their goal was to improve the transistor, the earliest semiconductor device, invented at AT&T's Bell Laboratories in the late 1940s. They wanted to put more transistor power into a smaller space. The obstacle was that the semiconductor material used in transistors, germanium, was not reliable at high temperatures. Germanium worked in small radios, which became the first mass application of transistor technology, but it didn't work well for big computers, where heat is a problem.

Their search for a substitute focused on silicon—highly refined sand. Silicon is brittle and hard to purify, but it can take the heat. Texas Instruments, a small startup company, assigned the project to two engineers, Gordon Teal and Willis Adcock. At a technical meeting in May 1954, Teal and Adcock displayed a small silicon chip hooked up to a record player. They turned on the player and dipped the chip into a pot of boiling oil. The record player continued to play. It was a turning point in the evolution of the information age.[5]

The race to exploit the new technology was on. Most of the competitors settled in an area south of San Francisco that was to become famous as Silicon Valley. In 1957, Robert Noyce, Gordon Moore, and others invested $500 apiece in a venture called Fairchild Semiconductor Corp. A decade later, Noyce and Moore broke away and founded Intel, now the world leader in advanced chips. (The name is a play on both "intelligence" and "integrated electronics.") The gains made by semiconductor technology since then can be measured by Intel's record in cramming more transistors on its fingernail-sized chips. The company's first microprocessor in 1971 contained 2,700 transistors. By 1996, its Pentium Pro chip held 5.5 million transistors. Intel is currently designing a dynamic random access memory chip that will store more than 1 billion bits of information. In more familiar terms, this gigabit chip will hold a quantity of data equivalent to Shakespeare's complete works ten times over.

Meanwhile, the U.S. semiconductor industry continues to ride the roller-coaster cycles of technological obsolescence and economic change that have marked it from its beginnings.[6] This includes increasingly strong competition from overseas chip producers. Clones of California's Silicon Valley have sprung up all over the world, from Scotland to Singapore. (The Scottish version is Silicon Glen.) The industry is remarkably ubiquitous in terms of where its production facilities are located. It is relatively free from the geographical constraints that bind heavy industry. At one point in the 1980s, Malaysia was the world's largest producer of chips. The industry's products are so small that a year's output of chips can be transported in a dozen large transport planes.

Chips are now embedded in almost every product that depends on electronics. In 1995, Ford Motors announced that the cost of chip-based electronic components in its cars averaged about $1,600—more than twice that of steel parts.[7] Dataquest, a market research firm, has estimated the world market for chip-filled automotive electronics at $57 billion by the end of the decade.[8] In 1996, Mercedes and IBM announced plans for a new generation of automotive electronics. In addition to managing a car's mechanical functions, the new system will give drivers access to satellite navigation systems as well as to computers controlling traffic in "intelligent highways." The system will also provide e-mail and fax links.[9]

The biggest users of chips, however, are Meganet and the machines attached to it, from telephones to TV sets. The growth of Meganet is the principle reason why the semiconductor market will more than double in size by the end of the decade, with $331 billion in annual revenues compared to $149 billion in 1995, according to the Dataquest survey.

Semiconductor market growth is impressive in itself. Equally remarkable is the rate at which the price of chips plunges even while their efficiency steadily improves. The result is a stunning paradox for the semiconductor industry and its customers. "The only thing that matters is if the exponential growth of your market is faster than the exponential decline of your prices," says George M.C. Fisher, chairman of Eastman Kodak. "Companies have to project out: 'How will I be competitive in a world in which technology will be virtually free?'"[10]

Despite these worries, the semiconductor industry's growth in the 1990s is limited generally by lagging production capacity. Although there are cyclical dips, rising demand usually outstrips supplies. The result is a race to expand production facilities throughout the world. New factories costing a total of $40 billion were on drawing boards or being built in 1996, topping the $35 billion spent the previous year.[11] The expansion is led by U.S. chipmakers, who have experienced a strong comeback from the late 1980s, when their share of the world market slid to 37 percent, down from 57 percent a decade earlier.

One of the newer installations is Intel's $1.8-billion factory on a high desert mesa in Rio Rancho, New Mexico. Opened in 1995 to produce sophisticated microprocessors for small computers, the plant has floor space equaling two dozen football fields. At its core is a series of "clean rooms," where the environments are more antiseptic than those in a hospital operating room. The tiniest speck of dust is a chip-killer. The assembly line's workers are suited up like astronauts in white Gore-Tex suits with hoods, goggles, boots, and latex gloves. Before entering work areas, they take a series of air showers to remove any dust particles. Cosmetics are removed at "wipe down" stations.[12]

The New Mexico plant is a critical element in Intel's strategy to maintain its lead as the world's most successful chip enterprise. David House, an Intel executive, declared, "Twice a second, somebody buys an Intel-based computer."[13] It is no idle boast. In the mid-1990s, Intel held more than 90 percent of the chip market for desktop PCs—the fastest-growing segment of the industry.

Given its investment in upgraded technology and new facilities, Intel's future may seem secure. But just like every other chip company it faces competitive challenges. This includes continuing inroads by foreign chipmakers, led by European, Japanese, and, increasingly, East Asian producers. After slipping behind in their race to dominate the global industry in the 1980s, Japan firms are challenging U.S. high-tech prowess once again.[14] Intel's 1995 announcement that it will develop a 1 billion–bit chip was matched by a similar announcement by Toshiba, the Japanese electronics giant.

These technical advances have spawned a new round of mergers and alliances among chip companies. The motivation is usually to share the staggering costs of technology research and production. In a typical deal, Motorola and Germany's Siemens joined forces in 1995 to build facilities for developing and producing advanced memory chips at a cost of $1.5 billion.[15] At the same time, Toshiba joined with IBM in a joint project to build a $1-billion advanced chip factory in the United States.

The increased demand for chips has created another problem—piracy. "Computer chips are the dope of the 90s," one industry observer pointed out. "They're easier to steal than dope. And for the people who steal them, here's the best part: once stolen, they're almost untraceable." The American Insurance Service Group, which monitors chip piracy, estimates that computer hardware worth $8 billion was stolen in 1994, primarily for their chips.[16]

The most certain prospect in the industry's future is that it will soon hit a technological wall. For all the advances of the past thirty years, chipmakers continued to rely on silicon-refined sand as the most important ingredient in their products. The key process in producing silicon chips is photolithography, in which circuits are etched by shining light through a patterned mask against a chemically treated silicon wafer. In the mid-1990s, transistors on advanced chips were spaced less than 0.5-millionth of a meter across. There is a physical barrier to reducing this much further. The U.S. Semiconductor Industries Association puts the limit at a 0.18-millionth of a meter, beyond which the technical barriers may be insurmountable. At the current level of chip development, this limit will be reached early in the new century.[17] Whatever the solution (or solutions) for a successor generation, the changeover will be difficult and expensive for the chip industry.

The most promising long-term option may be optical computing. The idea is to create optical switches based on tiny lasers, millions of which could be packed on a single chip. Linked together, these switches would move signals at the speed of light, much faster than the electrical impulses in present-day chips. Optical computing presents formidable engineering problems. Laser-based chips use up a lot of power and produce a lot of heat. The search for an efficient substitute for silicon chips, whether optically based or not, is under way. Meanwhile, the industry continues to press the limits of silicon-based technology.[18]

The changeover to more advanced technologies will take years, but it will have immense implications for Meganet and the machines attached to it. The new ultratech chips will vastly enhance the network's ability to deal with a full range of voice, data, and video capabilities—well beyond what is possible today. It will dramatically reaffirm Meganet's dependence on chip technology.

Semiconductor devices run the network's structure—the switches, cables, and satellites and the machines they connect. In less than three decades, chips have moved telecommunications networks from relative simplicity to stunning complexity. What was once "the phone system," used primarily for voice messages, is now a chip-filled transmitter of all kinds of information services.

This transition has been a very costly enterprise for telecom companies. One example is Nynex, which, before its 1996 merger with Bell Atlantic, was the regional phone company in the Northeast. In the 1980s, Nynex upgraded its network facilities in Manhattan by installing advanced fiber-optic cables. It replaced 33,000 tons of old cable along 3,000 miles of circuits, costing hundreds of millions.[19] Nynex's experience is being duplicated across the country as phone companies and their new cable-TV and satellite competitors make the transition to digitized, chip-filled equipment.

This upgrading is a Meganet imperative, and it is causing a sharp rise in global telecom equipment production. The United States continues to be the largest single market, propelled by political decisions to allow cable-TV and satellite firms to compete directly with telephone companies. Overseas, West European markets are expanding as new competitors challenge the former PTT monopolies, now being privatized under pressure from the European Union. New markets are also developing in Asian and Latin American economies, powered by a surge in investment funds from New York and other big markets. Telecom expansion in East Asia will soak up at least $200 billion in investment by the early years of the new century, according to Salomon Brothers, the New York banking house.[20] China alone plans to expand its telecom structure at a rate that will match the size of a U.S. Baby Bell every few years.

In this new global free-for-all, U.S. hardware companies have been losing market share to global competitors. Two decades ago, one U.S. firm, AT&T's Western Electric, produced half of the world's telecommunications equipment. Today, the U.S. share of the world market is about 30 percent.

This relative loss is due in part to the hollowing-out of large parts of the U.S. electronics sector as companies move production facilities abroad. Michael Dertouzos, director of MIT's computer lab, pointed out that more than 90 percent of all consumer electronics worldwide were produced in the United States in the 1960s. The U.S. share dropped to 5 percent by the 1990s, replaced largely by producers in

Japan and other East Asian countries.[21] Zenith was the last producer of consumer TV sets in the United States before it was bought up by a South Korean firm in 1995.[22]

The other factor came about as a result of the 1984 AT&T breakup, after which non-U.S. equipment firms tapped the U.S. market. The breakup agreement stipulated that Western Electric, AT&T's manufacturing arm, surrender its near-monopoly in telecom equipment production. Other U.S. firms began competing successfully in the newly competitive market. Unforeseen, however, was the rapid entry of European, Canadian, and Japanese firms, all seeking business in the world's largest market. A major entrant was Northern Telecom (now Nortel), which dropped its stodgy Canadian identity to become a major U.S. telecom equipment supplier. Another active firm was Germany's Siemens, which had fifty American units producing and marketing electronics equipment by the mid-1990s.

By 1991, the United States ran up a $1.9-billion trade deficit in telecommunications, much of it in network equipment.[23] In part, this imbalance resulted from trade barriers raised by foreign countries to protect local telecom equipment industries. This protectionism set off political alarms in Washington, resulting in congressional legislation that mandated sanctions against countries that discriminated against U.S. electronics exports. An epochal trade battle involved Japan's barriers to the importation of semiconductor chips. In 1986, when the negotiations began, foreign chips, largely U.S., made up a meager 8 percent of the total Japanese chip market. By 1996, after a decade of charges and countercharges, it was more than 30 percent.[24]

More recently, a new competitive surge by U.S. equipment firms has taken place in world markets. The telecommunications trade deficit has been lowered significantly.[25] In part this is due to congressional and White House pressure on foreign governments to open markets. Another factor is the advanced products and new market strategies developed by U.S. firms to compete more effectively. By 1995, this change had solidified the U.S. position as the leading supplier of telecom equipment, with a 30 percent share of the global market.[26]

The shift into high-gear competition was led by AT&T, which started with a strong advantage. It was the only telecommunications firm worldwide that served virtually the entire telecom equipment market, from Mickey Mouse phones to house-sized switching machines handling millions of calls each minute. AT&T's Bell Laboratories was a unique source of research breakthroughs, giving the company a strong technological edge. Despite these advantages, however, AT&T's equipment business was threatened by formidable competition at home and abroad. In the mid-1990s, seven of the world's top dozen equipment suppliers were European.[27] AT&T had dropped to third place worldwide in 1994, with only 10 percent of the market, behind Motorola and France's Alcatel Alsthom.[28]

This decline in market share was an important factor in AT&T's 1995 decision to split itself into three separate firms, one each for communications services, hardware production, and information facilities. The decision was a public acknowledgment that big was not necessarily better, that there were more efficient ways to organize a wide range of operations that earned almost $80 billion per year.

In deciding to split up the company, AT&T executives focused on the equipment business, which accounted for a quarter of the firm's revenues. They recognized that the most important buyers of AT&T equipment—telecom firms at home and abroad—were increasingly reluctant to do business with a company that competed with them in telecommunications and information services.[29] The new hardware company, Lucent Technologies, set itself the task of winning back old customers and attracting new ones. Lucent has been particularly aggressive in the market for cellular phone and other wireless networks, a booming sector in the late 1990s.[30]

Its strategic plan includes partnerships with foreign companies. In August 1996, Lucent announced that it would jointly develop a set of semiconductor chips with Japan's Mitsubishi Electric Corp. The chips are being designed specifically for digital high-definition television sets that will be marketed as replacements for standard analog sets later in the decade. The Mitsubishi alliance should put Lucent in a strong position to capture a significant share of what promises to be a lucrative equipment market.

It will be several years before the full effects of AT&T's decision to split off its hardware operations can be evaluated. When Lucent was being set up, AT&T brought in an outsider, Henry Schacht, chairman of Cummins Engine, to head the new venture. He came with a successful track record in competing against aggressive Japanese competitors in the diesel machine business. At Lucent, he has banked heavily on AT&T's brand-name reputation and the new company's financial resources. (Its initial stock offering in 1996 was one of the largest and most successful in U.S. business history.) Schacht's biggest long-term asset, however, may be Bell Laboratories, the R&D facility that had given AT&T its technological edge for almost seventy-five years. Most of Bell Lab's facilities were assigned to Lucent when AT&T divided in 1995. "With Bell Labs as the engine," Schacht said, "we can drive this company to be the most responsive in the world."[31]

Few industry watchers doubt Lucent's ability to compete effectively in the Meganet equipment market. The firm has set its sights on

France's Alcatel, which has held the global lead in the big-ticket equipment business for most of the past decade. Formed in the 1980s from a collection of French industries that were formerly government-owned, Alcatel moved aggressively into overseas markets with the advantage of already being the main supplier of telecom equipment to the French telephone system, the second largest in Europe. A few years later, the company raised its international profile even higher when it bought up the telecommunications assets of ITT, a longtime U.S. leader in marketing telecom equipment worldwide. This acquisition helped Alcatel in expanding further into overseas markets, particularly in Asia and Eastern Europe. By 1996, the company had fifteen joint ventures in China, competing directly against Lucent Technologies for a foothold in what may eventually be the world's largest telecom market.[32]

Lucent Technologies also faces stiff competition from Germany's Siemens, an electronics power for more than a century. Siemens has vied with Alcatel, AT&T, and Motorola for leadership in the global equipment market in recent years. It was aided by a restructuring of its operations in the early 1990s when it shucked off many of its old-line products and invested in new ones. Although its home base is in Europe, it has become an aggressive international player, with a particular focus on North American and Asian markets. In 1995, Siemens announced plans to invest more than $4 billion in its Asian production and marketing operations. The company set a goal of increasing sales in the region to $15 billion annually by the end of the decade. If this goal is reached, Siemens could pass Alcatel and Lucent Technologies in the Asian market.

In the meantime, Lucent and its front-running competitors are looking over their shoulders at other challengers. These include Canada's Nortel, NEC of Japan, L. M. Ericcson of Sweden, and Motorola. An unexpected competitor is Nokia, a small Finnish firm that has captured an impressive share of the equipment market with innovative products. In 1995, Nokia introduced a small, hand-held phone with a liquid crystal screen that provides access to the Internet's World Wide Web.[33]

Another firm to be reckoned with is Motorola. Starting with tinny-sounding car radios in the 1930s, Motorola has stayed ahead of the technology curve for decades, particularly in wireless communications. In recent years, it has led the field in building and marketing cellular phones and other wireless devices. It is also the prime mover behind Iridium, the sixty-four–satellite network that will link small wireless phones located any place on earth by the end of the decade. Motorola's wireless equipment reach is already global. Eighty percent of its wireless sales comes from overseas markets where annual growth is 35 percent—twice the U.S. rate.[34]

L. M. Ericcson, the Swedish electronics company, usually ranks in the top six or seven in the hardware competition each year. Ericcson is one of the diversified properties controlled by the Wallenberg family, which has dominated Sweden's economy for almost 150 years. The Wallenberg empire also includes holdings in such global enterprises as Saab, SKF, Electrolux, and the airline SAS.[35] From an established base of making plain old telephones, Ericcson moved nimbly into the mobile communications business in the 1970s. A decade later, more than 40 percent of all mobile phones worldwide were connected to Ericcson systems. Typical of the firm's global marketing strategy, in the mid-1990s it was the only company to produce wireless equipment that met all three of the contemporary technical standards used around the world.

Meanwhile, Japanese equipment firms are regrouping after a difficult period in the early 1990s. They were slowed down by a sharp appreciation of the yen, which affected their ability to price their products competitively in overseas markets. Along with other leaders in the equipment market, the Japanese face new challenges from firms in the "tiger economies" of Taiwan, Korea, Singapore, and Malaysia. After decades of producing radios and other low-tech goods for Western markets, the little tigers are becoming adept at building and marketing advanced equipment for Meganet.

An indication of this new aggressiveness was the 1995 decision by Samsung Electronics, a part of South Korea's largest industrial conglomerate, to buy a 40 percent stake in AST Research, a major U.S. PC manufacturer. It was the first significant Asian investment in a large U.S. computer firm.[36] A year later, LG Group, South Korea's third biggest conglomerate, announced plans to invest $10 billion in China, making it the group's biggest overseas manufacturing base.[37] LG Group's China focus will be on the production of electronic equipment, including TVs, VCRs, telecom equipment, and semiconductors.

Firms in China were also positioning themselves to be among the electronics powers. Small Chinese PC makers, offering high-performance machines at knockdown prices, were beating out foreign competitors in the country's burgeoning consumer market. Once thought of as lower in quality, local-brand computers accounted for 44 percent of the 1.5 million PCs sold in China in 1995, according to International Data Corp., a U.S. research firm.[38]

Another thriving part of the Meganet equipment business involves communications satellites. These high-flying "birds" transformed the network three decades ago with their ability to supply instant communications between any two points on the globe. Despite frequent predictions that its products would eventually be overtaken by advanced terrestrial circuits—particularly fiber-optic networks—the satellite equipment business is booming. According to the Teal Group, an industry consultancy, the value of payloads launched by U.S. firms will be $8.4 billion in the late 1990s.[39]

The first satellites had limited capacity: a few hundred phone calls to big, expensive earth stations. Today's advanced satellites can transmit a range of voice, data, and video services, including tens of thousands of phone calls. Most of them were designed to operate in geostationary orbit 22,000 miles above the earth where their footprint (their coverage area) can include one-third of the earth's surface. These satellites are "fixed" because their main job is to move massive amounts of communications traffic between fixed locations (large earth stations, in most cases). Their customers were mainly old-line telephone companies around the world who redistributed traffic to local subscribers. This has been the wholesale side of the global satellite business, the sector that accounted for most of the traffic and revenues.

The satellite business is, however, changing. One result is that equipment providers are being forced to adjust very quickly to customer demands for new services. The pace is being set by two fast-developing satellite sectors: direct broadcasting and mobile telephony.

Direct-broadcasting satellites are powerful birds that can deliver hundreds of channels of television and other services to small household dishes. The service was pioneered in the late 1980s by Astra, a Luxembourg commercial firm. Astra satellites now provide direct-to-home television broadcasts across a swathe of countries, from Ireland to Russia. In recent years, more than a dozen other DBS ventures have begun operations around the world. At least three networks will compete for customers in the lucrative U.S. market. The most extensive DBS operation is Star, controlled by media magnate Rupert Murdoch. Based in Hong Kong, Star's satellite coverage spans some fifty countries across Asia, from Ukraine to the Philippines. Its programming is an eclectic mix of news, American pop entertainment, and regional programs in different languages.[40]

The other new boom in satellite services: networks that link cellular phones and other mobile services. These services bypass, in whole or in part, traditional fixed communications lines operated by phone companies. In the late 1990s, a half-dozen mobile satellite networks were in various stages of construction, each with a different technical plan depending on the services offered. In the ensuing years, the hardware requirements for these and other systems involved an estimated $15 billion in satellite and launcher equipment costs.[41] These developments marked a trend toward very small, low-cost satellites to handle tasks formerly reserved for big birds. This new generation of *microsats* would rely heavily on advanced semiconductor capabilities to reduce size and weight. The ultimate goal would be to reduce all microsat electronics to a single integrated circuit, according to Rick Fleeter, founder of Aero Astro, a microsat startup company. The result would be, literally, a satellite on a chip that would weigh several hundred pounds and cost less than $100,000.

The prospect of thousands of swarming microsats in space is down the road, Fleeter admits. However, he and other microsat enthusiasts plan to have a transitional generation of smaller satellites in space before the end of the 1990s. These machines will have less power and fewer capabilities than larger satellites, but they should pay off in lower costs and the ability to handle specialized tasks.[42]

Microsats and DBSs illustrate the ways in which new hardware technologies are changing Meganet equipment patterns. For more than a century, telecommunications networks were controlled by national monopolies that offered voice telephone services and little else. These monopolies were eroding fast by the late 1990s, facing competitors marketing a range of new services requiring advanced hardware facilities. The remaining monopolies, which continued to control most Meganet resources, might have been inclined to embrace old ways, including old technology.

An apt analogy from another sector is the case of IBM. Once the kingpin of the computer industry, the firm stayed too long with its mainframe business while the rest of the industry shifted to smaller machines and services. The result was nearly a disaster for IBM, leading to a painful effort in recent years to regain a competitive position in a new kind of business environment.

Producers of old-line network equipment are now in danger of a similar slide into obsolescence unless they step up their adjustments to Meganet advances. Their standard products are still a necessary part of Meganet expansion. They are the machines, such as switches and circuits, that form the central nervous system of the network. But (to continue the metaphor) Meganet's focus is gradually shifting to the outer reaches of the nervous system, to the ganglia of specialized smaller grids that bypass, completely or in part, the core network. The long-term outcome of this trend for old-line equipment manufacturers will depend on their ability to adjust to these Meganet trends.

Increasingly, this means greater attention to the implications of what might be called the crossover equipment market. In this market, the distinctions between telecommunications equipment and the computerized machines they connect are being smudged. Until very recently, it was possible to distinguish clearly between the two, but no longer.

As MIT computer analyst Richard Solomon has pointed out, new technologies have dispersed much of the software-based intelligence needed to operate systems and services away from centralized networks controlled by big carriers. This intelligence is being transferred to machines such as PCs and workstations at the user end of the networks. In the process, the networks' consumers are gaining a greater measure of control over resources that were once closely held and very profitable domains of governments and other network monopolies.[43] This shift has been gathering momentum for the past decade and will continue to do so in future years.

Big business has been quick to take advantage of this particular Meganet development. The operative phrase is *bypassing the network*—avoiding all or part of the traditional grid. Their motive is only partly to save money. More often, it is to design their own network resources in ways that meet their particular needs, even if it is initially more expensive. Big corporations and institutions are using the new crossover equipment to gain control over their communications in the ways that MIT's Solomon described. In many cases, companies have been leasing circuits from the public carriers and fitting them into their own communications designs. In other cases, they are turning over their communications tasks to one of the many specialized leasing companies that have sprung up in recent years.

In newer communications designs, corporations are using crossover equipment to bypass the carriers completely. The new bypass route is in outer space, where satellite-based networks allow companies to link up their internal facilities and even to reach outside the company to their customers.

The technology used is known as very small aperture terminal (VSAT). Its basic tool is a small satellite dish, often less than two feet in diameter, and a box of electronics that can be linked to a company's computer, telephone, or video equipment. The system can serve a large network or a single computer. The data delivered via VSATs is assembled, packaged, encrypted, and transmitted from a satellite control center. Although most VSAT systems simply transmit data, increasingly they are being used to carry multimedia services combining video, text, speech, and graphics.

VSAT networks are well established in the United States, where more than 75,000 two-way systems were in use in 1996. These systems linked an estimated 250,000 terminals located in the tops of office buildings, factories, warehouses, retail outlets, and other corporate facilities.[44] Industry experts predict that the number of systems will increase to 100,000 by 1998.

The terminals are often the primary internal links for major corporations. Companies using VSAT systems include Chrysler, Chevron,

General Motors, Ford, and Toyota. Mobil Oil coordinates its world-wide operations with a satellite network that links 5,000 VSAT sites.[45] Federal Express uses the video capabilities of its 1,000 VSAT dishes to communicate with its widespread workforce. Joe Hopkins, FedEx's video production manager, described the system as "a very timely, impactful medium for getting critical messages, and just basic communications, out to an employee workforce of about 114,000."[46]

Meanwhile, VSAT use by overseas firms is growing. The European market developed slowly, but by 1997 more than 10,000 systems were in use. In a typical installation built by IBM, France's Peugeot/Citroen connects 4,200 auto dealers in eleven European countries. "We have a much closer relationship with our dealers," says Jean-Serge Bertoncini, Peugeot-Citroen's information technology director.

VSATs and other bypass techniques are a direct threat to the old-line telecom carriers. The corporate customer who uses thousands of VSATs, or even ten, is one who cuts into phone company revenues. This has led the carriers to develop varied strategies for turning around, or at least slowing down, the bypass trend. The most effective approach to date has been to promote one-stop shopping, offering business firms a package deal of communications services—voice, data, and video—that they claim will be cheaper and more efficient than other alternatives.

For the present, the use of alternate networks is limited largely to corporations and other large institutions. The next step will be to adapt alternate networks to the consumer market. By the late 1990s this was already happening, with major implications for Meganet's infrastructure and the machines connected to it. The pattern is being set by the Internet, and it is changing the way that Meganet will be used. A dozen years ago, the Internet was a simple data exchange grid, providing data communications among relatively small groups of professionals. It relied on "dumb" computers and ordinary phone lines. Today, the Internet is evolving into a mass information resource delivering video, voice, and data services. Many industry observers foresee the melding of telephone, television, and computer into a single *telecomputer*. Making and marketing these machines could provide the biggest single boost for the electronics hardware business in the next decade.

The transition to telecomputers will take a long time, and it may not happen in quite the way the current crop of industry visionaries predicts. The trend may turn away from complex desktop machines loaded with multimedia capabilities to simpler computers that offer nothing but screen, keyboard, and modem for connecting to the Internet. In short, the task of storing and massaging information inside a computer box would be transferred to the network. The Internet is, in its current format, too slow to make it a real substitute for software programs in the computer. A major obstacle is that the telephone network—still the vital link for Internet traffic—does not have enough capacity to deal with such a change.

The most promising prospects for change lie in software advancements that enhance the quality and the speed of the instructions inside computerized equipment and networks. After a century of relying on bigger and better machines, Meganet's future now depends heavily on the software bits and bytes that give it its operating instructions.

6

MEGANET TRADE: THE SOFTWARE BUILDERS

Software is Meganet's energy. It pulses through the network, providing Meganet's operating instructions and the information that flows through its circuits. The switches and wires that make up the network are inert objects until they are activated by software.

In the early years of computerization, the search for more efficient machines concentrated on improving hardware rather than on developing better software. Computers were regarded mainly as storage and calculating devices. This shortsighted view was corrected a generation ago by a group of scientists who were the intellectual founders of the information age. Among them were John Von Neumann, Claude Shannon, and Alan Turing, each of whom saw a much wider potential for the new machines. A special insight was contributed by an eccentric mathematician named Norbert Wiener. He was an authentic genius who had earned a Harvard doctorate by the time he was nineteen. Wiener's great contribution was to identify the importance of information controls (i.e., software) not only as a technical process but as the element that would give ordinary men and women mastery over the new information machines.[1]

Wiener called his concept *cybernetics*, from the Greek root meaning steersman. Today, software is Meganet's steersman, the component that sets its pace and direction. Wiener's theoretical formulations are the wellsprings for today's advanced information resources. Software has replaced hardware, technologically and economically, as the focus of attention for advancing global information development. An early turning point may have been IBM's decision in 1968 to stop giving away software with its computers and office equipment. One result of this decision was to make IBM the largest software company in the world, a position it still maintained in the late 1990s despite strong competition.

Software product sales have overtaken computer hardware sales in annual dollar volume.[2] Companies dealing in software and related services are Wall Street's darlings. Broadview Associates, a New Jersey research firm, tracks their performance on U.S. stock exchanges. In 1996, its index showed that these firms increased in market value from $663 billion to $1.8 trillion in the two years ending March 1996.[3]

The software sector is a bundle of paradoxes. It combines precise technical certitude with the free-ranging intuitions of a relatively small group of talented programmers. This mix of precision and hunch has produced brilliant innovations. It has also been costly and wasteful. A 1994 survey by *Scientific American* noted that "for every six new large-scale software systems that are put into operation, two others are canceled. The average software development project overshoots its schedule by half; larger projects generally do worse. And some three-quarters of all large systems are 'operating failures' that either do not function as intended or are not used at all."[4] This uneven record stems, in part, from an imbalance between the delicate precision of technical advances in computers and the heavy volume of software they must process. Software is code, and more code means more glitches. In the 1980s, the average word-processing program contained 15,000 lines of computer code compiled by a team of five programmers. By the mid-1990s, an equivalent program had at least 500,000 lines of code written by a team of fifty.[5]

In general, hardware technology has outpaced software development. As a result, software constraints often put limits on the capabilities of new computer designs. "The hardware guys giveth, the software guys taketh away," according to Chris Peters, a Microsoft engineer. Yet many software experts would argue that high failure rates for software products is the price that must be paid for advances in a field that involves the quirky combination of human intuition and mathematical certitude. Others would disagree. "It's like musket making was before Eli Whitney," said Brad Cox of George Mason University. "Before the industrial revolution, there was a non-specialized approach to manufacturing goods that involved very little interchangeability and a maximum of craftsmanship. If we are ever going to lick this software crisis, we're going to have to stop this hand-to-mouth, every-programmer-builds-everything-from-the-ground-up approach."[6]

On the one hand, handcrafted software is an affirmation of the role of human skills and imagination in expanding the potential of computerized devices. On the other, it is also an obstacle to progress in the

Meganet age, when computer-based systems depend on the technological and economic efficiencies of new software development.

Software's shortcomings show up in such projects as the baggage handling system at Denver International Airport, which opened for operations in the mid-1990s. A state-of-the-art system of 4,000 baggage bins ("telecars") was to be guided by 100 computers over twenty-one miles of steel track among the check-in counters, concourse gates, and baggage claim areas. That, at least, was the plan. But successful operation was frustrated by a rolling series of software errors. The opening of the airport had to be postponed for nine months, at a loss of $1 million per day, and even after the airport opened the baggage system continued to have periodic malfunctions.

Big glitches make headlines, but they have not stopped the boom in the software business. Rather, the steady expansion of the software sector is often cited as proof that the information age has arrived.[7] Software is arguably the fastest-growing sector in the global economy. The U.S. International Trade Commission estimated the annual world market at $277 billion in the mid-1990s, with production projected to expand 12 percent each year to the end of this century.[8]

Software design and production is overwhelmingly an American enterprise. U.S. firms supply 95 percent of the domestic market and about 60 percent of the overseas trade. European and East Asian firms, eager to compete, are behind the curve for the time being. Collectively, they produce only 20 percent of software goods and services while buying 46 percent of world output, most of it supplied by U.S. firms.[9] Because software technology changes so fast, however, it is a business with an extraordinarily high failure rate. "The software industry is so different than most other industries because the products shipping today will be obsolete in two years," according to Microsoft's chairman, Bill Gates. "The only question is, who will make them obsolete?"[10]

Software is not only the crown jewel of U.S. information age industries but also a spur to all other sectors of the economy, particularly information-intensive sectors such as education, the media, and banking. These are the major users of new software. They accounted for an estimated 85 percent of total U.S. investment in information technology since the 1980s, according to a 1994 National Research Council study. Besides energizing the U.S. economy and raising the level of U.S. exports, software-based technologies have propelled U.S. companies in all sectors to new levels of overseas operations. For each dollar earned from exports in the mid-1990s, U.S. firms took in nearly two from the sale of what they produced abroad.[11]

In an earlier era, trade followed the flag; today, it follows the expansion of advanced communications networks. Moreover, the mix of businesses taking advantage of these networks is changing. In the early 1990s, United Nations trade statistics showed that large multi-nationals accounted for about half of all cross-border assets. They held more than $1.2 trillion in total assets outside their home countries.[12] The big old-line firms still dominate U.S. international trade but not to the same degree as twenty years ago. Agile smaller companies are moving into overseas markets. Typical of these competitive companies is Dell Computers. Founded in 1984, it had annual global sales of $2 billion a decade later. Dell has shown well-honed skills in exploiting Meganet resources to expand its business abroad, a crucial element in its strategy for competing effectively with its established rivals.

Other firms, both the old-timers and the new challengers, have also leveraged Meganet and its software resources to gain advantages in fiercely competitive markets abroad. "There is no question that American companies are leaders in constructing and managing networks," according to University of Pennsylvania technology historian Thomas Hughes. "And there is no question that extensive use of networks, like factory systems in the 1920s, will be a key to establishing leadership in many industries."[13] Economist Robert Reich, secretary of labor in the first Clinton administration, stresses the role that information resources play in company strategies: "In their global operations, the new barriers to entry are not volume or price. . . . It is skill in finding the right fit between particular technologies and particular markets. Core corporations no longer focus on products as such; their business strategies increasingly center on specialized knowledge."[14] To implement these strategies, most companies have turned to a new breed of entrepreneurs who excel in managing and moving information. The expansion of Meganet traffic in the past twenty years has been heavily influenced by these information managers. As in other parts of the software business, U.S. firms have the largest share of this business, both as suppliers and users.

This computer services business has been dominated for years by one firm—Electronic Data Systems (EDS). It was founded in 1962 with a $1,000 stake by Ross Perot, marketing genius and erstwhile presidential candidate. EDS is no longer controlled by Perot; he sold it to General Motors in 1984. It was spun off from GM in 1996, although the automaker continues to be EDS's largest single customer.[15]

The newly independent EDS has annual sales of more than $10 billion. Its nearest competitor, Andersen Consulting, earns less than half that amount. The EDS strategy is to negotiate long-term service contracts, usually for ten-year periods. In 1995, EDS had such service contracts in-hand worth $60 billion.[16] Most of its dealings are with large corporations, particularly those with multinational operations. But it also manages the computer operations of Inland Revenue, the British government's tax collecting agency. Inland Revenue's 2,500 employees, once civil servants, are now part of EDS's 85,000-person workforce.

EDS and its competitors will market more sophisticated versions of their services in the coming years, expanding beyond the handling of printed data. Their corporate clients are moving from simple data-processing to multimedia services such as videoconferencing and graphics as part of their information strategies. 3M, the industrial and consumer products giant, has seventy-seven videoconferencing facilities at its production and marketing sites in Europe, Asia, and Latin America.[17] EDS and other data processors are now seeking out alliances and other linkups with telecommunications networkers to improve their prospects in this new multimedia environment. In 1994, EDS came close to an outright merger with Sprint, the number-three U.S. telecom carrier, but it pulled back before consummating the deal.

Eventually, EDS and other information service companies will move into a full range of multimedia operations. For the present, however, their core business is managing routine printed data. Their clients cope with a daily flood of electronic data that increasingly defines and directs their daily operations. Visa International, the world's biggest credit card company, is an outsized example. The firm handled more than 6 billion transactions per year in the mid-1990s, a figure expected to rise to 15 billion by the end of the decade.[18] Most firms are, in the industry phrase, data-rich and information-poor. "The fact is that information has now become a form of garbage," according to technology watcher Neil Postman. "We don't know what to do with it, have no control over it, don't know how to get rid of it."[19]

Companies handle data glut in different ways. Their common problem is that the old stuff-it-in-the-computer solutions no longer work. Many firms are adopting a new approach, known in corporate lingo as *virtual logistics*. It is based on tightly controlled networking of data in ways that integrate the production and marketing of goods and services anywhere in the world. Meganet resources thus become the essential tool in their management structure.

It is useful to take a snapshot of two industries—automobiles and fashions—each with very different needs but with a shared experience in adapting virtual logistics technologies to their production and marketing needs.

The U.S. auto industry had been operating overseas for more than seventy-five years, usually through autonomous units linked fitfully by telephone and telex with Detroit headquarters. Threatened with stiffer foreign competition in the 1980s, the big automakers not only restyled their products but also restyled their business practices to permit quicker responses to new market challenges. This involved a hard look at the ways they handled the information flowing through their operations.

As a first step, the industry turned to electronic data interchange (EDI) techniques—a mundane but effective system of dealing with ordinary business documents such as invoices and purchase orders. EDI replaces these paper documents with standardized electronic formats, moving information from one computer to another over the Meganet. EDI is now standard practice in the industry, enforced by the auto companies' refusal to do business with suppliers and sales outlets unless they adopt EDI procedures.[20]

With EDI firmly in place, the Big Three automakers—Ford, General Motors, and Chrysler—set up increasingly sophisticated company networks, relying heavily on satellite facilities. By 1996, General Motors had a network of small terminals at 9,000 sites throughout North America and 3,500 in Europe.[21] Chrysler's network links its North American factories and dealerships as well as assembly plants in nine countries abroad. A big step toward fuller use of Meganet resources was taken by Ford in the mid-1990s. The starting point was a company decision to merge its previously autonomous domestic and foreign operations into a single structure. The new framework, dubbed Ford 2000, utilizes Meganet circuits to integrate Ford's product development, production, supply, and sales operations around the world. Among other changes, the new system "delayered" the firm's traditional management hierarchy, cutting back the number of levels from fourteen to seven.

Ford's high-tech network has transformed the company from a multinational firm with regional profit centers into a global auto manufacturer organized by product line.[22]One result of this corporate makeover was Ford's highly touted "world car" experiment, a project a half-dozen years in the making at a cost of more than $6 billion. The first models were introduced in 1993 under different brand names— Mondeo, Contour, and Mystique. A small family car, meant to replace the company's Escort line later in the decade, is being developed in a half-dozen design labs around the world. The entire project relies on Meganet's advanced voice, data, and teleconferencing facilities to link Ford's research, production, and marketing units at home and abroad.

Meanwhile, the fashion industry has its own Meganet-based strategies for dealing with changing markets. No business is more subject to capricious consumer tastes. An arbitrary whim of fashion in material, cut, fit, or color can make or break a new product literally within weeks. The problem of fickle customers is compounded by the fact that the fashion industry is a global business. It is dominated by corporate conglomerates that design, produce, and market their products everywhere. Benetton, the Italian producer of pricy sweaters and fancy jeans, is a major international player, with 7,000 stores in more than seventy countries. The firm has expanded its manufacturing capabilities beyond its home base, with dozens of factories operated by contractors, mostly in low-wage Asian and Latin American countries.

Benetton pioneered the use of Meganet facilities to give it the flexibility to deal with changing customer tastes. The company collects sales data daily from its far-flung stores, primarily to track what is selling and what is not. The data supplies early-warning signals for adjusting inventories and product lines to match current trends around the globe. Benetton has integrated all its global network operations, right down to monitoring the productivity of the quarter-million sheep it raises in Argentina to supply wool for its clothing products.

Benetton's techniques have been copied, with variations, by other big fashion firms. Levi Strauss has installed "LeviLink," a computer system based on bar-coding and electronic data interchange standards to track production and retail operations. As a result, elapsed time between order placement and the receipt of goods in stores has fallen from fifty days to three.[23] Liz Claiborne is another industry giant that has adopted computer-integrated manufacturing, from original design to final production of its products. Meganet circuits transmit high-definition images of new designs from Claiborne's New York headquarters to production sites throughout Asia.

In 1995, the mass-market fashion trade as a whole took a big step toward full computerized integration of its operations by inaugurating a Meganet-based electronic network. Known as RagNet, the network links designers, manufacturers, and retailers. One of its services allows buyers to view high-resolution images of new fashions in their own offices, partially replacing the time-honored custom of visiting showrooms in New York and other international fashion centers.[24]

Meganet's impact on the automobile and fashion sectors pales before the changes the network is effecting in another major industry—financial services. Banks and other money centers are the most advanced examples of the global network's impact on business.

In most parts of the world, money is still represented by coin and paper. It is one of the reasons that almost half of all U.S. paper currency in circulation today finds its way overseas, stuffed inside boxes and under mattresses by people who don't trust any other currency, including their own. In Russia alone, central bank officials estimated in 1996 that 20 billion Yankee dollars were in circulation, compared with $12 billion in ruble currency at the then-current market rate.[25]

Paper money and coins will be around for a long time. Increasingly, however, they are being replaced by binary digits—bits—stored in computers and moved around on Meganet circuits. This digitization of money is part of what Walter Wriston, former chairman of Citicorp, called the new information standard—the electronic marketplace of ideas, goods, and services that recognizes no national boundaries.[26] Wriston was a pioneer in adapting Meganet resources to banking needs. He recalled that when he joined Citicorp's international division in the late 1950s the bank's rule was that you never sent a cable if a letter would do—and the letter was often sent by ship overseas. Citicorp took its first halting step toward the electronic age in the 1960s when it set up a telex line between its New York and London offices—a channel that transmitted about seven characters per second. Today, Citicorp is one of the largest private networkers on the Meganet, with circuits that routinely transmit data at thousands of characters per second among offices in more than fifty countries.

Other U.S. financial houses followed Citicorp in exploiting untapped banking and investment opportunities overseas. Global institutional investment funds rose to more than $14 trillion in the early 1990s, according to the World Bank.[27] Despite the strong presence of European and Japanese firms, it is a market dominated by U.S. financial houses.

They are, the *Wall Street Journal* reported in 1996, an "international juggernaut, adept at arranging loans, underwriting stock offerings and putting together multinational mergers."[28] U.S. financial firms have some built-in advantages, not the least of which is the ability to capitalize on the status of English as the global money market's lingua franca. But their day-to-day operations depend on how well they exploit the increasingly sophisticated information technologies of the global Meganet.[29]

Advanced Meganet resources are freeing international banks from the geographical constraints that limited them to a few money centers like New York, London, and Tokyo. Along the way, banks discovered markets that had been nonexistent or ignored, particularly in Asia and Latin America. As Morgan Stanley & Co. strategist Barton Biggs has pointed out: "If the five biggest emerging markets—China, India, Indonesia, Brazil, and Pakistan—accumulate just $400 per capita in mutual-fund and pension-fund assets over the next decade, this will create $1 trillion" for potential investment.[30]

The new electronic markets operate largely outside of banking's traditional old boys' network. Their prime resource is the computers needed to store and process bits and bytes of data. Paneled offices in the big financial houses have given way to trading floors the size of football fields crammed with computers manipulated (in the words of one observer) by twenty-two-year-old traders with ice water for blood.[31] Along with the financial houses, stock exchanges have been automated to handle larger trading volumes and the pressures of a round-the-clock global market. The New York Stock Exchange has spent more than a $1 billion to upgrade its technical capabilities, allowing market orders to be executed on the floor with a few computer keystrokes, replacing paper-and-pencil procedures.[32]

As computers replace clerks, the big financial houses and the stock exchanges are cutting back home-office staffs. Lower Manhattan lost 100,000 jobs, a fifth of its financial workforce, in less than a decade as banks and investment houses downsized and decentralized in the 1980s.[33]

At the same time, U.S. banks expanded their physical presence overseas. By the late 1980s, Citicorp had more branch banks in Brazil than in the United States. Routine operations, previously handled at headquarters, were shifted to low-wage developing countries in Asia and the Caribbean. The banks have flocked to so-called offshore banking centers (where the main attractions are friendly banking laws) newly combined with Meganet facilities that assure them they can be in instant touch with their money. A favorite Caribbean spot is Georgetown, capital of Grand Cayman, where about 20,000 financial groups are registered, roughly one for each inhabitant of the island. In 1997, Grand Cayman was the fifth largest financial center in the world, with 500 banks holding combined assets of more than $500 billion. Another popular money haven is the Seychelles, a ring of tiny islands in the Indian Ocean. The authorities there will give foreign investors who make a $10-million "investment subscription" a Seychelles diplomatic passport that will allegedly protect them from the snooping eyes of government bank regulators back home.[34]

International banks are fiercely competitive but they also rely on cooperative networks to assure the smooth flow of financial transactions over Meganet facilities. One of these networks is the Clearing House Interbank Payment System in New York, which balances out international accounts by the end of each banking day. Its daily turnover is $1 billion or more. Another bank-owned network is the Society for Worldwide Interbank Financial Telecommunications (SWIFT), which processes most large international payments. SWIFT handles more than 2 million transactions daily for its 5,000 member banks on all continents.[35]

The financial sector is bracing for more changes as Meganet-based transactions become more pervasive. The ability to do business almost anywhere is transforming the industry once more. In the United States, looser investment regulations are smudging the barriers among commercial banks (which lend and take deposits) and investment banks (which underwrite and trade securities). Big banks are merging with one another and taking over smaller competitors. As a result,

U.S. banking may soon be dominated by a dozen or so national financial "retailers" offering a full range of services. Industry watchers estimate that the number of U.S. bank employees in the United States will be cut one-third by the end of this century.[36] Others questioned whether traditional banks have any future at all. "Banks are dinosaurs," said Microsoft's Bill Gates. "Give me a piece of the transaction business and they are history."[37]

The very substance of money is undergoing a transformation as Meganet hastens the shift to cashless transactions. "We are moving into the electronic age where money will just be information about the wealth you have," according to Hans van der Velde, a Visa International executive. The new currency goes by different names—cybercash, virtual currency, digital cash, bit bucks, electronic money, or just plain e-money.

Whichever phrase eventually takes hold, the result is the same—bits and bytes replacing coins, bills, checks, and paper receipts at every level of economic activity from shopping at the local supermarket to multinational megadeals. E-money is cyberspace's coin of the realm, electronic cash moving along multiple channels, many of them outside the normal financial networks. There is no particular reason, aside from out-of-date banking rules, why a phone company could not market its own brand of e-money. We are, says one financial observer, going through the biggest revolution in currency since gold replaced cowrie shells. E-money can be backed by any currency or other asset. It is ideally adapted to the anarchic culture of the Internet as well as to Meganet's other information superhighway grids.

Even a partial transition to an e-money environment will take some time. It requires the dismantling and reconstruction of a financial system that has been doing business, with gradual variations, at the same stand for more than 500 years. Suddenly, e-money is here. As it becomes the currency of choice, it will undermine the stability of the dominant political organizations of the modern era: nation-states, whose power is based largely on their ability to issue money and control its value. This power is already being eroded by international money traders who routinely frustrate government attempts to control exchange rates.

Government controls can be routinely bypassed in the shift to e-money. "Over the long haul," according to Bill Frezza, president of the Wireless Computing Association, "this is going to lead to the separation of the economy and the state."[38] An early indicator of this trend can be found in the difficulties the fifteen members of the European Union are having in agreeing to plans for a common regional currency, a project they have been trying to implement for decades.

The shift to an e-money economy raises challenging questions. Who will issue e-money, and who will regulate the issuers? How will taxes be levied and collected in cyberspace? How will electronic payments be protected against fraud, money laundering, and high-tech counterfeiting?

The phrase "bank robbery" has already taken on new meaning. In 1994, a Russian hacker in St. Petersburg broke into a Citibank computer system in New York and transferred more than $10 million electronically to other banks around the world. Security experts estimate that in the mid-1990s there were three dozen instances of computer intruders stealing sums of more than $1 million each year in Europe and the United States.[39] Such abuses will continue to frustrate governments and financial institutions as the global economy moves further toward e-money.[40]

Until recently, e-money transactions were handled largely by big financial institutions, dealing among themselves or with well-heeled customers. The next step is the mass consumerization of e-money. This is beginning to happen. In 1995, 55 percent of all U.S. retail sales, by dollar volume, were electronic, primarily through credit card transactions. Round-the-clock automated banking services are now a routine part of consumer banking. Citibank has stated that its home banking services are busiest between 10 P.M. and midnight.

More than one-half of U.S. households regularly use ATMs, as well as computer and telephone home banking, around the clock. A new generation of ATMs can cash checks down to the penny. They can also dispense everything from postage stamps, traveler's checks, and movie tickets to up-to-the-minute bank statements. Moreover, ATMs can be located almost anywhere. Wells Fargo, the big California bank, had placed more than one-third of its ATMs in supermarkets by 1997.[41] Banking by phone has branched out in recent years into profitable specialties. TeleBank, in Arlington, Virginia, has no branches or checking accounts. Instead, its tellers are "telebankers," marketing certificates of deposit and money market accounts over the phone to customers across the country who have made a minimum deposit of $2,500. TeleBank's successful business is part of the 10 percent of all bank transactions made exclusively through telephone service centers in 1995.[42]

Consumers still tend to be cautious about the new services. Cash is the payment of choice for most U.S. consumers, still used in 54 percent of transactions. Credit cards are in second place at 38 percent, according to a 1996 Ernst & Young survey of spending habits.[43] It took most consumers more than a decade to embrace ATMs introduced in the 1970s. The same hesitation marks consumer reaction to more recent innovations in electronic banking. Remote telephone and computer banking still represent less than 1 percent of all consumer bank transactions. The pace is picking up, however, as banks push to make remote services attractive by assurances of convenience, reliability, and twenty-four-hour availability.

The American Bankers Association has estimated that the number of banks offering online services, 11 percent in 1995, will jump to more than 40 percent by 1998.[44] A big step toward developing national online banking was taken in 1996 when a consortium of fifteen large U.S. banks linked up with IBM in a project to build an advanced electronic network known as Integrion. The banks were following the advice of financial consultants who predicted that once customers get hooked on online financial services the companies that can reach the most customers electronically with banking and investment services will reap big rewards.

The Integrion network connects customers to banks that can electronically share data to facilitate services such as online check writing. Users of the new service dial a local telephone number to connect to IBM's network and then connect to the bank of their choice. Among the major banks initially participating in the network are Nations-Bank, BankAmerica of San Francisco, First Chicago NBD, and Royal Bank of Toronto.

Integrion is, in part, a preemptive move against Microsoft, which has developed software for home banking systems that operate on the Internet. Dozens of banks, brokerage firms, and financial services, including American Express, have signed up with Microsoft's online banking venture.[45] Other financial groups are experimenting with banking on the Internet. Hundreds of banks already sponsor World Wide Web pages to advertise services and handle inquiries. In 1996, three U.S. banks teamed up to launch Security First Network Bank, the first allowed by U.S. regulators to offer full banking services on the Internet.[46]

Killen & Associates, a consultancy based in Palo Alto, California, has estimated that $30 billion in financial transactions will be zipping across the Internet daily by early in the twenty-first century. "E-cash provides the necessary payment options to support new and low-cost products and services," according to the firm's president, Michael Killen, who also predicted a boom in the number of services that will take advantage of these cheaper transactions. For the present, however, minting e-money is no guarantee for making profits on the Internet. A number of early entrants in the field have lost money attempting to help banks do business on the Internet.[47]

Although such online services are, for the present, limited largely to North America and Europe, they will become normal practice on the worldwide Meganet in the coming years.[48] The road to large-scale consumer cyberfinance is, meanwhile, uphill and winding. People still like to see and to touch their money, whether it is stored in piggy banks or popping out of ATMs. There is a long way to go before most people feel comfortable about invisible cash.

Electronic transactions will continue to expand, however, because of their compelling efficiency and convenience. These are critical factors as financial services firms try to stay competitive. Ironically, it is this competitiveness that will relegate these firms to a remote presence at the other end of a Meganet circuit.[49] The Main Street bank is already a fading anachronism, giving place to remote ATMs and banking kiosks. Huntington Bancshares of Ohio, a big regional bank, uses videoconferencing kiosks that allow customers to contact a banker face-to-face electronically any hour of the day or night to discuss bank services, from mutual funds to mortgage loans.[50]

Meanwhile, some banks are beginning to market *smart cards*, sophisticated versions of credit cards that go beyond familiar credit and debit functions. Semiconductor chips embedded in the cards can be "loaded" with e-money, ready to be withdrawn for a purchase in a store or even at a Coca-Cola machine.

A smart card is an "electronic purse" that makes paper money and coins obsolete. An early example is prepaid phone cards. By 1997, smart cards packed the processing power of a 1980s-era PC. The target market—people who use bills and coins for small purchases—is potentially huge. According to Visa, cash transactions amounted to $8.1 trillion of the $14 trillion in total world personal spending in 1993.[51]

Smart cards caught on first in Europe, where a British card, Mondex, has taken a lead position. Both MasterCard and Visa (which are owned by banks) are adopting smart card technology. Both began test marketing the cards in U.S. cities in 1996, emphasizing their convenience in making small purchases. Their primary test site was a thirty-block area of Manhattan's Upper East Side, where stores were equipped with the machines needed to service the cards.[52]

Visa and MasterCard are also exploring the prospects of using smart cards for purchases over the Internet. The marketing problems are formidable. Internet users will have to buy extra equipment in order to use a smart card. Another barrier is the extra security measures needed to ensure safe transfer of cash over open telephone networks. "Internet commerce will probably be the final frontier for smart cards," according to Cary Serif, a spokesman for the banking industry's Financial Services Technology Consortium.[53] Smart cards and other e-money projects will impact Meganet in the future by expanding demand for its circuits to accommodate the heavy data traffic e-money will generate.

The software industry is already feeling the force of these demands. Its ultratech products, the ones that make the Meganet run efficiently, are being upgraded accordingly. But the biggest change will be in consumer software, most of it embedded in the 100 million or so small computers plugged into global Meganet circuits.

The software for these machines has been dominated for more than a decade by so-called *Wintel* standards set by Microsoft *Win*dows and In*tel* microprocessors. Wintel is the technology at work in more than 80 percent of the world's small computers. Its popularity was confirmed when Microsoft sold 40 million copies of its upgraded Windows 95 software within a year after it was introduced in August 1995.[54] Wintel standards will dominate small-computer uses into the twenty-first century. By then, Microsoft and Intel will likely be feeling the pressure from new challengers.

The software that their competitors are counting on is, in industry lingo, *object-oriented.* In the first generation of small-computer software packaging, up to and including Windows 95, software programs and data were rigidly separated. Object technology turns this approach on its head. Data and the software needed to manage data are merged into a specific task, or set of objects. Instead of investing in expensive software upgrades, often with a number of features most consumers don't want, they can buy (or rent) little bits of software (*applets*) for specific tasks as needed. Many applets are throwaway items, intended for one-time use and then discarded.

The Internet will be a crucial element in the object-oriented software environment. Many object-oriented software programs are being configured as *webware,* aimed at the growing number of World Wide Web users. Internet enthusiasts foresee webware operating on inexpensive, stripped-down "network computers" that will serve as the Web browser. One prototype, demonstrated by Sun Microsystems, includes a microprocessor and computer memory but no storage disc. It is essentially a Web browser terminal that fits into a box measuring five by nine by two inches. Users can connect to the World Wide Web for a variety of computer chores. The Web will operate as a huge virtual disk drive, capable of handling all forms of multimedia information, available at a mouse click on a blue hypertext menu. IBM took the lead in marketing a desktop network computer in 1996, pricing it at about $700, less than half the price of most desktop PCs.[55]

At present, Web-related products are still a blip on the software industry's radar screens, involving less than 1 percent of the $100 billion–plus global market. But the future looks promising. Despite the dominance of Wintel software, many software companies are gearing up to get webware products on Meganet circuits. Sales of Internet-based programs are doubling annually, with the prospect of reaching $4 billion by the end of the decade, according to Hambrecht and Quist, a computer consultancy.[56]

The parallel growth of Internet networking and object technology is happening while growth in other software applications is slowing down. The rush of millions of PC users into cyberspace has triggered a spate of startups, mergers, and alliances in the industry, most of them aimed at making Internet-based programs part of corporate strategies. Software with offbeat names like Navigator, Java, and Yahoo! are being marketed to meet rising consumer demand.

These competitors are taking aim at Microsoft's overall market dominance. "The new programs are a direct assault on Microsoft's whole paradigm," according to Robert Aston, president of Market Vision, a California research firm. Lawrence Ellison, head of Oracle, echoed this in saying that Windows 95, Microsoft's most successful upgrade, marked the zenith of the PC industry.[57] These are brave words, directed at a company that has achieved near mythical status in U.S. industry with its familiar story of how Bill Gates and other college dropouts turned a software technology known as DOS into an overwhelming marketing success. In the mid-1990s, it appeared as if Microsoft had stumbled when it underestimated the Internet's impact. An upstart rival, Netscape Communications, seemed to be on its way to creating a huge new market in Internet-navigating "browser" software, a friendly kind of software that makes it possible for technophobic citizens to overcome their fears and join the crowd on the World Wide Web.

The new Web software developed by Netscape, Oracle, IBM, and others threatened to make Windows irrelevant. But Microsoft responded with impressive speed and ferocity to protect its Wintel advantage. The campaign began with a determined R&D effort ($800 million in 1995) to upgrade older technologies and reposition Microsoft as a major player in the new software environment. Microsoft has moved quickly to integrate Internet components and communications links into every Microsoft product, including Windows. "The Internet is the primary driver of all new work we are doing throughout the product line," Bill Gates announced in 1995. "We are hard-core about the Internet."[58]

By 1997, the company was well on its way to offering a full range of competitive, Internet-based services.[59] Meanwhile, three Microsoft rivals—Silicon Graphics, Netscape, and Sun Microsystems—announced an alliance to develop a Web system that will provide three-dimensional graphics, among other new features.[60]

As the U.S. software sector sorts out corporate winners and losers in this contest, it faces new competition from overseas. Software is evolving as the quintessential global enterprise. It is borderless and ubiquitous. Software production doesn't need large amounts of natural resources, big factories, or proximity to markets. Its products can be moved around on small disks or over Meganet circuits. The industry's basic resource is talented men and women sitting in front of computer screens, a combination that can be assembled almost anywhere.

U.S. firms enjoyed a head start in this process, but others are beginning to catch up. Large parts of low-end software production have already migrated abroad, particularly to India and other emerging economies. This migration also included advanced software, directly challenging the near-dominant role U.S. industry has enjoyed for a generation.

The strongest competitors in sophisticated software are found in West Europe and Japan. The Europeans mounted a major R&D software effort in the early 1980s aimed at catching up with the Americans. Funded by the European Community (now the European Union), the project involved investments in more than 200 advanced projects employing more than 3,000 researchers.[61] The project helped fuel growth in the European information and communications technology sectors in the 1990s, reaching an annual growth rate of 8.3 percent in 1995. The expansion of the European market attracted U.S. firms, who accounted for five of the top-ten software companies in sales by the early 1990s.[62] Despite these changes, a 1997 survey of West European information technology (IT) resources by U.S. corporate executives found that the region was falling behind the United States and Asia in exploiting these resources. "The problem in Europe is an unenthusiastic use of IT resources," according to Intel chief Andrew Grove. "Technologies such as electronic mail are just not part and parcel of the way in which European companies work. IT is largely incidental to the way managers work."[63]

The story in Japan turned out to be somewhat different. Japan long dominated many parts of the global electronics industry, but it has lagged in the software sector. Its industry was slow to respond in the early 1980s when the powerful Ministry of International Trade and Industry declared that software was a strategic national industry. A decade later, the most profitable software companies were Nintendo and Sega, a pair of video game firms that were highly successful but not cut out to lead a national assault on U.S. software dominance. This led MITI in 1995 to set up a public-private consortium in an attempt to spur development of advanced software.[64] A year later, MITI set up a special series of tax breaks for companies that agreed to focus on developing innovative software for Japanese industry.

Many observers believe that full expansion of Japan's software capabilities will require a change in corporate culture. The country's electronics sector is dominated by lumbering conglomerates that are better at producing high-quality electronic hardware; software remains a secondary concern. Thus, a new kind of Japanese entrepreneurship might be needed, one that appreciates software's primacy in today's economic environment. A good example is Masayoshi Son, who made a small fortune selling Japanese video games while studying economics at the University of California during the 1970s. Son now runs Softbank Corp., a $2.6-billion software empire headquartered in Tokyo. Softbank is involved in a wide range of multimedia programming, software networking, and Internet-access ventures. The company is also the biggest computer publisher in the world, with eighty magazines.[65]

Western Europe and Japan will be increasingly formidable competitors in global software markets, aided by Meganet. But a newly significant market presence is a handful of fast-growing Asian and Latin American economies—the so-called big emerging markets (BEMs). Most of them began modestly, in software-based information services in which low-wage workers processed data for U.S. corporations. American Airlines was an early user of these services, sending sales data for processing to Caribbean countries. Offshore data processing continues to be a steady business in several countries, including China, South Korea, and Ireland. In one operation in China, for instance, hundreds of data-entry workers sit before computer screens, punching in numbers from U.S. phone books for transfer to CD-ROMs and other electronic storage devices.

More recently, software trade has taken a high-tech turn in Asia and Latin America. This was first demonstrated a decade ago when U.S. electronics giant Texas Instruments set up its first software production facility in Asia. It chose Bangalore in southern India. After coping with India's Byzantine regulations, the Bangalore facility became one of Texas Instruments' main production units, turning out world-class software created by low-wage Indian engineers. (A 1993 World Bank–funded report estimated that the average monthly wage for programmers in India was $225, compared with $2,500 in the United States.) Satellite dishes on the roof of the Bangalore facility transmit its software production in milliseconds to company plants in Europe and the United States.[66]

This success story typifies the steady globalization of the software business, as well as the agility of U.S. firms in exploiting this option. In recent years, a dozen major U.S. companies have set up shop in Bangalore. Other companies have done the same thing in Singapore, Taiwan, Mexico, and Malaysia, either as wholly owned company units or in partnerships with local firms.

This economic colonization has benefited all of those involved. U.S. firms have honed their competitive edge by lowering production costs and moving closer to fast-growing markets in Asia and Latin America. Meanwhile, they have created a potentially formidable set of competitors abroad. Countries that had heretofore not developed software production industries have been emerging as world-class players, first as production outposts for U.S. and European companies and, more recently, as independent producers of their own software.

In the late 1990s, the leading example of this trend was India. In 1985, India's software industry was worth $10 million. By 1997, it had a turnover of $1 billion. This is less than 1 percent of total global software output, but the significant fact is that India's software output was growing at four times the average rate worldwide.[67]

India's software industry still depended heavily on Western companies who outsourced software development projects. This changed as software firms were set up by local entrepreneurs, many of whom learned their trade with foreign firms and then moved out on their own. Like the imported Western companies, companies in India can take advantage of the technical competence, low costs, and reputation for prompt delivery that characterize its software sector. They also benefit from government decisions to ease tariffs and other restrictions, subsidize software technology parks, and dole out five-year tax exemptions to Indian software exporters.

Other countries are adopting similar software development strategies. The Republic of China on Taiwan has a national program for matching its strong computer hardware sector with expanded software production. The government is building a $300-million software park near Taipei. The Taiwanese are concentrating their efforts on Chinese-language software. They hope to benefit from what promises to be an exploding market on the mainland once political tensions between the two countries are lowered.[68]

Other countries in Asia and Latin America are also jumping into the software race. Brazil recently surpassed Japan as a software producer. Mexico built up strong capabilities as U.S. companies outsourced more software production there. Korea, Malaysia, Thailand, and the Philippines are all moving into the field, usually starting as production outposts for Western companies, then developing their own production capabilities.

As the global software industry grows, so does its biggest problem: piracy of products on and off the Meganet. According to a 1995 U.S.

International Trade Commission study, U.S. companies were losing more than $12 billion per year through electronic theft. Piracy is generally regarded as an overseas problem, but it occurs at home, too. About 35 percent of business software in the United States is pirated, according to the Washington-based Business Software Alliance (BSA). Piracy is also a problem in Western European, where it cost software producers $6 billion in 1994. Software theft is not confined to back-street, Mafia-type operations. The first computer users to be imprisoned for software larceny in Europe were executives of a staid Finnish engineering firm who were caught using illegal copies of AutoCAD, a computer-aided design package. In another widely publicized case, Microsoft sued Argentina's government for allegedly using Windows illegally in 90 percent of the country's public-sector computers.[69] In the West, Turkey heads the piracy league. Ninety-seven percent of software sold in Turkey is copied illegally, according to BSA. Software piracy is more rampant in Asia, where BSA estimates that three countries—Indonesia, Thailand, and Pakistan—have a 99 percent piracy rate.

A typical example of copycat capabilities in Asia was the introduction of Windows 95. Weeks before the product was put on the world market in 1995, copies were being hawked by street vendors in China for $6. Despite its losses in China, Microsoft is cooperating with government agencies there to expand its product lines in what can be potentially one of the largest software markets in the world.[70]

Meanwhile, production of illegal software in China has reached the point where it exceeds domestic production. Illegal Chinese software is now exported around the world. In 1993, the U.S. government launched a major trade negotiation with the Chinese to combat copyright violations. The resultant 1995 agreement included U.S. technical assistance to help the Chinese enforce their own copyright laws. The Chinese followed up with a highly publicized shutdown of some illegal operations. This proved, however, to be a hollow gesture. There were reliable reports in 1996 that Chinese pirates had actually expanded their illegal operations.

Software theft will continue to bedevil the industry as it expands economically and technologically. The problem is complicated by the fact that electronic software raises a question: Who owns information? For centuries in the United States, the answer was relatively simple. Information, whether in a book, a song, or a theatrical play, belonged to the individual or the organization that created it. One of the great achievements of the U.S. Constitution was to accommodate this principle by granting Congress the power to legislate a system of patents and copyrights.

As the world neared the end of the twentieth century, software ownership was in disarray. All forms of information had become merged into electronically delivered bits and bytes delivered over the Meganet. Communications scholar Anthony Smith argued that in the new digital age the property rights that go with information would wither. Anne Branscomb, a lawyer specializing in information issues, noted: "We must redefine the boundaries between public and private information clearly and unambiguously. We need to establish a global system of electronic signs. Electronic travellers need to know on whose electronic domains they are entering and what rules prevail on these electronic highways. We need warning signs and clearly established rules of 'netiquette.'"[71]

For information-intensive societies like the United States, new rules covering intellectual property are needed. The old protections afforded by patents, trademarks, brand names, and copyrights are eroding. The issue affects all industries: Consider the lengths that Coca-Cola goes to in protecting its "secret formula" or the speed with which the Disney Company rushes to court when it spots unauthorized images of Mickey Mouse, Donald Duck, or other denizens of its corporate menagerie. The *Financial Times* of London pointed out that "intellectual property is increasingly at the heart of business success in the developed economies. . . . [It is] the central debate, with other trade issues secondary." Establishing new legal protections for software and other digitized information products will be a critical factor in Meganet's evolution.

THE POLITICS
OF MEGANET

The ongoing pull and tug of Meganet expansion has released powerful political forces. This reality shows itself in different ways:

- When Nelson Mandela was released from prison into house arrest in 1990, he asked for a fax machine, as well as an e-mail connection. With these resources, he was able to direct the last phase of the African National Congress's successful assault on racial *apartheid* and minority white control in South Africa.
- In the 1970s, Iran's Ayatollah Ruhollah Khomeini was exiled in France, safely blocked from direct political activity. But he produced a regular series of antigovernment sermons that were smuggled into Iran on audiotapes and broadcast in mosques. Within a year, he returned home as the leader of a fundamentalist Islamic revolution.
- In Mexico, Zapatista rebels, fighting government forces in Chiapas, make their communiqués and other information available over the Internet from their jungle headquarters. The rebellion, said Mexican foreign minister José Angel Gurria, has become a war on the Internet.
- During the 1996 U.S. presidential campaign, e-mail, fax messages, and Internet Web pages channeled a flood tide of partisan appeals to millions of potential voters cheaply and effectively.
- Reacting to Communist Chinese threats to reclaim Taiwan by force in 1996, Taiwanese activists set up an Internet Web page, "Keep Your Bloody Hands Off Taiwan," urging fellow citizens to send e-mail protests to Chinese government officials.
- An Arab dissident organization in London uses fax machines, electronic bulletin boards, and toll-free phone calls to distribute information in Saudi Arabia aimed at fomenting an Islamic revolution there.

These are random examples of the political impact of ordinary Meganet resources—telephones, fax machines and audio tapes. Meganet is not only the creation of political institutions. It is also a force in reshaping them. These effects will intensify as Meganet resources are made available to billions more people in the coming years.

Politics has dictated the pace and direction of Meganet's growth since the first telephone and telegraph lines were installed in the nineteenth century. Governments were quick to take over the new networks as an extension of their traditional claim to control information resources. (The exception was the United States, which opted for light government regulation of private networks.) Electronic communications became a powerful weapon in the arsenal of the modern nation-state.[1]

This situation went unchallenged for more than a century. Today, it is in disarray, eroded by more powerful forces. Advanced technologies make it increasingly difficult to maintain a centrally directed network monopoly. There are too many options for bypassing any single network arrangement. Political authority over information is dissipating as huge waves of digitized bits and bytes rush through networks at the speed of light.[2] Government telecommunications monopolies have become industrial era dinosaurs, incapable of adapting to information age realities. They have been run by conservative bureaucracies who served a narrow segment of businesses and upper-class customers. They also served government purposes by being profitable, supplying a steady cash flow to national treasuries.

In the Meganet era, this pattern is changing as a broader range of claimants demand communications access, particularly to the more advanced telecom facilities that most governments do not provide. Business firms lead the pack, aware that high-tech communications are necessary tools for anyone hoping to compete in today's markets, either at home or abroad. Close behind these business leaders are ordinary citizens who simply want a telephone.

Pressures from all these claimants are insistent and increasingly effective. The French showed a particular aptitude for organizing popular efforts to improve phone service, using a satiric slogan: "Half of France is waiting for a phone; the other half is waiting for a dial tone." An astute politician, Valéry Giscard d'Estaing, got the message when he ran for president in the mid-1970s. He won the election in part on a pledge to improve the phone system. It was a promise on which he actually delivered, and he was reelected.

This scenario is being replicated, with local variations, in dozens of other countries. The turnaround has been sweeping in scope and dramatic in effectiveness. Twenty years ago, government telecom monopolies were the rule in almost every country, the United States excepted. Today, some element of private-sector competition has been introduced in more than fifty countries. By the year 2010, old-style government monopolies will be virtually extinct.

This political shift is the main impetus for Meganet's current expansion, both geographically and in its technical capabilities. Meganet growth is most visible in the spurt in ordinary telephone service. The world's current stock of about 800 million phones will double in the next decade. The drive to deregulate and privatize national phone systems is essentially unstoppable, despite rear-guard actions by many governments to keep all or part of their monopolies. The political fallout from this development is substantial. Even though governments still have considerable power over Meganet resources, they must now face voters who understand, for the first time, that there are alternatives to the old monopolies.

There are no firm guidelines for bringing order out of the current communications disarray. The United States is the most advanced example of a society that has accepted the challenge and consequences of universal access to advanced communications resources. The U.S. experience in dealing with information age resources is not, however, a model that can be readily transferred the rest of the world. Few other societies have a political tradition of information freedoms to match the First Amendment, or the economic structures that allow these freedoms to be translated effectively into social resources. Other countries will take different and usually slower paths to a more open communications environment.

The one clear lesson the United States offers is that communications and information resources are redefining national power. The old benchmarks—natural resources, military forces, industrial output—are being modified by information age realities. What are the new benchmarks? How can relative strength be measured in today's Meganet terms? Some economists use a simple yardstick: *teledensity*, the number of telephones per person in a country. Teledensity has been adopted by the International Telecommunications Union (ITU), a United Nations agency, as the most easily quantifiable measure of communications penetration throughout the world. It is a useful rough measure; the United States usually rates second only to Sweden.

A more sophisticated measure is a country's production of electronic data, a basic information age product. The U.S. lead in digitally stored information is decisive. In the mid-1990s, it had 4,956 major electronic databases, almost twice as many the rest of the world combined. Great Britain was a distant second with 641 installations.[3]

The most exact measure of information power is the binary digit. Today, every society on earth, including the most economically backward, has its share of bit power. But this power is wildly disbursed and unequally distributed. By any standard, the United States is the binary digit superpower, the largest generator of the digitized information that flows through Meganet. It arrived at this preeminent position because of a series of historical events.

The foundation for the U.S. lead is the First Amendment. There is a direct and powerful connection between the Founders' decision to prohibit government restriction of free speech and today's Meganet.[4] This connection is reflected in the curious, often naive, American faith in the fusion of technology and democracy. Benjamin Franklin, kite in hand, may be the best-known symbol of the search for an electrically powered paradise. The invention of the telegraph and the telephone led to the first visions of a "wired" nation. Alexander Graham Bell wrote in 1878 about the potential of his new telephone as a universal link in words that would delight any of today's information highway enthusiasts: "Are all the nations communing?"[5] Walt Whitman asked after the invention of the telegraph, "Is there going to be but one heart to the globe?" This is the rhetoric of the technologically sublime, and it runs like a golden thread through the national uplift literature.[6]

Nineteenth-century enthusiasms led to ambitious projects to wire the North American continent. These projects were the first, primitive working models for a Meganet-scale global network. Telegraph lines reached across the country by the 1870s. Telephone expansion occurred more slowly. At the beginning of the twentieth century, all U.S. phone numbers could be listed in one directory. By 1914, however, there were 10 million phones—70 percent of the world total. A year later, a New York–San Francisco link had been established.[7]

In those early days, the U.S. focus was on building a domestic network. There was curiously little interest in links with other countries. Cyrus Field, the U.S. sponsor of the first transatlantic cable, had to rely on European investors for funds to complete the project. It was the British, and later the French, who saw the need for global networks, primarily to reinforce their control over colonial possessions in Asia and Africa. By 1890, they and other European powers had established telegraph links that stretched as far as China and Japan.

For decades, U.S. communications companies were minor players in the race to build international networks. The government in Washington was, moreover, wary about foreign attempts to establish cable links in the Western Hemisphere, seeing them as an electronic intrusion that challenged the Monroe Doctrine. At one point, the U.S. navy turned back a British ship trying to land a telegraph cable on a Caribbean island. The United States initially refused to join the International Telegraph Union, which was set up to establish compatible technical standards for the new global telegraph and telephone networks, fearing that the European-dominated group might try to regulate U.S. communications.[8]

This isolationism could not last. The United States was emerging as an imperial power in need of global communications. U.S. companies began looking for business abroad, with government encouragement. After World War I, the U.S. navy helped create a chosen-instrument company, the Radio Corporation of America (RCA), primarily to establish an overseas U.S. presence in communications networking and in equipment manufacturing. Simultaneously, AT&T expanded its overseas phone and telegraph circuits. Another important player was ITT (the International Telephone and Telegraph Co.), which at one point owned or controlled most of the telephone companies in Latin America.

These initiatives led to a new U.S. strategy in international communications. Beginning with negotiations for the Treaty of Versailles ending World War I, U.S. delegations argued the case for assuring open access to all international communications resources. In part, their efforts were aimed at curbing the European powers who then controlled most international circuits. Behind this economic motive, however, was a wider purpose—to promote an international version of First Amendment freedom of communications. These early negotiations laid the ideological basis for U.S. policy in dealing with the more complex problems of assuring the universality of today's advanced Meganet.[9]

Four events in the past half-century mark the ascendancy of U.S. leadership in global communications. They are, chronologically, the emergence of a U.S.-built global military network during World War II, the evolution of communications satellites in the 1960s, the breakup of AT&T in 1984, and the enactment of landmark telecommunications legislation in 1996.

The first of these transforming events took place during World War II. The overseas networks then controlled by Britain and other European countries were effectively put out of commission in the fighting. They were replaced by a vast U.S. military network, built by the U.S. Army Signal Corps to support troop operations worldwide. As a result, the United States emerged from the war as the unchallenged communications power. Taking advantage of this new situation, AT&T and other companies moved quickly to expand their overseas operations, utilizing a new generation of submarine cable technology, which permitted reliable transoceanic telephone connections. By the mid-1950s, U.S. communications companies dominated global networking.

The second development that advanced U.S. global communications power was the advent of communications satellites in the 1960s.

These satellites were a uniquely American achievement. The technology was developed in U.S. laboratories and the first machines were built in U.S. factories. Equally important, the United States took the political initiative to sponsor Intelsat, the international organization that still operates the main global satellite network.

Intelsat was a crucial political breakthrough in the evolution of today's Meganet. It created a global network capable of linking any two places on earth. The network was completed less than eight years after the first experimental satellite was launched in 1962. The early satellites were technologically primitive by today's standards, but they changed the nature of world communications.

The global satellite system that had emerged by 1970 was a stunning exercise in U.S. political power. When the first experimental satellite, developed by AT&T, was launched in 1963, the Kennedy administration faced two choices. One was to build a U.S.-dominated worldwide monopoly. The second was to devise a political formula for sharing the network's ownership and operations with other countries. Both views had strong support in industry, Congress, and other power centers. The decision, made by President Kennedy and confirmed in congressional legislation, was to develop a cooperative international system under nominal United Nations sponsorship. The system would be owned by the countries that used it.[10]

The result was a unique, profitable global institution formally known as the International Telecommunications Satellite Organization. Intelsat is essentially a cartel of more than 140 countries who have voting shares proportionate to their use of the network. Collectively, these countries represent more than 97 percent of global communications traffic. Intelsat is consistently profitable, assuring its owners a comfortable 20 percent annual return on their investment. The United States has always had the largest ownership share and is consequently the biggest voice in the organization's affairs.

Intelsat's share of global traffic has declined in recent years with the expansion of commercial fiber-optic cable networks. The organization also faces growing competition from private-sector satellite networks. These developments have led to proposals for privatization of parts of Intelsat's operations to deal more effectively with the new competition. This restructuring is now well under way. A partially privatized Intelsat will continue to be an important part of the global Meganet structure. Over and above its day-to-day operations, Intelsat has given convincing proof that the imbalance in world communications can be reduced, if not entirely eliminated. Intelsat was a major step toward creating today's advanced Meganet.

The events surrounding Intelsat's creation in the 1960s forced the United States to articulate a coherent global communications policy.

The subject had previously been addressed in a casual manner, relegated to the lower levels of the bureaucracy. The decision to build Intelsat involved a dozen federal agencies, with no central coordinating point. The first step toward introducing some coherence to the process was taken by the Nixon administration in 1971. The Office of Telecommunications Policy (OTP) was set up at the White House level, headed by a young engineer, Clay (Tom) Whitehead, who moved into the Washington bureaucratic scene from the heady atmosphere of California's Silicon Valley.

Under Whitehead's leadership, OTP's mission was to develop a credible approach to national telecommunications policy. In addition to its primary job of advising the president, it produced some of the first serious policy research on the economic and social impacts of technological changes in U.S. communications. Inevitably, the agency became involved in political controversy. One of its early studies suggested a national disaster communications network reaching down to households. The proposal was attacked by opposing Democrats as "a blueprint for a government-operated propaganda and spy system."[11]

The OTP's effectiveness in policy formation ended when it got caught up in an administration-inspired project to punish the New York television networks for their alleged anti-Nixon bias. The White House eventually backed down, but the OTP's influence withered. In 1977, the new Carter administration relegated some of its functions to the third level of the Department of Commerce. Since then, international communications policy has been largely left up to a bureaucratic coalition of a dozen federal agencies dominated by the Departments of State and Defense.

The FCC has also had a role in forming fundamental policies on Meganet-related issues. The FCC's charter is to monitor and regulate domestic telecommunications. Beginning in the early 1970s, it issued a series of landmark decisions aimed at introducing more competition to the U.S. telecommunications sector.

The FCC acted to effectively reduce regulations that no longer fit economic and technological realities in the communications sector. New companies, led by MCI, were allowed to compete against AT&T, the firm that for decades had been the U.S. version of a government telephone monopoly. By the late 1970s, AT&T was fighting a rearguard action to keep itself intact. The FCC continued to nibble away at AT&T dominance while Department of Justice lawyers pursued an antitrust suit designed to break up the company.

The result was the third big breakthrough in strengthening U.S. leadership in global networking. In 1982, AT&T struck a deal with the Department of Justice to end the antitrust case. The company agreed to give up the largest part of its Bell system business—local telephone service. In exchange, it was given permission, long denied under government regulations, to enter the fast-growing information services sector. The Bell system companies were restructured as seven regional conglomerates. This consent decree was announced in Washington on a cold, wet day in February—the day, as one wag put it, when all Bell broke loose. The divestiture of the Bell companies went into effect in 1984.[12]

The AT&T divestiture reinvigorated U.S. telecommunications. The decisive action moved the entire sector out from under the shadow of a giant monopoly into a sunnier era of more open competition. The result was the longest running period of rapid growth ever enjoyed by any U.S. industry—a pace that in the late 1990s showed no signs of slowing down. Thousands of companies entered the business while the older ones continued to prosper. Any fears that AT&T's power would be diminished in the new competitive shuffle were soon dispelled. It remained the dominant corporate force in U.S. communications—the big gorilla, in industry parlance—even after splitting into three separate companies in 1995.

The agreement that broke up AT&T had a strong effect on global Meganet development as well. U.S. companies, from AT&T on down to the agile newcomers, moved overseas looking for business in newly deregulated national and international networks. Today, U.S. firms are involved in telecommunications trade and investment projects in more than seventy-five countries on every continent.

The agreement was also a pragmatic response to changing circumstances, and in balance it has proved to be an effective one. The divestiture of AT&T's Bell system removed a major stumbling block to full U.S. participation in building advanced Meganet facilities at home and abroad. It also stepped up the pressure for further political decisions to resolve other communications problems that needed to be addressed.

This increased regulatory activity led to the proliferation of communications industry lobbies and political action groups in Washington and in state capitals. During its long years as a monopoly, AT&T had been the most powerful of the Washington lobbies. Suddenly it was joined by scores of competitors, including local phone companies, cable firms, and the media. All jockeyed for position to influence further government deregulatory actions in the wake of the AT&T breakup. But by 1985 it was clear that the AT&T divestiture plan was coming apart. Economic pressures and technological advances were outpacing the plan's objective of setting a pattern for the U.S. telecommunications sector into the new century. New political decisions were needed. Moreover, the costs of delay in changing the rules were increasing.[13] Pressures mounted for political actions that would end, or at least modify, the ambiguities that threatened to slow down expansion in the communications sector.

The psychological turnaround took place during the 1992 presidential election campaign pitting George Bush and Bill Clinton. Until that time, the debate over communications policy roused little interest outside the industries directly involved. The Clinton campaign decided to highlight the issue, focusing on concerns about the country's future in a high-tech information economy. It was an astute move, aimed at younger voters who were increasingly involved with computers and other information age devices in the workplace and at home. Also, the 1992 presidential election was the first in which computer-based facilities were fully integrated into campaign strategies, including digitized polling, e-mail, fax distribution, Internet pages, and electronic "town hall" meetings.[14]

Clinton's high-tech theme caught on, particularly since its upbeat message contrasted with the lackluster issues of the Republican campaign. Given the American penchant for reducing big ideas to bumper-sticker simplicity, the theme became "the information highway." Once Clinton took office, the administration pressed the issue. The initiative was led by Vice President Al Gore, who as a U.S. senator had sponsored some of the earliest legislation supporting information age advancement, including mass use of the Internet.

The White House became computer-friendly, with its own World Wide Web page (www.whitehouse.gov) and a heavily used e-mail facility. It also sponsored demonstration projects in schools and hospitals across the country, showing the advantages of computer-based networking in health and education.

The Clinton administration stepped up the use of Internet and e-mail facilities in federal agencies. Web sites proliferated. The State Department set up one site to provide travelers with a list of countries where they should be alert for possible terrorist threats. A Bureau of Land Management Webpage listed the requirements for adopting a wild horse or burro. In 1995, the federal government inaugurated a program to make it easier to assure personal privacy in dealing with agencies through the World Wide Web. The program used plastic "key cards" with special cryptography to assure privacy in citizen transactions.[15]

Behind the information highway hoopla, the Clinton White House showed real political savvy in developing the first coherent national strategy for the Meganet era. The administration gained industry support by emphasizing that the government's role would be to support private-sector efforts to build the highway.[16] The Republican opposition in Congress scrambled to get on the information highway bandwagon, motivated in part by surveys showing registered Republicans were the heaviest subscribers to online services. Strong support for Meganet development came from Republican Newt Gingrich, a self-described conservative futurist who became Speaker of the House after the 1994 Republican takeover of Congress. Gingrich challenged Vice President Gore as Washington's leading cheerleader for information highway programs.[17]

These initiatives were useful in publicizing the information highway idea, but the work of realizing it—then as now—has taken place outside the Beltway. The prime force has been competitive private initiatives aimed at exploiting the business opportunities that beckon along the highway. State and local governments have also played a role, largely as part of plans to improve their competitiveness in the new information-centered economy. Among the states developing advanced networks, Iowa was an early leader. Its state grid consists of 3,000 miles of fiber-optic cable, linking schools, hospitals, and other institutions in every county. More recently, Louisiana launched TeleMed, a video linkup between urban and rural hospitals. By 1997, every state was developing similar networks.[18] Municipal governments also began to sponsor advanced communications facilities. In the mid-1990s, Anaheim, California, was a pioneer with an ambitious plan to reverse its declining economy. The city voted for a $200-million modernization budget that included building a fifty-mile fiber-optic network, part of which supports fire, police, and other municipal services. The city gained a new revenue source by leasing the network's excess circuits to private firms that sell telecommunications and information services.[19]

Such public- and private-sector activities underscore the need for a more comprehensive national telecommunications strategy. The details of such a strategy have been hotly contested. The different sectors of the communications industry, particularly the phone and cable-TV companies, each had an agenda. The public's new interest in information highway themes, actively promoted by the Clinton administration, provided an incentive for breaking the logjam. While battling aggressively for their particular agendas, everyone concerned—from the White House to the communications and other industries—piously extolled the glittering benefits of the information highway. This rhetoric got attention, but it did not provide instruction on how to speed up telecom development.

Many of the barriers were still embedded in outdated congressional legislation: the Communications Act of 1934, which touched only three industries—telephone, telegraph, and radio broadcasting. The legislation was designed primarily to protect these industries from outside competition. It gave AT&T a virtual monopoly over the national phone system. Despite its flaws, the 1934 law had effectively expanded First Amendment rights to cover electronic technologies. It did this by establishing the principle of universal access to telephone and broadcasting resources and by mandating its fulfillment. By and large, this goal had been achieved.

The 1934 law was amended over the years to accommodate new technologies, including television, satellites, and computer networks. These changes, however, kept the basic regulatory divisions between these technologies without regard to the technological convergence that was making such rigid separations irrelevant. Inevitably, the 1934 law became an anachronism in a computer-driven era when digitized information resources could be delivered down a common "information pipe." Rules of the road had to be revised to guide both government and industry into the new era.

The 1984 AT&T breakup was an attempt to meet this need for a new set of guidelines. It modified the dominant monopoly and introduced a greater measure of competition. It did not, however, resolve the larger issue—the increasing irrelevance of regulatory barriers that divided the product lines of communications suppliers, including phone companies, cable systems, satellite networks, and broadcasters. The FCC, led by its aggressive chairman, Reed Hundt, in the mid-1990s stepped up its efforts to dismantle some of these barriers.[20]

These were piecemeal efforts to accommodate outmoded laws. What was needed was a new approach, one that radically changed the old rules set up sixty years ago in a technologically innocent era. It took twenty years to finalize that new approach. The first congressional hearings to revise the 1934 legislation were held in 1976. The process was completed in 1996 with passage of landmark congressional legislation that redefined U.S. national policy in the new Meganet environment.

The Telecommunications Act of 1996 was a bundle of compromises wrapped into 180 pages of small type. Essentially, the law drastically reduced, and in many cases eliminated, the regulatory barriers between telephony, cable TV, satellites, and broadcasting in ways that permitted open competition among all digitally based services.[21]

The law was the outcome of an epic political battle that was waged for the most part outside of public view. Hundreds of lawyers and lobbyists were mobilized by phone companies and other communications firms to influence the legislation. Corporate lobbying and congressional logrolling were key ingredients in arriving at a consensus in which each of the industry's sectors got a respectable share of what it wanted.

The process of forming this consensus was a latter-day affirmation of Bismarck's observation that one should not look too closely at how sausages and laws are made. The road to final agreement on the legislation was paved using massive slabs of corporate funds. By conservative estimate, lobbying costs exceeded $50 million, including generous donations by political action committees. Larry Pressler, the South Dakota Republican who headed the key Senate committee, collected almost $500,000 in such funds during one six-month period in 1995.[22]

This largesse was shared by Democrats and Republicans alike, for the differences between their positions were minimal. What mattered was which industry lobby had the inside track with which individual member. Little attention was paid to the efforts of public interest groups such as the Consumers Union, which sought legislative assurances of open access to advanced Meganet facilities for ordinary citizens. Except for some rhetorical language, this factor was largely ignored in the 1996 legislation. The result was a flawed law. It established ground rules for a more competitive environment in the telecommunications sector. But their impact was marred by special interest provisions that benefited particular corporations or sections of the industry.[23]

It is still too early to assess the full effect of the Telecommunications Act of 1996. Although congressional authors claimed that the law was comprehensive, many critical issues were left open—either undecided or ignored altogether. Large sections of the legislation were purposely written in vague language, with the blanks to be filled in later. More than eighty provisions in the law were referred to the FCC for clarification.[24] Full implementation of the law could be delayed by a flood of legal challenges designed to limit the impact of the law's liberalized provisions on communications companies' traditional privileges. The regional Bells, for example, have mounted an assault on provisions that open the nation's local phone monopolies to competition.[25]

Despite its flaws, the 1996 law has set a new political tone in U.S. Meganet development. The thrust of the law was to recognize that regulatory micromanagement could no longer keep pace with technological and economic changes. Most regulations unravel as quickly as they are enacted. By removing barriers to digital coordination of most communications services, the new law signaled a shift away from the century-old practice of omnibus regulation of individual business sectors.[26]

To prepare themselves for this new era, communications and media companies are scrambling to strengthen their respective competitive positions through joint ventures, mergers, and buyouts. "These joint ventures are literally all over the map, across borders and across industries," according to Eli Noam, a telecommunications expert at Columbia University. "They have ended the notion of territoriality within business segments. Managers used to eat the other guy for breakfast; now they are inviting him over *for* breakfast."[27] In many cases, this involves negotiating mergers and other alliances to take advantage of cross-sector business opportunities now open to them.

Merger mania broke out in the phone industry. In the West, two regional Bell companies, Pacific Telesis and Southwestern Bell, joined forces in 1996. Bell Atlantic and Nynex made the same move in the East. In both mergers, the purpose was to consolidate management and technical resources in order to compete more effectively with AT&T, MCI, and Sprint in long-distance markets that were opened to the regional Bells by the new legislation. GTE, the largest provider of local phone service in the country, with 17 million customers, expanded into long-distance operations. Meanwhile, the three long-distance companies were restructuring themselves to compete in local telephone markets.[28]

The 1996 law has also affected overseas Meganet developments. Although it was binding only in the United States, the law tripped the wires that sent signals for changes in the pace and direction of Meganet expansion worldwide. The new law marked the first legislative acknowledgment by a national government of comprehensive digital age realities. Sooner or later, other countries will have to follow suit. The price of putting off such governmental decisions will be marginalization economically, if not politically and culturally.

The fifteen-nation European Union reacted to the new U.S. law by stepping up its schedule for liberalizing telecommunications regulations within Western Europe. The U.S. initiative also prompted the Japanese government to increase its efforts to loosen traditional controls over telecommunications. In brief, the 1996 law put other countries on notice that the U.S. telecom industry was positioning itself to compete globally at all levels—technological, economic, and political.

How will the new regulatory flexibility in the U.S. telecom sector affect global operations? U.S. companies probably have a five-year window of opportunity to press the advantage. But this lead may be temporary given the quick pace of Meganet development. The question is this: Will U.S. companies take advantage of the opportunity? Some observers have suggested that many U.S. firms will concentrate on new opportunities in the U.S. market, rather than exploit overseas investment possibilities. Other observers have suggested that it is more likely they will continue to pursue offshore opportunities as extensions of their domestic operations.

Global trade expansion is a matter of great interest to U.S. telecommunications policymakers. With $500 billion in U.S. overseas sales, goods and services produced by the communications sector represent the biggest, most rapidly expanding export area. London's *Economist* has projected that growth in the global information business will reach $3 trillion by the end of the decade, or roughly one of every six dollars of worldwide gross national product.[29] Overall, the Americans dominate this market. In the mid-1990s, for instance, U.S. information services firms had a 46 percent share of global trade and an annual growth rate of 13 percent.[30] Protecting this lead has been an objective of U.S. trade policy for more than a decade and will continue to be a policy focal point for as long as anyone can predict.

U.S. industry is confronting increasing foreign competition in its home market. Siemens, the giant German electronics firm, had eighty factories in the United States by 1996. Nokia, an obscure Finnish company, grew to be the second largest marketer of cellular phones. Canada's Nortel has challenged AT&T's traditional position as the largest domestic producer of telecommunications equipment.

Meanwhile, U.S. firms are striving to increase their share of overseas markets. They have enlisted the federal government's aid in lowering trade barriers that limit U.S. exports in Meganet-related areas. The mantra recited by Washington trade officials: the level playing field. They are pursuing tough negotiations to force governments to open their markets to U.S. products. This diplomatic offensive gathered steam during the Reagan and Bush administrations and reached full force during the Clinton era. The new emphasis was on expanding electronics and other high-tech exports, an objective that fits well with domestic information highway initiatives.

In the first Clinton administration, the tone of the new high-tech litany was set by a mild-mannered Berkeley economist named Laura D'Andrea Tyson, chair of the White House Council of Economic Advisers. She criticized what she called the rigged game of international competition in a book published just before Clinton took office in 1993: "The potential strategic threats posed by foreign ologopolistic control in some high-technology industries should be the cause of policy concern . . . especially when this control is exercised by the Japanese."[31]

Tyson's partner in carrying out tougher trade rules was a feisty Los Angeles lawyer named Mickey Kantor, head of the White House Office of the U.S. Trade Representative (USTR). (In 1996, he was appointed Secretary of Commerce.) At USTR, Kantor played the self-styled "tough cop" in negotiating for favorable trade opportunities in the communications and information sectors. The enormous market potential of mainland China was a particular target. In July 1994, a

White House mission to Beijing, which included the chief executives of twenty-five large U.S. corporations, resulted in joint-venture agreements worth almost $6 billion, including $620 million in communications and information products.[32]

The new trade strategy was a combination of carrots and sticks, promises and threats. It involved negotiations at three levels. The first level was direct discussions with individual countries, aimed at reducing their national trade barriers. These bilateral talks were, in part, the result of heavy congressional pressure to force individual countries to lower barriers. The 1988 Omnibus Trade Act mandated sanctions against countries that specifically discriminated against the import of U.S. telecommunications goods and services. The legislation set up a strict schedule for negotiations to remedy alleged discrimination, with specific sanctions should the talks fail. It was aimed directly at Japan and Germany, the biggest markets that maintained import limitations on U.S. communications goods and services.

The second level involved regional negotiations. By the early 1990s, regional economic blocs had assumed new importance. Canada, Mexico, and the U.S. signed the North American Free Trade Agreement (NAFTA), laying the groundwork for unrestricted trade among the three countries. In Europe, the twelve-nation European Community moved decisively to complete its goal of a regional free trade area. The newly industrialized Asian countries formed the Asia Pacific Economic Cooperation forum (APEC) and held initial discussions for creating a permanent regional economic organization.

In dealing with these regional groups, U.S. trade negotiators fought attempts to set limits on Meganet-related trade. In 1995, the United States and the European Union agreed to negotiate the phaseout of all tariffs and trade barriers to information technology products, including computers, semiconductors, and software, by the year 2000.[33] In Asia, the United States made a similar proposal to APEC in 1996, urging that tariffs on trade in information technology and products in the region be eliminated by the turn of the century.[34]

Meanwhile, Mickey Kantor and his USTR colleagues turned their attention to a larger issue: reform of global trading rules. These negotiations took place in the major forum for international rulemaking, the General Agreement on Tariffs and Trade (GATT). For more than forty years, GATT had applied mainly to trade in manufactured products. This left out the largest and fastest growing global businesses—service industries such as banking, tourism, and insurance, data services, and telecommunications traffic. U.S. business was clearly interested in including these in any new trading rules. Services are the chief U.S. export sector. In 1996, the services sector accounted for virtually all net job growth, as had been the case in eight of the previous sixteen years.[35]

U.S. negotiators had lobbied since the early 1970s to add trading in services to GATT. It was an uphill fight, as most GATT signatories resisted a change they regarded as primarily advantageous to the United States. Nevertheless, it became obvious that any new GATT-type agreement would have to include services. Agreement to take up the subject was finally reached in 1986 during negotiations known as the Uruguay Round, which set the agenda for reforming GATT's entire structure.

The GATT reform negotiations dragged on for seven years. Proposals dealing with services were a main source of contention. Most countries balked at making significant concessions that would open their borders to greater services competition, particularly in telecommunications and information trade. Nevertheless, by the time the Uruguay Round ended in 1993, negotiators had agreed on general trade rules for services. No agreement was reached, however, on how to deal with specific service sectors, including telecommunications. This setback threatened U.S. prospects for competing in the lucrative business of building the global Meganet. For U.S. interests, being shut out of the world market for basic telecommunications services just as it was feeling the swell of increasing telecom privatization was unacceptable. Intent on ending what it saw as unreasonable trade restrictions, the Clinton administration pressed for negotiations in the newly created World Trade Organization.[36] The result was a February 1997 agreement in which the United states and sixty-seven other countries endorsed liberalized rules that will open their telecommunications systems to greater competition among domestic and foreign carriers.[37]

Trade growth will continue to be a critical element in U.S. Meganet strategy in the coming years. Meanwhile, there are other issues that fit into the mosaic of U.S. Meganet policy. Although they seldom make headlines, they make for highly charged politics.

Take, for instance, the volatile issue of intellectual property rights— the protection of ideas and products, including patents, copyrights, trade secrets, and trademarks. Defending intellectual property rights is increasingly important because violations threaten high-tech U.S. industries at home and abroad. Theft and leakage of corporate and industrial secrets trebled during the mid-1990s, resulting in losses of $24 billion per year, according to a 1996 study by the American Society for Industrial Security.[38]

Industrial larceny was once a simple business, usually involving stolen documents. In a digital age, valuable secrets can be compressed onto a compact disc or moved across borders on Meganet circuits without leaving a trail. In most cases, no physical property is stolen, making detection untraceable and successful prosecution unlikely.[39] Acquiring advanced technology without paying for it is routinely encouraged by many overseas governments, either through covert spy operations or more open methods (e.g., requiring foreign companies to turn over secrets as the price of doing business in the country).[40]

The U.S. government has tried to stem intellectual property losses, without much success. In the cold war days, Washington was reasonably effective in pressuring other governments to halt the export of ideas and products to the Soviet Union, China, and their allies. But cold war incentives no longer hold. The new struggle is for economic advantage. Many cold war restrictions remain, but they are resisted and often flouted, even by U.S. companies.

One area where U.S. companies have opposed federal restrictions is the ban on export of advanced encryption technology. Some firms use ingenious methods to get around the regulations. Sun Microsystems, a major California software company, decided to use a foreign system, rather than fight the restrictions. The company turned to a world-class group of experts: unemployed Russian cryptographers whose previous job had been developing advanced Soviet codes.[41] Meanwhile, computer industry executives have warned that failure to allow greater use and export of advanced computer encryption could severely impair high-tech U.S. exports. A congressional inquiry into the subject in 1996 suggested that the computer industry could lose up to $60 billion by the year 2000 if it continued to be barred from selling cryptography products abroad.[42]

Despite such frustrations, protecting the U.S. lead in advanced technologies has remained high on Washington's agenda. In the negotiations leading to the inclusion of services in the World Trade Organization, the Clinton administration lobbied successfully for enforceable protection of patents, copyrights, trade secrets, and trademarks. It has also called for digital age regulations to replace out-of-date rules developed by a United Nations agency, the World Intellectual Property Organization (WIPO). These changes may help, but the most effective approach is the threat of trade sanctions against governments that actively support piracy of goods and services. Often this approach fails, as exemplified by the continuing attempts to enforce sanctions against flagrant violations by China.[43]

There is another trade-related area that has affected Meganet prospects: technical standards. Meganet works efficiently when all countries agree on the technical rules for its operations. In a simpler era, such standards were easier to determine. Many of them were set by the two U.S. corporations that dominated their industries: AT&T

in telecommunications and IBM in computers. In the more complex digital era, such simplicities have gone by the board.

Obtaining international agreement on standards has often been politically difficult. One example: the ten-year effort to set rules for a universal telephone numbering system that would make it easy to dial up any phone anywhere electronically, without benefit of an operator. Negotiations, sponsored by the ITU, took a decade to arrive at an elegantly simple solution. Every telephone number on earth now has, in addition to its own number, a country code as well as a code for the region within the country. Thus, a businessman in New York can dial 49-511-978800 to reach a company in Langenhagen, Germany. Most technical standard solutions, however, are not so simple. Politics intervenes as countries try to protect technological and trade advantages.

Standards decisions carry heavy economic overtones. Whenever a single country or company is able to dictate an industry standard, competitors are put at a disadvantage. A familiar example is Microsoft's Windows technology, which is found in 80 percent of computer operating systems, giving the company an enormous advantage in marketing its products. Ongoing international negotiations deal with technical standards in such areas as digital video discs, telecommunications connection standards, the radio spectrum, computer operating systems, and video games—with billions of dollars riding on the outcomes of each decision.[44]

Technical standards are part of the mosaic of issues that collectively make up U.S. communications policy in the Meganet era. It is only in the last decade or so that a coherent idea has emerged as to the impact of communications resources on U.S. strategic interests. The subject was given its first public airing in a 1984 report entitled *America's Hidden Vulnerabilities: Crisis Management in a Society of Networks*, which was based on research conducted at the Center for Strategic and International Studies in Washington.[45] The report documented in detail the extent to which U.S. society was vulnerable to serious disruption of its communications systems by terrorists and other enemies.

The problem has become more acute since that 1984 report. Its current dimensions are summed up by CSIS scholar Walter Laqueur:

> There is little secrecy in the wired society and protective measures have proved of limited value. . . . The possibilities for creating chaos are almost unlimited even now, and vulnerability will almost certainly increase. Why assassinate a politician or indiscriminately kill people when an attack on electronic switching will produce far more dramatic and lasting results. The switch at Culpeper, Virginia, headquarters of the Federal Reserve's electronic network, which handles all federal funds and transactions, would be an obvious place to hit. If the new terrorism di-

rects its energies toward information warfare, its destructive power will be exponentially greater that any it wielded in the past—even greater than it would be with biological and chemical weapons.[46]

This vulnerability of communications systems is now a priority concern in the U.S. government's national security agenda. The concern ranged from sophisticated terrorist threats to the disruptive activities of computer hackers. In 1996, a twenty-two-year-old Argentine student, using a PC, was charged by U.S. authorities with breaking into sensitive government computer networks via the Internet. His entry point from his home in Buenos Aires was a computer installation at Harvard University.

As a follow-up to this incident, the Department of Justice succeeded, for the first time, in getting a court order to monitor private electronic communications. This led to a new form of "cyber-sleuthing" in which law enforcement officers spend their working hours at computer terminals, sifting through webs of electronic leads, rather than knocking on doors or doing paperwork. "This is," said Justice Department attorney Donald K. Stern, "a glimpse of what computer crime-fighting will look like in the coming years."[47]

In terms of national security, the problem has implications that go well beyond the antics of hackers. There are basic questions about the nature of military force in an evolving information age. The subject has created its own vocabulary of clichés—cyberdeterrence, digital battlefields, netwars, and information warfare. At one level, the new role of military force involves exploiting information technologies to defeat an enemy on the battlefield. As a Pentagon-sponsored study noted: "The computer chip and digital systems for ground combat are as radical as the machine gun in World War I and the blitzkrieg in World War II; they permit standoff attacks rather than closure to rifle range, decreasing U.S. casualty rates and increasing the tempo and breadth of the battlefield."[48] Two Rand Corporation researchers, John Arquilla and David Ronfeldt, have taken a wider strategic view of what they call cyberwar:

> The information revolution implies the rise of a mode of warfare in which neither mass nor mobility will decide outcomes; instead the side that knows more, that can disperse the fog of war yet enshroud an adversary in it, will enjoy decisive advantages. At a minimum, cyberwar represents an extension of the traditional importance of obtaining information in war: having superior command, control, communication and intelligence and trying to locate, read, surprise and deceive the enemy before he does the same to you.[49]

These military options are clearly dependent upon the continued expansion of Meganet resources. But the decisive struggles in twenty-first-century information warfare, as Walter Laqueur pointed out, could take place elsewhere than on traditional battlefields. This war may be aimed primarily at civilian communications targets: cable lines, microwave towers, and the like. The physical fragility of most communications networks makes them highly susceptible to hostile actions that can paralyze a city—or even an entire nation. This is especially true of the most vulnerable of electronic information resources: computers, which can be disabled by invisible viruses.[50]

This weakness in computer-driven communications systems has been exposed on a number of occasions. A software bug in one of AT&T's regional switching centers brought down the company's long-distance network for nine hours in 1990. Such disruptions could have a devastating effect on the Pentagon's communications traffic, of which 95 percent is carried by nonmilitary circuits.[51] This very concern has led U.S. government officials to create the Information Warfare Technology Center, a unit of the National Security Agency, to defend military and intelligence computer installations against break-ins.[52]

Protecting classified electronic information is a formidable problem. In 1993, the Pentagon's Defense Information Systems Agency assembled a team of in-house hackers to test the vulnerability of military computers. The team was able to take control of 88 percent of the 8,400 Pentagon machines they attacked, with only 4 percent of the penetrations noted by computer operators. Commenting on these weaknesses in computer security, former CIA director John Deutsch noted: "This is a very important subject ... which we really don't have a crisp answer to. Understanding that we have a vulnerability and knowing what to do about it are two different things."[53]

There is a growing consensus among strategic planners inside and outside the military that advanced Meganet resources enhance U.S. power to influence global events. This new factor is America's information edge, reinforcing its conventional military and economic strength, according to Harvard University political scientist Joseph Nye: "Knowledge, more than ever, is power. The one country that can best lead the information revolution will be more powerful than any other. For the foreseeable future, that country is the United States. America has apparent strength in military power and economic production. Yet its more subtle comparative advantage is its ability to collect, process, act upon and disseminate information, an edge that will almost certainly grow in the next decade." Professor Nye has pointed out that U.S. negotiators now have an advantageous capability in providing (or withholding) information, particularly high-tech data, that other countries need to cope with information age problems.[54]

Meganet's effect on U.S. security in a changing world order is only beginning to be sorted out. The process calls for new kinds of strategic thinking. Meganet resources are already overriding comfortable but older political and economic practices. One example, discussed in Chapter 6, is the way in which controls over the flow of money, a critical prerogative of governments, are being bypassed by electronic transfers over the Meganet. As Walter Wriston, former chairman of Citicorp, has pointed out: "No matter what formal decisions a government makes, the 200,000 screens on the world's trading rooms will continue to light up, the news will march across the tube, traders will make judgments and a value will be placed on a currency that will be known instantly all over the globe."[55]

These Meganet-based developments raise questions about the continued relevance of the nation-state, the strongest political unit in the modern era. This strength has been measured by geography, natural resources, military strength, and, not least, control over communications and information resources. This latter power is slipping away fast in the early Meganet era. National governments cannot control even the simplest information outlets such as telephones or Internet access. What kind of world will it be when information has no boundaries. Does the nation-state have a future? If so, what is that future like? Can the U.S. democratic structure cope with these information age complexities?[56]

There are no easy answers to these questions. What can be hoped for is a working consensus by Americans on how best to reorder their democratic institutions to meet the challenges of the information age. That means identifying appropriate ways of protecting the interests of a free and open society at home. It also means finding ways to set an example for other societies seeking similar benefits for themselves.

8

INTERNET: THE MODEL FOR MEGANET?

A rough model for an advanced Meganet exists: the Internet, the free-form network of networks that links tens of millions of computer users around the world. As it expands, the Internet provides us with early-warning signals of both the opportunities and the barriers that lay ahead in building a worldwide information network. In this chapter we look at how the Internet relates to the Meganet currently and potentially.

While in its early stages of development, the Internet means different things to different people:

- Nicholas Negroponte, director of MIT's Media Lab, measures its impact as "10.5 on the Richter scale of social change."[1]
- Bill Gates, the Microsoft wunderkind, believes that it holds out the promise of a golden era of "friction-free capitalism."[2]
- Novelist William Gibson, who coined *cyberspace*, thinks the Internet is "the great anarchic event that defies conventional commercial exploitation."[3]
- James Gleick, author of *Chaos*: "The hardest fact to grasp about the Internet and the I-way is this: It isn't a thing, it isn't an entity; it isn't an organization. No one owns it; no one runs it. It is simply Everyone's Computer . . . the most universal and indispensable network on the planet somehow burgeoned without so much as a board of directors, never mind a mergers-and-acquisitions department."[4]
- Astronomer Clifford Stoll deplores all the rosy visions of an Internet world: "It is an overpromoted, hollow world, devoid of

warmth and human kindness. . . . No birds sing. For all the promises of virtual communities, it's more important to live a real life in a real neighborhood.[5]
• Anatoly Voronov, a Russian computer expert, sees the Net as a dark Yankee plot, a brooding presence whose heavy American content makes it "the ultimate act of intellectual colonialism."[6]

The Internet is too new, too varied and too fast-moving to be measured accurately. Its sheer size is daunting. As London's *Economist* has pointed out:

> It is more populous than 49 of the 50 American states; its population is growing at a rate to make a pope blush; all its citizens have a degree of functional illiteracy. Its size, complexity and rapid growth have made the world's largest network of interconnected computers, the Internet, a great place for chat, idle and otherwise. They could make it a great marketplace, too. The Internet offers new ways to share work, to make contacts, to provide the information on which markets thrive.[7]

These contrasting estimations of the Internet reflect its unpredictable impacts on conceived notions of how an advanced global Meganet might be developed and managed by governments and corporations. The Internet has speeded up the timetable for Meganet development and has challenged the plans of Meganet builders. The Internet is, in the biologist's language, a sport, an accident that both defies and validates the norms. So far, the Internet is not controlled by any vested interest. It operates under few rules beyond those imposed by its relatively simple technology.

In a curious way, the Internet is reversing the Meganet pattern. The Meganet project is being planned, built, and managed from the top down by a political and economic establishment. The Internet has emerged from below. It operates on Meganet facilities, but its strength has been the unconstrained ways in which its users have shaped its development. It works largely because it was ignored for many years, regarded as the plaything of computer buffs and academics.

Internet's achievement is that it has responded to a powerful, unmet need: easy, economical access to previously unavailable information resources. It is Meganet's wild card, an unexpected demonstration in miniature of what a truly open information utility might look like in the future.[8]

For the present, conventional Meganet services and the Internet are developing side by side in a kind of symbiotic relationship. Both are powerful resources in meeting global information needs. The Internet is sufficiently strong that it cannot be ignored as an early model for

Meganet as a universal information network. It is instructive, therefore, to look at the Internet's current activities and to assess its future as part of the larger Meganet.

First, a word of caution: For all the hype generated about the Internet, it is still a minor blip on the global communications screen. Its effect on the growth and direction of a global Meganet is largely in the future. The Internet's audience now comprises less than 1 percent of the world's population. Overwhelmingly, this small group lives in one region: North America.

For the present, the Internet's technical capabilities are largely limited to providing data information with some graphics. Eventually, the Net will be a large-scale supplier of audio and video services, but this prospect is some ways down the information highway. Another limitation is that most of the traffic on the Internet is in English—the language of less than 15 percent of the world's population. As one South Korean computer expert has pointed out, "It's not only English you have to understand, but American culture, even slang. All in all, there are many people who just give up."[9]

One day, English or some sort of computerized "unicode" may dominate. One prospect is the development of a language-translation capability. A primitive version of such a device was put on the market in 1996 by a Virginia-based firm, Globalink. The software allows a user to click a "translate" button on the screen to get a rough translation of a foreign-language text.[10] For the present, however, language has remained a significant constraint to the Internet's global expansion.

Today's Internet is a transitional phenomenon. It began as an experiment by young technocrats who wanted to create an alternative to conventional information networks. It operates within the existing telecommunications structure, but it is also independent. There is no organization that is in charge of the Internet, or even speaks for it. It is self-propelled. The closest to an institutional voice is a group of national Internet societies whose membership consists mostly of computer buffs interested in preserving the Net's philosophy of open-ended access to information resources. The Internet societies—there are several dozen scattered around the world—meet annually to debate the Net's future and to discuss its technical needs. They do not, individually or collectively, control the network. The Internet's explosive growth in recent years caught the big telecommunications and information companies off-guard. Belatedly, IBM, AT&T, MCI, Microsoft, and others are adjusting their corporate strategies to Internet realities. By 1997, they were on their way to replacing the influence of the loose confederation of Internet societies that had been responsible for setting the Net's working rules.

Under this corporate influence, the Internet is moving rapidly away from the electroanarchic visions that motivated many of its early promoters. The Net began, paradoxically, as a cold war military project. In 1962, Paul Baran, a researcher at the Rand Corporation in Santa Monica, California, was studying ways to maintain Department of Defense (DOD) communications in the case of a disruption due to nuclear attack. He came up with the idea of packet switching—breaking up messages into small, digitized packages and sending them along the established military network, often by circuitous routes, for reassembly at the intended destination. Package switching is still the basic technology underlying Internet operations. The same technology is also used now by much of the other traffic flowing through Meganet circuits.

Four years after Baran's breakthrough, DOD's Advanced Research Projects Agency (ARPA) budgeted $1 million to build a small packet data network. Several dozen companies bid on the project. One of the hallowed bits of early Internet lore is that IBM declined to bid, claiming that such a network could never be built. IBM has long since reversed its doubts about the Internet, making it a centerpiece of its production and marketing strategies in the 1990s.[11] The ARPA experiment was a success, in large part because a group of graduate students developed software, known as TCP/IP, which is the common language understood by computers on the Internet. One of the graduate students was Vinton Cerf, who later became a leading proponent of the Internet. Another was Doug Engelbart, who invented the computer mouse.[12]

The new "Arpanet" spread rapidly, linking military and civilian research installations. In 1983, a decision was made to divide the network between military and civilian circuits. The civilian grid—the Internet—was funded by the National Science Foundation, largely as a result of congressional pressure, which was led by an up-and-coming U.S. senator from Tennessee, Al Gore. The new Internet linked fewer than 300 host computers. In 1993, this had increased to more than 1 million linkups. In 1996, there were more than 10 million, not including the millions of individuals who have access to the Internet through America Online and other consumer services.[13]

These statistics are estimates, like most numbers that describe the Internet. Describing the network tends to be an inflated exercise in numbers. A cottage industry has sprung up in which consultants make educated guesses about the size, shape, and direction of the Internet. The few reliable statistics they come up with are generally outdated before they are published.

Meanwhile, the Internet continues to grow, with no signs of leveling off. Veronis, Suhler & Associates, a New York consultancy, sees compound growth in interactive digital media, including Internet services, averaging 33 percent annually in the late 1990s, totaling $6.1 billion in 1999.[14] Perhaps the most accurate index of Internet growth is sales of Internet-related hardware. Web servers are a critical enabling technology for the Internet's World Wide Web: Industry figures show that 300,000 servers were sold in 1995, triple the number sold the previous year.[15] Sales have also boomed for the makers of other Internet hardware. The three leading Internet equipment makers— Cisco Systems, 3Com, and Bay Network—rose from obscurity in the early 1990s to a combined market capitalization of nearly $38 billion by 1996.[16]

The biggest statistical gaps are usually seen in attempts to determine the number of Internet users. Estimates vary widely. Vinton Cerf, the network's pioneer, stuck a pin in the statistical balloon by pointing out that if one were to make an estimate based on the network's rate of expansion during the mid-1990s, everyone on earth would soon be on the Internet, an unlikely prospect. By 1997, most estimates put the number of online Americans at about 30 million. A 1996 IBM survey predicted that there would be 500 million Internet users by the end of the decade.[17] However, these figures have been skewed by the fact that for years analysts assumed an average of ten users per Internet host computer, which can be a single PC with one user or a network server with hundreds of users. Moreover, as Mark Lotter of Network Wizards, a California Internet service company, has pointed out, an increasing number of Internet host computers are "hidden" by security system firewalls.

Even less is known about the demographic profiles of Internet users—age, sex, race, occupation, or personal interests. A classic *New Yorker* cartoon depicted two dogs, one saying, "On the Internet, nobody knows you're a dog." The problem is compounded by the fact that many users are known only by their cybernames. It was months before the sexual come-ons of "Fabulous Hot Babe" on an Internet chat line were discovered to be the creative musings of an eighty-three-year-old man living in a Miami nursing home. Most Internet users are more conventional.[18] A decade ago, they tended to be college-educated males. A 1996 Nielsen survey indicated that this pattern was changing. Women now make up 40 percent of Internet users. The percentage of users with college degrees had dropped in a few years from 56 percent to 39 percent; that of users living in households with incomes exceeding $80,000 fell from 27 percent to 17 percent.[19]

The majority of Internet users seek information and entertainment resources. Others wend their way through the Internet's electronic maze to make contact with like-minded human beings. This explains the tens of thousands of informal subnetworks on the Net that link, for example, Barbie collectors, Illinois Democrats, fly fishermen, or Shakespeare buffs, among others.

Much of this searching is lightweight and transitory. Some of it meets deep-felt human needs. One such network on the World Wide Web links families who are caring for relatives with Alzheimer's disease. The Alzheimer's Center at the University Hospitals of Cleveland sponsored a twenty-four-hour Internet support group, standing as an excellent example of the network's ability to link people with special, sometimes desperately real needs. Michelle Slatal, who has tracked the development of the Alzheimer's network, had this hypothesis: "It is 3 a.m. Your Alzheimer's spouse won't let you sleep. A month ago, you'd be sobbing uncontrollably. Instead you turn to your keyboard, knowing that you can connect to someone who is also up, also dealing with the same tragedy. When people talk about community on the Net, this is what they really mean."[20]

The Alzheimer's network is part of the World Wide Web, the fastest growing service on the Internet. Created in 1989 by Tim Berners-Lee, a British high energy physicist, the Web has vastly simplified access to Internet sites. Berners-Lee saw the Web as "a seamless world in which all information, from any source can be accessed in a consistent and simple way . . . on any type of computer from any country, using one program."[21] His vision has had a profound effect on the Internet's development. Because of it, the network's resources are made available to even the most technically impaired users by allowing them an easier means of access, much like television channel–surfing. A report by the Massachusetts-based consulting group Forrester Research noted, "The World Wide Web has almost single-handedly transformed the net from a members-only sandbox into a gigantic crossroads with strip malls, noveau info-publishers and EDI depots."[22]

Professor Berners-Lee's purposes in developing the Web were strictly academic. He wanted a user-friendly way to connect nuclear energy researchers around the world. Academic exchanges are still an important Web activity. A major use is the Human Genome Project, a global effort by biologists to decode DNA genes. From small beginnings in 1992, by 1996 the Human Genome Project's webpages were receiving more than 12,000 queries per day.[23] The Web has also turned more conventional educational institutions, from graduate schools down to kindergartens, into Internet users. U.S. school districts spent an estimated $4 billion on educational technology during the 1995–1996 school year, much of it on Internet-related equipment and services.[24]

Webpages include an indiscriminate jumble of subjects, from the profound to the frivolous. These disparate subjects coexist in electronic equality, using the same format and covering a wide range of interests. It is less than a decade since the Web first appeared, but no one can say with any certainty how many webpages it contains. In 1995, when Digital Equipment, a computer group, developed high-powered software to search and index information on the Web, it identified 30 million; a year later, there were 50 million.

The expanding number of Webpages is astonishing, but most of them are seldom activated. Per Bilse, head of EUnet, Europe's largest Internet service provider, estimates that 90 percent of Web traffic can be traced to about fifty sites.[25] The U.S. government is a major (and popular) presence on the Web, from White House webpages to the those sponsored by the Department of Interior's Fish and Wildlife Service.

The Web is the electronic home of a wide range of organizations, including religious groups. The Jewish community in England sponsors a webpage that reaches out to the worldwide dspora. By means of it, twelve-year-old boys in isolated areas can prepare for their bar mitzvahs. When the Vatican joined the Web during Christmas 1995, Pope John Paul II received 300,000 "hits" from seventy countries within two days. Many of them offered remedies for a bout of flu that had prevented him from celebrating Christmas mass. He was advised to drink lots of liquids, including chicken soup.[26] The Dalai Lama, spiritual leader of Tibetan Buddhists, is also on the Web (www.tibet.com).

The Web is a huge electronic tent in which all kinds of organizations have set up displays of information, ideas, and opinions. The greatest activity surrounds sites for doing commercial business, which industry people call *electronic commerce*. Futurist George Gilder sees the Net emerging as "the central nervous system of global capitalism."[27] This development is occurring in many ways, at different speeds and levels. As is true in estimating numbers for other aspects of the Internet, it is difficult to nail down quantifiable facts. Prophets outnumber practitioners in defining the future of electronic commerce on the Web. There is, however, no doubt as to the speedy, upward direction of the trend.

By 1997, there were more than 2 million Internet host computers registered under the network's .com suffix, the domain for commercial sites (different suffixes mark other important domains, e.g., .edu for educational sites and .gov for government sites). Almost half of publicly traded U.S. companies with annual sales of more than $1.5 billion had a presence on the Internet by 1995, according to the U.S. Internet Society (ISOC). ISOC estimated at the time that about 60 percent of Internet traffic is commercial in origin. The Standish Group, a Massachusetts consultancy, has projected that half of all global electronic transactions will take place over the Internet by the end of the decade.[28]

BOX 8.1 SURFING THE WEB: AN ECLECTIC COLLECTION OF WORLD WIDE WEBSITES

Subway Maps—metro.jussieu.fr:10001/bin/cities/english. Maps subway routes in cities around the world.

Wine Tasting—augustcsser.washington.edu/personal/bigstar-mosaic/winde.html. Includes a virtual tasting group.

Arizona Hang Gliding Association—azstarnet.com/~azhg/AHGA.html. The webpage warns: "Do not bet your life on the information contained here."

Net Banker—netbanker.com. A listing of the leading financial services websites.

Girl Scout Cookies—cookies.openmarket.com/GSstore. Cookies can be ordered on this webpage.

United Nations—undcp.or.at/unlinks.html. Encyclopedic information about the world organization.

Sherlock Holmes—bcpl.lib.md.us/imoskowi/holmes/html. Information about the great detective, including electronic versions of all the Sherlock Holmes novels.

World Map—pubweb.parc.xerox.com/map. Zoom in to a map of any spot on earth.

Horticulture—btw.com/urls/toc.html. Tips for home and garden.

Legal Beat—wired.com/justin/dox/law.html. Current legal cases dealing with cyberspace.

Internet Games—wcl-rs.bham.ac.uk/gamesdomain.

American Marketing Association—ama.org/gem. Information on latest trends in marketing strategies.

The White House—whitehouse.gov. Presidential greetings, texts of official statements, and menu of other government information sources.

Virtual Frog Dissection—george.lbl.gov/ITG.hm.pg.docs/dissect/info.html.

Fed World—fedworld.gov. Your tax dollars at work.

NASA Jet Propulsion Laboratory—jpl.nasa.gov. A catalog of the space agency's activities, including color photos from the space shuttle.

Hard@Work—hardatwork.com. An "online water cooler" dedicated to discussions of getting ahead in the corporate world.

Virtual Meet Market—wwa.com:1111. Cyberspace bar scene. Men outnumber women ten to one.

San Francisco Hotels—hotelres.com. Booking reservations at the city's hotels.

Other Net watchers are more cautious about the Internet's business offerings. For the present, these offerings consist mostly of what can best be described as corporate billboards, where companies describe themselves and their services. Traditional retail marketing is developing more slowly on the Internet. Goldman Sachs, the New York banking house, believes that retail sales consummated over the Internet will reach $382 million in 1997, up from $7 million in 1994.[29] The increase is significant, but it is still a blip in the $6-trillion U.S. retail economy.

Cautious projections of the Internet's commercial prospects have not noticeably slowed down the business community's interest in cyberspace markets. Companies are looking for the "killer application," the formula that will make the network a profitable business location. The failure rate for companies that have tried various formulas has been high; most of them rushed onto the Net with little or no economic analysis and without any business plan.[30] Other firms have done well. The companies benefiting most from the Internet's rapid growth are those that facilitate access to the network. From the Internet's earliest days, signing on has often been a frustrating task, even for the computer buffs who were the network's original audience. The problem has become more acute as the Internet attracted millions of consumer users, most of whom were not computer "experts." Network circuits were often gridlocked. Responses to user commands became intolerable during these "brownouts." By the mid-1990s, software executive Mark Garver could complain, "The U.S. Internet is about as reliable these days as the phone system in Russia."[31] As Anthony Rutkowski, a network pioneer, pointed out: "Using the network is still too complicated right now for anyone but moderately skilled geeks. What we have to do is almost reduce it to the ultimate no-brainer potentially anywhere in the world, over just about any medium."[32]

Dozens of companies have rushed in to offer solutions for easier access. The most familiar are consumer services such as America Online, CompuServe, and the Microsoft Network, who have opened up the Internet to more than 15 million subscribers in North America and abroad. Less known are the commercial service providers whose customers are corporations and other large institutions. Collectively, they represent an industry that for all intents and purposes did not exist ten years ago. By 1995, it was a $1.07-billion sector, with an estimated monthly growth rate of 67 percent.[33]

Internet access firms began in the early 1990s as mom-and-pop operations. The age of innocence lasted only a few years. Today, the sector has been taken over by large firms. The smaller ones (known as "toaster nets" in the industry) are being bought off or pushed out. It is a fiercely competitive business, rife with price wars. In 1996, California-based Netcom On-Line Communications Services was the largest independent provider of Internet access, yet it could not turn a profit.[34]

Netcom and other startup firms are hard-pressed by bigger companies with deeper financial pockets, among them AT&T, IBM, MCI, and the regional phone companies. AT&T's 1996 announcement that it would supply Internet access service at favorable rates to its 80 million long-distance customers sent shock waves through the industry. Another potent competitor is Hughes Network Systems, a General Motors subsidiary whose national satellite network offers DirecPC access, including Internet services, to home computer users.[35]

The Internet access providers set the stage for the network's next major development: its use as a commercial marketplace. Companies began to look at the Internet as a place to do business. The short-term prospect was an opportunity to reach the millions of younger, more affluent men and women who were already Internet users. Further down the road, the Internet held out the promise of access to a larger mass market.[36]

The Internet's commercial buildup has been slow but steady in the late 1990s. The network does not fit easily into traditional mass-marketing patterns. An important difference is that Internet users cannot be identified statistically, with the kind of demographic numbers beloved by marketing executives. Nevertheless, the potential rewards for setting up electronic sites to advertise themselves and their products have been too strong for many companies to resist.

A few firms began cautiously, buying advertising space on consumer access services such as America Online and Prodigy. Increasingly, however, companies are setting up their own pages on the World Wide Web. These began as low-key "electronic store windows" in which firms displayed general information about themselves and their services. In most cases, the results were institutional and boring, full of self-congratulatory prose.

Some companies learned to use their corporate billboards more imaginatively. An early example was Time Warner, which set up Pathfinder pages that offered excerpts from its publications. By 1995, the Pathfinder site was averaging 2 million hits weekly. Canada's Molson Brewing Company ran a successful contest on the Web to publicize a new beer. The prize was a trip to a "beach party" 100 miles from the Arctic Circle. General Electric used its Web billboard to supplement its toll-free telephone service for answering customer queries. Federal Express, which makes 2 million deliveries every day, lets customers know the status of their packages at any given time. Procter & Gamble has sites (headaches.com, underarms.com) to explain how its products can ease your problems.[37]

In 1996, General Motors launched an innovative marketing site on the Web. It is a cyberspace showroom where prospective customers can choose the combination of features they want in a car or truck, then take a virtual ride that allows the "driver" to get 360-degree interior and exterior views. "The idea is to create a 'buzz' so that Internet users will tell each other 'you've got to check out the GM site,'" says Phil Guarascio, a GM marketing executive.[38]

Corporate billboards are now a prominent feature on the Internet. By 1996, they accounted for an estimated 70 percent of new Web-pages.[39] More recently, they are being developed well beyond their original role as showcase for companies and products. The Net is becoming a direct marketing instrument, supplementing sales made through retail stores, catalogs, toll-free telephone numbers, and direct mail. As with most aspects of Internet commerce, these direct marketing efforts are relatively new and untested. Experience with them is anecdotal, and hard numbers on their effectiveness are hard to come by. There have already been many failed experiments, mainly by companies who saw the Internet as a low-cost marketing outlet. But the Internet is not a bargain basement. The cost of entry into Internet advertising can be quite high, reaching upwards of $1 million for a major campaign.[40] Moreover, most Internet users are skittish about buying products on the Web, with justified concern about giving out credit card numbers, or even addresses and telephone numbers, on an open network.

Despite these drawbacks, consumer retailing on the Web is growing. The initial beneficiaries have been sellers of computer software and machines, presumably because computer-wise Internet users know and trust these sellers. In 1996, Microsoft announced plans to make its software products widely available for purchase over the network. "We want to be where our customers want to shop," says Johan Liedgren, a Microsoft marketing director.[41] The company estimates that 10 percent of its software sales will be distributed electronically via the Internet by 1998. Forrester Research, the Massachusetts consultancy, predicts that by the end of the decade as much as 50 percent of all software will be delivered online.[42]

The prospects for Internet marketing are being watched closely by newspapers and other mass media. They see a threat to their current operations in the Internet's ability to deliver massive amounts of information and entertainment to homes. These concerns are most immediate for the print industries—newspapers, magazines, and books. Internet video and audio services are still too technologically limited to be a threat to Hollywood or the television networks. The print publishers' initial reaction to the Internet was to seek customers on the World Wide Web. A website, the Electronic Newsstand, was set up in the early 1990s, offering excerpts from hundreds of publications together with inducements to subscribe online. The project was a failure, in part because 30 percent of those who did subscribe didn't pay up.[43]

More recently, publishers have begun marketing more aggressively on the Internet. Time Warner's Pathfinder pages began charging for access to the company's publications in 1996, after initially offering it free. *USA Today* has brought its snappy news style to the network, specializing in sports scores and features. Subscribers initially paid $14.95 per month for three hours' usage, with lower charges for additional hours. The *San Jose Mercury News*, owned by Knight-Ridder, charged $4.95 per month for access to its website (current newspaper subscribers paid only $1).

The most extensive test of Internet media marketing was inaugurated in April 1996 by the *Wall Street Journal*. The *Journal's* Interactive Edition is a bet by Dow Jones, the *Journal's* publisher, that its readers will pay a hefty annual subscription fee to get the paper delivered electronically. The online edition is aimed at the large number of business executives among the *Journal's* nearly 2 million subscribers who use personal computers. In addition to receiving the paper's daily news and features, subscribers can track the current status of their personal investment portfolios through the Dow Jones electronic data service.[44]

The most controversial electronic publishing project has been *Slate*, a Web magazine edited by Michael Kinsley, a Washington journalist. Funded by Microsoft, *Slate* is a relatively highbrow weekly review of opinion, politics, and the arts. Kinsley had high hopes that the publication would set a trend: "My measurement of our success or failure is, in an odd way, financial. I would like to demonstrate that a magazine of serious journalism can be self-supporting on the Web and that this new technology can be used in a way that serves democracy."[45]

Most media observers doubt there will be a significant shift of readers to electronic pages any time soon. As Richard Harwood, the *Washington Post* media critic, pointed out, the market prospects are still very limited: "This is probably a major reason that the *Washington Post* and the *New York Times* are investing hundreds of millions of dollars in new presses and that the press moguls at Gannett, Knight-Ridder and other companies are on the prowl for newspapers to buy. That's where the bucks are: $36 billion in advertising revenues last year as against less than $5 million from the Internet."[46]

Meanwhile, Internet marketing of goods and services is advancing on other fronts. Companies are setting up "interactive departments," to explore cyberspace marketing prospects. They are also taking a closer look at the actual size and nature of the Internet audience. One survey, conducted by Thomas Miller, publisher of the newsletter *Interactive Consumer*, suggested that less than 15 percent of Internet users can be classified as active prospects for consumer sales. The rest come to the Internet from corporations, academia, and the government, primarily for professional reasons.[47] The Internet is no quick road to marketing success. Nevertheless, most analysts see more consumer-oriented marketing opportunities on the network as the number of home computer users increases.

The businesses that have the highest hopes for cashing in on these prospects are in the financial services sector. More than any other industry, financial services firms have transformed their internal operations through electronic networking during the past thirty years. They now see another opportunity to extend their electronic reach to retail consumers, shifting them from old-fashioned transactions to full service through the Internet.

Banks and other financial services advertise the convenience of electronic transactions. Customer convenience may be one benefit, but their primary interest is in the potential cost savings from consumer networking, specifically in keeping customers at electronic arm's length from their employees. In the mid-1990s, the average cost of each customer-teller transaction was almost $3. An ATM transaction cost $.27. Transactions on the Internet promise to be considerably cheaper.[48]

The Internet is the next big step in wiring up consumer money markets. Financial services firms currently account for the largest number of new business registrations on the Internet, with banks leading the way.[49] Their aim is not only to lower transactions costs but also to hold on to customers being lured away by competition from outside the banking industry. These nonbanks include AT&T, the second biggest domestic provider of credit cards; it has its own Internet facilities to service them. A 1996 Booz Allen & Hamilton survey predicted that by 2000 more than 16 million households will bank via the Internet. The study also projected that 1,500 banks would have Internet sites by 1999 and that at least 500 of these would offer full-fledged banking capability.[50]

Despite the Internet's attractions, financial firms are cautious about moving too quickly into cyberbanking. Most still limit themselves to Webpages that advertise services. More recently, other financial services firms have been migrating to the Internet. One of the largest U.S. mutual fund groups, Fidelity Investments, has relied heavily on Internet marketing to reach old and new customers. By 1996, its website was receiving an average of 20,000 hits daily.[51] Discount brokerage houses have also moved aggressively to the Internet, facilitating stock trades, providing information about customer accounts, and offering real-time or delayed stock price quotations. In 1996, an estimated 800,000 investors had such online accounts—a small but growing segment of the 60 million more conventional accounts held by U.S. investors.[52]

The Internet's big challenge for financial services groups will be its ability to process real-time credit card transactions for online shoppers. Their target is the more than 150 million credit cards held by U.S. consumers. The technology is largely in place. The problem is the Internet's vulnerability to fraud. One 1996 survey estimated that there was an Internet security breach every twenty seconds.[53] In February 1996, the two largest global credit card firms—Visa International and MasterCard International—announced an agreement on technical specifications for secure transactions.[54] Despite these assurances, online shopping is not about to replace visits to the local mall in the foreseeable future.

Meanwhile, other business uses of the Internet will flourish. The most heavily used Internet feature is the network's oldest service: electronic mail. Recent technological breakthroughs allow companies to create Intranets, in-house versions of the Internet that give employees quick access to one another, as well as efficient ways to tap into company databases and to place orders with suppliers. By 1996, Intranets were the fastest growing commercial application on the Internet. A survey of Fortune 1000 companies at the time indicated that two-thirds either had an Intranet facility or were planning to install one.[55]

Electronic commerce is still a small part of overall Internet traffic, but it is expanding fast. Its future growth will depend on many factors. Not the least of these is overcoming a troubling Internet handicap in reaching potential customers: the difficulty of helping customers select what they want from among the network's vast resources. There were, conservatively, more than 50 million webpages by 1997, with numbers more than doubling every year.

Searching out information resources can be a daunting task, even for experienced computer buffs. The time when the network's resources could be indexed manually, like a library's Dewey Decimal System, was passed years ago. The alternative is reliable, user-friendly electronic catalogs that will be, in the words of one Internet enthusiast, "the ultimate index of all human knowledge."[56] The odds against a quick solution to this indexing problem are high. Even after the adoption of satisfactory cataloging systems, there will be a huge backlog of information on the World Wide Web that has not yet been indexed. By one estimate, the number of webpages is expanding so fast that fewer than half of them have been identified by indexers.[57]

The potential financial reward for developing a reliable Web catalog has attracted dozens of companies. They are the so-called search services, a new breed of Internet entrepreneur. Although their solutions vary, each offers programs that scour the Internet, record everything they find, and then store it away in big databases. This is done by search engine software, variously known as *crawlers, worms, spiders,* and *robots.* Spider is emerging as the word of choice, given its affinity with the World Wide Web. Spiders move around the Web, looking for key words in the title or body of digitized documents, simultaneously scanning all other Web documents to track down any related references.

The race to market efficient search engines has begun with a corporate scramble that may spin off the Internet's biggest moneymaker of the decade. The competitors all started from scratch in the mid-1990s. Companies with names like Yahoo!, Netscape, Open Text, Web Crawler, and Alta Vista have become, collectively, the main gateways to Internet resources.

The earliest and best-known firm is Yahoo!, started in 1994 by two Stanford graduate students, Jerry Yang and David Filo. Their first product was a primitive electronic indexing system named Dave & Jerry's Guide to the Web. For several years, they distributed their guide without charge before deciding to go commercial in 1995. A year later, Yahoo! became the instant symbol of the search engine boom when it floated its first stock offering. Yahoo! had total revenues of only $3 million in its first commercial year, making an operating profit in only one of four quarters. When the company floated its initial stock offering in April 1996, investors pushed the stock up to $848 million on the first day it was offered.[58] Several months earlier, a Netscape initial stock offering experienced a similar boom, jumping from $28 to $160 per share, making the firm's cofounder, Mark Andriessen, then twenty-four years old, worth more than $100 million.

This speculative bubble has since been deflated, with search engine stocks settling down to more realistic prices. The industry is still small, earning an estimated $80 million in 1996 with projected forecasts of a $1-billion market by the end of the decade.[59] In 1996, Netscape, the most popular service, claimed customers used its service an average of 45 million times every day. Because it got started earlier than Microsoft, its major rival in offering Internet access services, Netscape could claim at the time that more than 85 percent of the people surfing the Net used its software.[60]

Although the new search services are helpful to all Internet users, they are critical for the operators of commercial databases. Services such as Reed Elsevier's Nexis-Lexis, Knight-Ridder's Dialog, and Dow Jones News Service's financial data archives have been in business for decades, using slower search technologies. The new search engines give them the boost they need to handle the growing flood of information on the Internet. By 1996, Dialog's massive database contained more than 6 terabytes of information—the electronic equivalent of 6 million books.[61] By way of comparison, the Library of Congress contains about 16 million books.

Search engine companies and other cyberspace commerce are concentrated in the United States. This reflects the fact that in the late 1990s more than one-half of Internet users and a similar share of online providers (using the usual measure of websites) are in the United States. But the network is also an international phenomenon. In one form or another, the Net was available in more than 100 countries and territories in 1997. Internet connections are stronger in Western Europe, and their number is growing rapidly in Asia.[62] Usage trails off sharply in most of the rest of the world. Only a handful of the fifty African countries, with populations of more than 500 million people, have even minimal access to the network.

The pace of Internet growth is relatively slow abroad, even in economically advanced countries. Often, these countries do not offer the kind of government encouragement that triggered the network's initial growth in the United States. But there are other reasons. As new-media expert Mary Modahl pointed out, half-jokingly: "There is not the love affair with technology the way there is in the U.S. We're kind of like the Borg—the bizarre people on *Star Trek* who are half machine, half human. We are the Borg of the world community."[63] Cultural barriers also slow down the spread of the Internet, but they do not stop it. Aggressive marketing by U.S. companies is ferreting out a receptive audience for their services. Yahoo! claims that more than 30 percent of its users came from outside the United States by the end of 1995.[64] America Online, CompuServe, and other consumer-oriented access companies were well established in Western Europe before their first regional competitor, Europe Online, began operations in 1995. Europe Online could not compete, and it shut down one year later. America Online has teamed up with Bertlesmann, a major German media company, to strengthen its marketing position in Europe.[65] In 1996, two of the largest U.S. software companies, Microsoft and Netscape, signed an agreement with France Telecom, the dominant French telecommunications carrier, to develop a national Internet grid.[66]

European commercial firms have been slower than their U.S. counterparts to take advantage of the Internet. Many of them have opted to share common facilities for Internet access. A leading example is London's Telehouse, a state-of-the-art communications facility shared by British and other European companies. Telehouse handles 85 percent of Internet traffic, largely commercial, between Europe and the United States.[67]

The pace of Internet growth is much faster in the expanding economies of East Asia. Bringing up the rear, however, is Japan, the region's biggest communications power. (In a 1995 global survey that correlated the number of Net hosts with gross national product in individual countries, Japan ranked below Ecuador and Slovenia. At the time, Japan had fewer than 100,000 hosts, compared with 2 million in the United States. Less than 10 percent of Japanese computers were plugged into a network of any kind.)[68]

Many Japanese Internet users have problems in coping with the network's heavy use of English, a language in which relatively few are proficient. "The Japanese language is isolating Japan in the age of the Internet," says Wataru Hanayama, a Tokyo software publisher. Some hope of easing the problem is promised with new Japanese-created translation software designed to overcome the English-language barrier.[69] Consequently, Internet use is expanding in Japan—but at a slower pace than in most other industrialized countries.

Other East Asian countries are moving faster, yet the number of Internet users in Asia remains low. Until recently, there were relatively few computers in those countries with the necessary modem equipment to link up with the network. Internet growth in the region has usually proceeded unhampered by government censorship or other political restrictions. One exception is Singapore, where laws require organizations posting political or religious information on the World Wide Web to register with a government agency. The Singapore government has also introduced "antipollution measures" to clean up alleged violations of morality on local Internet screens. Curiously, the government allowed access to the Online Graffiti site, where users can scribble a message on what is, in effect, a virtual bathroom wall.[70]

The biggest potential pool of Internet users is in China. For the present, access is severely limited while the country's communist rulers debate the advantages and risks of expanding the network. According to official Chinese sources, there were only 120,000 Internet users (out of a population of more than 1 billion) in 1996.[71] Although the Internet has been a readily available, inexpensive channel for domestic networking as well as for linking with the rest of the world, it has also been a destabilizing factor in its potential for compromising government information controls. As Chinese authorities have already found out, there is no simple way to control Internet traffic, particularly that of computerwise users who have learned to get around the restrictions.

In 1995, China's government decided to legalize limited Internet access, primarily to keep a better eye on who was using the network and what they were using it for. Two government-controlled Internet circuits were opened, one from Beijing and the other from Shanghai. The rush of users alarmed authorities to the point where they issued new regulations in February 1996 designed to limit access to overseas data resources.[72] More recently, several Internet access services have been started that are roughly similar to America Online and CompuServe. The new services walk a careful line between official toleration and the danger of being shut down at any time. In addition to World Wide Web access, they offer e-mail, chat sites, job listings, and a dating service.[73]

In September 1996, Chinese authorities made clear their intent to maintain tight restrictions on Internet use. They cut off access to more than 100 World Wide Web sites they considered obscene or politically dangerous. The action came after the government discovered that Chinese employees in international firms were using company computers to get information on the Internet. The censored sites included those linked to exiled dissident groups. Another banned page featured *Playboy* magazine pinups. Other sites featured materials from U.S. news media such as the *Wall Street Journal, Washington Post, Los Angeles Times*, Voice of America, and CNN.[74]

In Russia, computer buffs are flocking to the Internet. They are heavy users of the Net's *elektronnaya pochta*—the e-mail that lets them bypass the country's haphazard communications system. "E-mail succeeds here in part because everything else fails so badly," says Anatoly Voronov, director of Glasnet, one of the first post-Soviet computer networks.[75]

Internet use has been slower to develop in the rest of the world. Progress has been thwarted in many Latin American countries, partly because of the reluctance of many government telecommunications agencies to support the service.[76] The situation is worse in Africa: By 1996, only four of the forty sub-Saharan countries possessed full Internet access.[77] In many Middle East states, access is officially restricted because of the objections of Islamic fundamentalist groups to the network's contents. However, there is a considerable flow of clandestine Internet traffic.[78] One reportedly popular activity, in countries where women are veiled from head to toe, is downloading pictures of *Playboy* centerfolds.

Internet use will expand, in fits and starts, around the globe in the coming years. Questions about its role in the overall growth of the larger Meganet will become more persistent. The Internet is one information network among many that make up the Meganet, but it is more than that. Its technology, ease of use, and range of resources set it apart from all other networks. Of all the Meganet components now operating, the Internet is singularly well suited to creating an "open marketplace of ideas," well beyond anything that Justice Oliver Wendell Holmes could have envisioned when he coined the phrase early in the century.

This vision has helped power rapid growth of the Internet. The concept of the network as an electronic marketplace of ideas was originally defined by a small fraternity of computer buffs two decades ago. Since then, the Internet has become a mass facility, a potential resource for hundreds of millions of people. Eventually, billions of people will be Internet users.

Can the transition to a mass-scale, more commercialized resource be accomplished without compromising the Internet's essential value as an open electronic forum of ideas and information? Will this ideal be lost to governmental or corporate control? Many of the original sponsors of the network have been defensive about maintaining the network as a more or less private preserve, walled off from too much outside pressure. Their defensiveness rose as the number of first-time users—"newbies," in Netspeak—expanded in the 1990s. Many of the Internet's pioneers saw the change as paradise lost. Others took a more activist approach, particularly in resisting the trend toward commercialism on the network.

There was a curious episode in 1994 when Internet computer buffs tried to prevent a commercial invasion of the network. Their target was not a megacorporation but a small law firm in Phoenix. The firm went on the Net to advertise its services to immigrants, especially help in obtaining "green card" work permits. An electronic uproar was heard across the network as Internet loyalists protested the ad. They jammed the law firm's Internet mailbox, but their protests were in vain. The lawyers prevailed. The main result of the incident was to heighten interest in the Net as a good place to do business.

Already, the furor raised by the Phoenix lawyers seems quaint. The Internet is becoming big business at many levels. The marketers of information products now count it as a newly important part of their corporate strategies. Bill Gates has proclaimed, with mantralike repetition, that the Internet is central to Microsoft's strategy. IBM has adopted a "netcentric" vision for its global operations that embraces Internet technology and practices. Thousands of other companies see the network as an expanding marketplace for their products.

The Internet's siren song may be leading many of these firms toward rocky shoals. The Internet is not a shortcut to commercial riches and fame. Even at this early stage of its commercialization, the network's limitations are apparent. It is one marketing resource, and it calls for special skills and cautions just like any other.

Some Internet enthusiasts fear that the network will be co-opted by Big Business. But this is unlikely. Internet resources are capacious enough to accommodate a wide range of uses. An apt comparison is with the public telephone system, which has expanded over the years to meet new demands, from teenage gossiping to toll-free services. Commercial transactions may become a major, even dominant part of the Internet, but they will not crowd out the already bewildering array of other uses by individuals and by public-service organizations such as schools, libraries, and government agencies.

Rather than blight the Internet, commercialization may strengthen it. Consumer access firms like America Online and search services like Yahoo! have opened the Internet to millions of users who would otherwise have been shut out. The rush to market goods and services on the Internet will speed up the introduction of advanced video and audio services on the network. The Internet has the technical capability to provide a full range of such services to computers and television sets, although their availability is relatively limited at present. Developing the infrastructure for these resources will require heavy investments from the business sector.[79] The range of services will expand with the increase of pressures from businesses looking for multimedia-based strategies to market products on the Net. These new services will also benefit other users, namely individuals and noncommercial organizations.

Commercialism will change the Internet, but it does not have to dull its promise as an open forum for the free exchange of information and ideas. There are other concerns, however, that could set limits on this ideal. One of them is the limited pool of actual Internet users, individuals who have a modem-equipped computer and access to reliable telephone lines. By 1997, these users added up to fewer than 2 percent of the world's population. This ratio will improve. But how much? And how fast? Physical restrictions on Internet access will persist well into the next century. The Internet is not immune to the large—and growing—problem of social and economic divisions between the information-rich and information-poor. Economist Robert Reich pointed out: "No longer are Americans rising or falling together, as if in one large boat. We are, increasingly, in smaller boats." If current trends continue into the next generation, he noted, the top 20 percent of U.S. earners will account for more than 60 percent of all earned income; the bottom fifth, for 2 percent.[80] Media critic Terry Curtis has suggested that we are moving toward a computer-generated caste system.[81]

Beyond the question of correcting the imbalance in access to the Internet, another issue affecting the network's growth is the matter of political controls. As we have seen, government restrictions on access to the system exist, particularly in authoritarian countries abroad. Calls for such restrictions are also a matter of debate in the democratic West. There is already concern in some quarters about the large number of counterculture organizations who have webpages. Some of these groups are potentially dangerous, such as the ones that offer instructions on how to build bombs.

Others are simply oddball. The American Patriot Network proclaims on the Web that the postal ZIP code is a conspiracy to subject the innocent to federal taxation. The Sovereign Citizen Resource Center's webpage denies that there is such a thing as U.S. citizenship and offers citizenship in the "Washitaw" nation, promising freedom from all taxes and regulations for a $65 fee that includes a passport and driver's license.[82] Most proposals for Internet censorship deal with pornography, real or alleged. In most cases, the restrictions are based on voluntary measures administered by Internet access providers. Unipalm Pipex, Britain's largest access company, agreed in 1996 to government proposals to block some pornography materials, using software that requires a password.[83]

The most extensive U.S. attempt to impose legal limits on Internet materials was the Communications Decency Act, passed by Congress in February 1996 as part of its overhaul of national telecommunications regulations. The legislation makes it a crime to transmit "obscene, lewd, lascivious, filthy, or indecent" images via computer networks. The law was immediately challenged as a violation of First Amendment rights in a court case brought by a broad coalition of civil rights organizations and media industry groups.[84]

Legal controversies over pornography and other sensitive matters will continue to entangle the Internet. They are an inescapable part of maintaining and expanding the network's ideal of open access to information and ideas.

The Internet is based on a capacious technology that can accommodate an almost limitless range of multimedia information. It began as a free-form, helter-skelter haven for data information. The coming years will see this capability expanded to audio and video materials. Meanwhile, the network will evolve as a mix of commercial and noncommercial resources. It will segment into different levels of services. This trend was demonstrated in 1996 when MCI and British Telecom announced they would offer a premium Internet service that uses high-capacity network facilities that bypass the slow-moving telephone lines that often create gridlock on the regular network. Sprint, which is the world's largest carrier of Internet service, provides a similar service to corporations.[85]

The Internet is also evolving beyond simple data transmissions into a multimedia channel. The first nondata medium to break into the Net was radio. Radio transmissions are possible because of the development of audio-on-demand software. Until recently, sound files on the Net had to be fully downloaded before they were played, which made live broadcasting impossible. Newer technology allows radio stations to transmit data from the station's computer server to users' PCs. Receiver software then converts the data to audio that plays through the

PC's soundcard. By 1997, there were more than seventy radio stations broadcasting on the Net twenty-four hours a day in the United States.[86] They are beginning to target audiences on the Web. The first all-sports Web radio station went on the air in August 1996 from Fort Lauderdale, Florida, transmitting a Penn State football game.[87]

Internet video is a little more complex, but it involves the same basic technology. In 1996, MTV, the pop music network, launched a twenty-four-hour cable television channel that offered simultaneous viewing on PCs and webpages containing related data. This and similar developments have led to the production of "cybersoaps," digital versions of TV soap operas. One cyberserial, *Techno 3*, is a takeoff on the 1970s' *Charlie's Angels* series, in which three well-shaped ladies are controlled by a cyberterrorist.[88]

Another fast-developing Internet innovation is telephone calling. Talking over the Net is not as simple as picking up the phone. Establishing a connection can be tricky. Both parties must be logged on to the Internet to connect the call, usually meaning that calls can be placed only at prearranged times. Once a connection is made, the sound quality is often poor.

Yet Internet telephony is compelling, if only because of the economics involved. Net phone calls can be made anywhere in the world for the price of a local call. Thousands of Internet buffs have logged on to this prospect, despite the complications of placing calls. This in turn has led to a scramble by telecom companies to deal with what could be a major shift in telephony, the biggest single use of Meganet. The problem centered on the need for technology that will make Net calling more user-friendly. Microsoft and Intel have jointly announced that they are developing software standards to do this.[89]

The telephone companies have not ignored the threat. They are taking a two-pronged approach. The first is to try to limit the expansion of current Net phone calling until they develop their own strategies for exploiting Internet telephony. In March 1996, long-distance companies petitioned the Federal Communications Commission to restrict the sale of Internet telephone software. They also asked that Internet service providers be made to pay the charges that long-distance carriers pay to local phone companies for originating and terminating calls.[90]

The phone companies' other strategy is to prepare for the day when Internet telephony will be a regular, hopefully profitable part of their operations. AT&T has already moved in this direction with its Internet service, and the regional Baby Bells are following suit. The result could be the most dramatic, if not traumatic, shift ever in the ways the old-line phone companies do business.

These multimedia developments will bring changes in the Internet's tradition of free information. Increasingly, access to Internet resources will involve a fee, whether or not those resources are supplied by commercial firms. Information is not a free good. Some of it is, in the lawyer's phrase, intellectual property, a concept that includes an obligation to compensate its creator. In a digital age, most of the old-line copyright and patent laws will have to be modified to assure that this principle extends to cyberspace resources.

The Internet tradition of largely cost-free information will change accordingly. Economic barriers to access will necessarily result. The network no longer will provide the free ride most of its users have come to take for granted. More important, these new costs will affect the network's reach to hundreds of millions of new, less affluent users around the world.

The question of assuring open access to the Internet is essentially a public policy matter. In the United States, the issue is comparable to the earlier one of assuring universal telephone service. In 1934, Congress mandated such a goal, and it was met through a mix of government regulations and industry practices. However, history never repeats itself. Internet resources are much more complex than plain old telephone services. The basic problem, however, has remained the same: how to create a consensus on an effective balance between public- and private-sector interests in ways that ensure open access to communications resources.[91]

In the United States, a general consensus has already developed on how to build information highway resources, including the Internet. The Clinton administration's initiatives in this area have emphasized that the lead role will be taken by the private sector, with government support. The federal and state governments have contributed heavily to Internet development through research funds and subsidies for educational public network operations.[92] Public authorities could also promote regulatory practices that encourage Internet access without interfering with content. One such example is an April 1996 FCC proposal to set aside radio frequencies for community computer networks to link to the Internet and other information resources.[93]

In the long run, the prospect for Internet expansion is tied to the concept of a civil society in which access to information is given a high value. In a democratic culture, there is no one-size-fits-all solution. The many decisions Americans must make regarding universal Internet access will shape America's future as an information age society. It will also resonate on the future of the worldwide Meganet. The Internet is setting a constructive tone for the mix of networks that will eventually make up this advanced network. The Internet can help democratize Meganet.

9

TELE HAVE-NOTS: MEGANET IN THE DEVELOPING WORLD

The global Meganet is less than one-half built. Its facilities are concentrated along a narrow geographic band in the Northern Hemisphere, roughly from Tokyo eastward to Berlin. Meganet resources are still scarce throughout the vast regions to the south, in Asia, Africa, and Latin America. Here, the six-lane information highway becomes a dirt road.

The challenge in the next decade is to "build out" Meganet's resources to reach the 4 billion people who live in the so-called developing areas. For the present, they are the *tele have-nots*. Most of them have never talked on a telephone, much less used any of the advanced gadgetry that has been transforming communications in the world's richer nations.[1] In the mid-1990s, northern industrial democracies possessed 10 percent of the world's population and more than 70 percent of Meganet's circuits. The issue of popular access to telephones and computers is much more than a question of convenience. A full-service network available only to the rich is a long-term threat to global stability.

The disparity can be overcome, and there is a good chance that it will be. This prediction is based on promising developments that are already under way. Ordinary telephone services are spreading at an impressive rate in developing economies. Phone lines in these countries have been increasing 11 percent annually in the late 1990s, compared with 3 percent for richer countries.[2] But it will still take another decade or more to bring most Third World telephone resources up to minimal standards.

Twenty years ago, the United Nations set a goal for developing a worldwide network. The objective was to provide a telephone within an hour's walk of every town and village on earth by early in the twenty-first century. It is now clear that this goal will be reached much sooner in most of the developing economies, but progress is uneven. Meganet expansion is booming in some areas, falling behind in others. São Paulo, Brazil's largest city, has more mobile phones than Paris. China boasts more pagers ("beepers") than any other country in the world. Singapore has, per capita, the most sophisticated national communications resources on earth. In contrast, some African countries have actually experienced a decrease in per capita telephone availability. Booming population growth is only one of the obstacles standing in the way of a timely build out of Meganet facilities in Asia, Africa, and Latin America. Another is the heavy capital investment required. Providing basic telephone lines alone will cost tens of billions of dollars. Expanding into more complex Meganet services will raise the investment ante to $1 trillion or more.

The roots of the disparity problem go back a century, when large parts of Asia and Africa were colonial outposts of European powers. Colonial administrators built limited telegraph and telephone systems designed to help them control their territories. This pattern was continued during the post–World War II era, when most colonies became nations. The new nations were, in most cases, governed by authoritarian leaders whose political interests were best served by small, centrally controlled communications networks. The old colonial systems were readily transformed into tight national monopolies.

Telecommunications was given low priority in national development schemes. This need was largely overlooked while the World Bank, the United States, and other countries poured aid into the new countries. Local politicians showed indifference toward the potential of telecommunications and information resources in promoting economic growth and advancing national development. These resources were not high on the priority lists of aid-giving organizations. The tone was set by a World Bank policy, adopted in the 1970s, that stressed aid in three "basic human needs" sectors—agriculture, health, and education—without considering the role of adequate communications in meeting these needs.

The process was complicated by cold war rivalries. The Americans, the Soviets, and their respective allies dispensed funds to developing countries according to an ideological litmus test. Given the general disinterest of local rulers in expanding communications systems, funding resources drew little support in most of the new nations. As late as 1995, the International Telecommunications Union identified forty-eight countries, mostly in Africa, whose telecommunications resources, on a per capita basis, were actually declining.[3]

Attitudes toward communications resources began to shift during the 1980s. The need for encouraging telecommunications infrastructure projects was documented by a group of World Bank economists. They charted how the introduction of a single telephone in a remote village could tip the balance toward economic and social well-being.[4] Another landmark study, issued in 1985, was sponsored by the ITU. The report sharply criticized the policy of supporting inefficient government phone monopolies. The Maitland Report, named for the group's chairman, British diplomat Sir Donald Maitland, went beyond the usual pieties about the importance of communications resources and laid out a specific program for giving their development higher economic priority. The report recommended better management of existing facilities and the loosening of monopolistic controls, together with marked increases in investment, including opening up the local networks to foreign investors.[5]

The Maitland Report was a good blueprint for change. Its recommendations not only made sense but came at the right time. Technologies such as satellites and wireless networks opened new prospects for communications resources more adaptable to developing needs. At another level, the breakup of AT&T in 1984 made a strong impression abroad by demonstrating the positive effects of competition. Finally, the end of the cold war signaled the beginning of the end of ideologically inspired foreign aid programs. Development strategists could now take a more realistic look at telecommunications and other previously neglected areas.

Economic pressures also played a role in supporting the changes recommended in the Maitland Report. World trade, which expanded steadily during the 1980s, required better communications facilities. It became clear that developing countries would be left behind if they were not plugged in electronically to the new global economy, at home and abroad. Increasingly, foreign investors were giving greater weight to communications facilities when making decisions. Moreover, the increasingly competitive environment in Meganet communications gave investors new choices. The alternatives were outlined by AT&T chairman Robert Allen in a 1992 talk to foreign business leaders: "Customers have power, and they have options. They can shift their investments to countries where the telecommunications system provides competitive choices. Or, if they choose, the technology gives them the option of bypassing national networks."[6]

In short, the squeeze was on. Disadvantaged countries had to improve their communications structures or be left behind economically. And so the advanced industrialized countries began restructuring their own communications resources, abandoning state monopolies for more competitive strategies. The United States made the most radical choices by way of a series of steps that opened its national structure to full competition. Europe followed with a plan to open up most of its communications networks to full competition in 1998. Japan tagged along reluctantly, slowly dismantling its monopoly structure in the late 1990s.

The problems in raising networks to even minimal Meganet standards were more difficult for developing countries. Most were saddled with antiquated networks run by resistant bureaucracies. The financial requirements for even modest improvements in these networks were daunting. Nevertheless, the pressures to improve the networks were hard to ignore. Some came from local business firms anxious to compete in expanding markets at home and abroad; others came from ordinary citizens who simply wanted a workable telephone.

Increasingly, these pressures have been working, as there has been a sharp rise in communications facilities throughout the developing world within the past decade. The rise has been steepest in East Asia and Latin America. Progress has been much slower in the Middle East and Africa. There is no standard pattern for the 130 or so countries involved. Each is dealing with a mix of political, economic, and technological forces that varies from country to country.

Nevertheless, the overall pattern is one of positive change. The countries involved can be divided into two general categories: the fast-trackers and the laggards. The fast-trackers are those countries that have taken decisive action to begin to bring their national systems up to global Meganet standards. By rough count, there are about thirty of them. The laggards are those that, for various political and economic reasons, have trailed behind. They are the majority, and they pose some intractable problems.

Identifying the fast-trackers can be tricky. The selection tends to be arbitrary, often not following the usual measures of political importance, economic development, and geographic size. Singapore is on every fast-track list even though it has a smaller population than New York City. China is also on all lists, although it ranks among the poorest countries in terms of per capita communications assets. But China is the third largest economy in the world, and it is carrying out an impressive program to upgrade its communications systems.

A pragmatic attempt to identify fast-track economies was made by the Clinton administration in 1992 as part of its global trade initiatives. Telecommunications resources ranked high among the indicators used to identify the big emerging markets. The Clinton list of BEMs has served as a useful guide to the new telecommunications movers and shakers in the developing areas: In Asia, they include South Korea, Indonesia, India, Thailand, Malaysia, the Philippines, Vietnam, Brunei, and the China Economic Area (China, Hong Kong, and Taiwan); in Latin America, Mexico, Brazil, and Argentina; in the Middle East, Turkey; in Eastern Europe, Poland; and in Africa, South Africa.

These countries are largely responsible for sustaining the developing world's growth rate of almost 5 percent per year in the late 1990s, which doubles that of the industrialized West.[7] They are, moreover, the engines of economic growth in their regions, far outstripping neighboring countries and, increasingly, offering commercial challenges to the United States and other advanced trading nations. And they are leading Meganet growth in Asia, Africa, and Latin America.

Latin America is in a race with East Asia to be the first region in the world to meet advanced Meganet standards in the coming decade. Whichever region wins, both will be transformed. For its part, Latin America has more than forty national communications systems that are currently in various stages of disrepair and obsolescence. With 8 percent of the world's population, Latin America has just 3 percent of global telephone access lines.

There is, moreover, a wide disparity in communications resources among the region's economies. Argentina has a per capita telephone rate of 17 percent, whereas in Peru it is 3 percent. The region's telephones are heavily concentrated in the bigger cities. They are still a rarity in rural areas, where most people live. The price tag for upgrading Latin America's ramshackle phone systems is very high. The Organization of American States estimated the cost at upwards to $130 billion in the next few years just to *maintain* the current telephone lines per capita.[8] Expanding into advanced Meganet facilities could double this investment requirement in the early years of the twenty-first century.

The prospects for upgrading the region's telecommunications are encouraging nevertheless. They are based on trends that are transforming Latin America well beyond merely improving its phone systems. The most basic of these is the new wave of democratization that has, in most countries, sent the leaders of military juntas back to the barracks or into exile. Their replacements are sometimes weak and prone to backsliding. But, in general, the political changes have set a hopeful new tone throughout the region.

All this has positively affected Latin America's economic development and, by extension, the prospects for improved telecommunications. The image of Latin America as an economic backwater, shipping out coffee and bananas, is being revised. There are optimistic plans for setting up a hemispheric free trade area linking newly competitive national economies in the early years of the twenty-first century. This goal is ambitious, and it will probably have to be adjusted considering the disparities in Latin America's economic development. In the 1996 annual ranking of competitive national economies issued by the authoritative International Institute for Management Development, only one Latin American country—Chile—was ranked among the top forty worldwide.[9]

The other critical factor favoring these changes is the influence—geographic, political, economic—of the United States. This influence includes a direct hand in the region's telecommunications development, dating back a century or more.[10] Early in the twentieth century, the U.S. government actively supported an electronic extension of the Monroe Doctrine, identifying the region as the preserve of the U.S. communications industry. By 1929, one U.S. company, International Telephone and Telegraph, controlled two-thirds of the telephone facilities in the region.[11] ITT's dominance ended in the years following World War II, when most of its Latin American ventures were nationalized and reverted to the PTT monopoly models common in the rest of the world. A general decline in both the quality and availability of telecommunications services throughout the region soon followed.

By the 1980s, the lack of good phone services had reached critical proportions. There were few new phone lines, and the older ones were overloaded. Dial tones were hard to come by, and telephone burglary was rife. For a price, thieves dressed in black—*hombres de araña* (spidermen)—would scale a wall at night, cut loose a phone line, and run it through alleys into a different house or apartment. The old subscriber would have a dead line in the morning. The new "subscriber" would have a phone connection, thus avoiding the long wait for installation of a legitimate line.[12]

Such tactics are less common now. The backlog of ordinary telephone service orders is being reduced in most Latin American countries, and advanced new services such as mobile phones are being introduced. The primary reason for these improvements is that governments are slowly but steadily abandoning the old PTT monopoly models in favor of more efficient privatized or liberalized operations. Privatization—the sale of government assets to the public—is occurring at a steady, if somewhat uneven, pace. In Chile, full privatization has been completed; in Brazil, the government is still majority owner of the national network. Liberalization—opening up previous monopoly markets to competition—has moved more slowly.

In the past decade, every large and medium-sized Latin American country has moved in the direction of privatization and liberalization. (The significant exception has been Uruguay, where a proposal to partially privatize the local PTT was turned down in a 1992 national referendum.) In most cases, the move has meant turning over a significant part of the revamped enterprises to private investors, who previously would have been sent their money out of the country to safe-haven banks in Miami and Geneva as a hedge against domestic inflation, confiscatory taxes, and political upheaval. Suddenly, for local investors, the local phone company looked like a better place to put money; foreign investors are beginning to agree with them. Kenneth Bleakley, a Colorado-based telecommunications consultant, estimated that foreign companies were spending $10 billion per year on network expansion projects in Latin America.[13]

A large share of this funding has come from U.S. investors. The first big infusion came in December 1990, when a controlling interest in Telmex, Mexico's national telephone monopoly, was turned over to a private Mexican consortium and two foreign partners—Southwestern Bell, a regional U.S. phone company, and France Telecom, France's national phone monopoly. The newly privatized company agreed to a tight timetable for upgrading the national network. As a result, more than two-thirds of the network has been converted to digital standards. Telephone penetration has increased from six to ten main lines per 100 inhabitants. In January 1997, Telmex faced direct competition in basic services when its long-distance monopoly ended. Its new competitors—AT&T, GTE, and MCI—each teamed up with Mexican investors.[14] The interest of the U.S. investors was spurred in large part by the fact that the volume of telecom traffic between the United States and Mexico was greater than traffic between any other two countries, except for the United States and Canada. In 1997, Telmex took steps to improve its cross-border links with U.S. networks when it applied to the FCC for an operating license in the United States.[15]

The 1990 Telmex privatization energized similar deals throughout the region. Chile's government had taken the first steps in 1988 when it privatized its long-distance phone service. More recently, Chile extended privatization and liberalization throughout its telecom system, making it by far the most open telecommunications system with the highest phone per capita ratio in the region. It also became the most advanced technologically. In 1993, it was only the third country in the world to possess a totally digitized telephone network.[16]

By 1997, more than thirty countries in South America and Central America had privatized their networks or were well on their way to doing so. Most of their plans included foreign participation, with U.S. companies as the lead investors. However, the Americans no longer dominated as they had in the past. The French are major investors: In addition to their investment in Mexico's Telmex, they own a major stake in Argentina's privatized network. The largest single investment

in Latin American phone systems is held by Spain's national phone
system, Telefonica, which has interests in a half-dozen networks
throughout the region. By 1997, the company held such a dominant
position in the region's telecommunications structure that major U.S.
firms, including AT&T, were negotiating to invest in its operations.

The rush to modernize Latin America's phone systems is in full
swing. The message has gotten through that erratic phone service not
only hurts local business but also dulls prospects for foreign investment. Trade ministers seeking to lure new investors now boast about
their countries' ability to supply a reliable dial tone. Moreover, they
are adopting a new attitude of cooperation with one another to improve phone services throughout the region. A subject that was dealt
with rhetorically a few years ago is now being treated seriously.

The first steps in this direction were taken in the late 1980s when
Mexico, Canada and the United States negotiated the North American
Free Trade Agreement. Agreement on eliminating communications
trade and regulatory barriers among the three was difficult, largely because of Canada's and Mexico's sensitivity toward U.S. dominance.[17]
NAFTA included a series of cautious provisions to reduce cross-border
telecommunications barriers over a period of years. The progressive
reduction of these barriers has led to a steady rise in communications
traffic among the three countries.

Although NAFTA involved only one Latin American country, its
impact was felt throughout the entire hemisphere. The agreement
clearly played a role in encouraging Mexico to step up its plans to privatize Telmex. NAFTA has also influenced other countries to cut back
trade barriers in communications and information services. The agreement was hailed as a model that could be expanded southward to include the entire hemisphere. This prospect ran into some stubborn realities. One was the legacy of trade protectionism in Latin America,
which has been based on suspicions that the United States would
dominate the hemispheric economy if trade barriers were removed.
Another factor was the protectionist mindset of some U.S. politicians,
who issued apocalyptic warnings about the flood of cheap Latin American imports that would follow any lowering of trade barriers.

The result was a tactical retreat and a moving away from free trade
plans on a grand design. The new regional approach focuses on smaller
agreements designed to open up trade in telecommunications and other
areas. An important initiative has been taken by Mercosur, the common market established by Southern Cone countries Brazil, Argentina,
Paraguay, and Uruguay. By concentrating on a series of slow, practical
steps, Mercosur has reduced trade barriers among member countries

that combined have more than 200 million inhabitants. Similar trade promotion moves have been made by a group of Andean countries, as well as by countries in Central America and the Caribbean.[18]

These subregional efforts are being pulled together in a wider effort. Known as the Free Trade Agreement for the Americas, the proposal included provisions for reducing barriers to advanced Meganet services throughout the hemisphere. The most hopeful aspect of this wider initiative is the inclusion of private business representatives in the negotiations along with government officials, a break with Latin American diplomatic tradition.[19] This inclusive approach is both pragmatic and promising as a way to reform out-of-date trade practices.

It is doubtful that hemispheric free trade planners will meet their 2005 deadline, the official target date. A major cause of the delay is the continuing weaknesses of Latin American economies, including high inflation, low investment, corruption, and poor money management. After Mexico teetered on the verge of fiscal default in 1982, it took eight years before most Latin American countries regained normal access to commercial international capital. Mexico delivered another economic shock to the region when it devalued the peso in 1993. Among the industries affected was the newly privatized Telmex phone system, which took a pretax foreign exchange loss of $765 million the following year.[20] The 1993 Mexican devaluation set off the "tequila effect"—ripples of economic insecurity in other countries throughout the hemisphere.

Despite these setbacks, Meganet expansion will continue throughout the region. Latin American planners project a 10 percent annual telecommunications growth rate through the late 1990s.[21] Consumer pressures for better communications services are strong. The political scene is more stable. The financial climate is favorable. Telecommunications is getting the lion's share of the new funds invested in the region's rickety infrastructures.[22] Much of this investment will be used to upgrade current facilities, still hobbled by decades of neglect. (When the new managers of Argentina's privatized phone system took over several years ago, they found switches that were eighty years old, and there were no diagrams of the system's circuits.)[23]

Finally, the entire Meganet modernization process is being speeded up by new technologies. The old, slow methods of building out a telecommunications system with wires and telephone poles are being replaced by newer, more efficient technologies. Communications satellites provided a groundbreaking example of this thirty years ago. Within a few years, countries in the region had the first reliable links with one another and with the rest of the world. Satellites are now being used for domestic communications in Brazil, Mexico, Argentina, and other countries. About a dozen Latin American countries lease circuits on Intelsat, the global satellite network, to supplement their inadequate terrestrial networks. Private satellite companies, led by U.S.-based PanAmSat, have begun to deliver services in the region.[24] More recently, there has been a boom in direct-broadcast satellite services, using small dish antennas to supply entertainment programming to a potential market of 80 million television homes in the region.[25]

The other technology that is changing Latin American communications habits is cellular telephony. From a slow start as the elite businessman's toy in the early 1990s, mobile phones are spreading like wildfire throughout the region, threatening to overtake old-fashioned wire telephony in some countries. Middle-class Latin Americans can now bypass the long waiting list for ordinary telephone service. Along with the Internet—the innovation that gives them access to global information resources—they are entering the advanced Meganet world through a technological backdoor.

Meganet modernization is happening fastest in the newly privatized economies of the BEMs—Mexico, Argentina, Chile, Venezuela, and Colombia. The exception is Brazil. It has the biggest telecommunications system in Latin America, the fifteenth largest in the world, but it ranks thirty-ninth in phone penetration. A good part of the problem is a phone monopoly, Telebras, that is tied up in Byzantine complexities. Telebras is a holding company for twenty-seven companies that supply almost all telecom services in the nation. Although much of Telebras is already in private hands, the government is still the majority owner.

Changing the Telebras pattern will be difficult. Since the early the 1990s, Brazil's government has sold more than forty-five state companies worth $12 billion, but not its telecom holdings. They were pointedly excluded from the privatization process, primarily for political reasons. Labor union opposition was intense. Another inhibiting factor was the 3,000 senior-level jobs in Telebras that are political plums, controlled by Brazilian government officials. After years of political maneuvering, the government took the first step toward liberalization in 1996 by allowing competition in mobile phone services.[26] One of the new competitors is AT&T, which is part of a joint venture that includes Globopar, the investment arm of Brazil's biggest media group, and Bradesco, the country's biggest private bank.[27]

Nine out of ten people in Latin America still have no telephone access. And even where local networks are capable of supplying service, most people are too poor to afford it. Despite the dramatic improvements in overall services, there is a long way to go to bring the region up to standard as part of an advanced global Meganet system.

Meanwhile, another area of the world—Asia—is moving ahead with tremendous energy. In the 1990s, the growth center of Meganet has shifted to the vast arc of countries from Korea to Pakistan. The region's thirty countries now make up the largest global market for telecommunications products and services, according to the ITU. The potential Asian market comprises 3 billion people, most of whom have still not used a phone, and half of whom are under the age of twenty-five.[28] The recent surge in Asian telecommunications is part of what is sometimes called "the Asian miracle," the wave of economic growth now being experienced in the region's BEMs.

In the past decade, the East Asian BEMs have together raised their per capita incomes by nearly 6 percent per year—more than twice the rate of increase of their Western counterparts. "Never before has so broad and diverse a group of countries grown so fast for so long," according to London's *Economist*.[29] This achievement masks big economic differences among countries. In the mid-1990s, Japan's gross domestic product was $37,000 per person. The comparable figure for India was $370. Similar gaps separate the very rich and the very poor in most Asian countries. Nevertheless, the most important societal change taking place across the region is the emergence of a middle class, eager to enjoy the benefits of a modern economy.

These benefits include telephones, computers, fax machines, and the other Meganet paraphernalia. The demand for them accounts for a huge increase in new communications and information resources within Asia in recent years. Telephone density—the most common measure—is five per 100 Asians, compared to a world average of twelve. As with overall economic development, the disparities between countries is striking. Japan has forty-eight telephone lines per 100 persons, the Philippines less than two.

These gaps are beginning to narrow. This involves upgrading or junking networks that were neglected for decades. It also means reorganizing local phone systems to deal with new demands. Since 1990, more than twenty Asian countries have privatized all or part of their PTT monopolies. Typically, they are also opening up their systems to outside investment and competition. Communications has become a magnet for foreign direct investment in the late 1990s.[30] A 1997 survey of global investment patterns by Arthur Andersen, the accounting and consultancy firm, estimated that by 2002 Asia (excluding Japan) would replace Western Europe as the most important region for corporate inward investment. Telecom will get a large share of this expanded investment.[31]

This trend involves big numbers. Some 148 million new phone lines are planned in the region by 2000, at an average cost of $1,500 per line.

By simple arithmetic, this involves a $228 billion price tag.[32] The timetable may slip, but in all likelihood new phone resources equivalent to all those in the United States east of the Mississippi will be added in Asia early in the twenty-first century.

There are several reasons for optimism. They include relative political stability, a generally pragmatic mix of favorable government economic policies, and the amorphous but powerful combination of traditional cultures and Western-style modernization. A special factor is East Asia's evolution as an electronics power. That process began thirty years ago when U.S. and Japanese firms relocated production sites for TV sets and other consumer goods to Asian countries where they could get skilled labor on the cheap.

It was a profitable move for the foreign companies involved. Its greatest long-term effect, however, was to give Asian economies the technical and management skills to make it into the global electronics game. They are in the game now, and they are no longer turning out just radios and TV sets. They are becoming direct competitors of Western industries in high-tech computer and telecommunications equipment.

Asia now has the basic industrial resources to supply most of its own needs in building an advanced regional Meganet. Its economies are less dependent on exporting to the West. By 1995, trade within the region outpaced exports to other parts of the world. This has created a new sense of common interests among the region's economies. In 1995, the leaders of eighteen Asian Pacific nations agreed to an unprecedented regional trade plan, which was designed to achieve free and open trade by 2010 for industrialized countries and by 2020 for developing nations.[33]

Asia's Meganet prospects depend mainly on the three regional giants: Japan, China, and India. Japan's postwar role has been that of an exporter of both capital and manufactured goods. More recently, Japan has raised its economic profile through strategic control of technology throughout the region, with an emphasis on telecommunications and information technology.[34] By solidifying its lead in technology, Japan is assuring itself a strong role in regional Meganet development, challenging competitors in the United States and Europe as well as those in newly resurgent local economies across Asia.

The most formidable of these regional competitors will be China. Already a looming presence, China will dominate Meganet developments in Asia for decades to come. It is home to one in five of the planet's inhabitants. It may be true, as China watcher Lucian Pye observed, that China is a civilization pretending to be a state. But it is a civilization that for millennia has seen itself as the Middle Kingdom, the society to which all others should defer.[35]

China is still essentially an agricultural society. Two-thirds of its population lives in rural areas. In many ways, it is a country in the first stages of industrialization. Per capita income level is in the lowest Third World range. Nevertheless, China is on a forced march toward an advanced economy, intent on catching up to the United States, Japan, and Western Europe.

Ordinary telephones are crucial to this effort. In the late 1980s, China was close to the bottom of the list of nations in teledensity, with less than one phone for every 200 inhabitants. In a determined turnaround, the Beijing regime has developed plans to build an advanced phone network that will be the largest national system in the world within the next fifteen years. Implementation of these plans is well under way, with an annual growth rate approaching 50 percent in the late 1990s.[36] Mobile telephony plays an important role in Chinese plans. By 1997, more than 6 million mobile phones were in use, with the prospect that cellular penetration will reach 40 million by 2000. China is then expected to replace Japan as the world's third largest cellular phone market, after the United States and Europe.[37]

The Chinese government's commitment to this effort was highlighted in its latest five-year economic plan, covering the years up to 2001. Telecommunications was singled out as a high-priority sector. The plan envisaged adding 64 million phone subscribers to the 40 million who had phones in 1996. Every rural village would have at least one phone under the plan. Looking beyond the plan deadline, the government forecast that 420 million lines would be available in 2010—a network almost three times the size of the current U.S. phone system.[38]

This may not happen quite as planned. Official Chinese statistics tend to be fantasy exercises, designed to impress. As with all previous five-year plans, current goals for economic growth, including telecommunications, are targets. It would be a mistake, however, to underestimate the pace and scope of China's telecommunications effort. There is every indication that eventually China will put together an advanced Meganet system that will include high-tech fiber optic networks, microwave channels, and an extensive domestic satellite system.[39]

Chinese planners clearly recognize the telecom imperatives in sustaining the strong economy they are determined to build.[40] For the present, network expansion is focused on big population areas. These include the "special economic zones," which Chinese authorities have set up as havens of free market capitalism in an economy still hobbled by communist theories.

The country's Meganet development is directed by the Ministry of Post and Telegraph (MPT), a sprawling bureaucracy with 1.5 million employees. MPT oversees a system that is an aggregation of dozens of provincial, district, and village networks linked to one another with varying degrees of success.[41] MPT's dominant position was somewhat modified in 1994, when the government authorized a second national network, Unicom, to compete with MPT's facilities. The move was hailed by some outside observers as a market-oriented reform that followed the trend toward privatization and competition occurring elsewhere in the world. They were wrong. Unicom is controlled by three powerful government ministries, led by the Ministry of Electronics Industry. Its creation was less a reform in the usual sense than a change in national industrial policy intended to ease the political and economic pressures brought on by rapid communications expansion.

Nevertheless, Unicom has introduced a competitive note, albeit a tentative one. The company moved quickly to establish itself as an alternate service. One year after it was founded, it began offering cellular phone services in China's largest cities in competition with MPT's network. It aimed to capture a one-third share of China's burgeoning cellular market by the end of the decade.[42] Meanwhile, it has begun to build its own national network, which was designed to end its current reliance on circuits controlled by MPT. Unicom will undoubtedly become one of the world's telecom industry giants early in the twenty-first century.

All this will cost money. Unicom plans to spend $11 billion on its expansion plans by the end of the decade. MPT's investment schedule is even higher. An increasing share of the funds to pay for this expansion will have to come from abroad. Of all the developing countries, China is the largest recipient of foreign direct investment—$153 billion since it opened its markets to outsiders.[43] Fortunately for the Chinese, foreign enthusiasm for giving them money to expand their telecom facilities is contagious. Banks, investment houses, and communications companies have fallen over one another in the rush to be a part of what promises to be the biggest telephone sweepstakes of all.

They are right—up to a point. The market potential is enormous. But this potential is also hedged by the hard realities of doing business with a totalitarian regime. The rules for entry are strict. Foreigners are banned from managing or operating networks. Returns on investment can only be in the form of a fixed payment or of profit sharing over a specific time period. Moreover, the Chinese usually insist that agreements include the transfer of advanced technology as well as assistance in expanding local manufacturing capacity.[44]

Despite these hard bargains, Japanese and Western investors have generally prospered in the new Chinese telecom market. The first major foreign investment occurred in 1984 when Alcatel, the French manufacturing giant, entered a joint venture to produce central office switching equipment. The enterprise held one-third of the market in the mid-1990s. Among U.S. companies, Motorola has been successful in building manufacturing facilities in China. Its advanced semiconductor factory in Tianjon, near Beijing, has competed with other large microchip joint ventures involving Japanese and Korean firms.[45] AT&T, MCA, Sprint, Northern Telecom, Microsoft, and IBM have also negotiated large joint ventures in recent years.

China's communications resources are still lopsided. As the country approached the turn of the century, 90 percent of its households did not have telephones, and 99 percent lacked access to networked computers. Such deficits will be chronic for a long time in rural areas, where official statistics listed the average annual income at $190 in 1995.[46] For the present, these needs are largely ignored as the new networks focus on strengthening the economy.

China's communist leaders have gambled that they can continue to channel the new networks largely toward economic development as they expand. The evidence is mounting that they cannot. Inevitably, the network spreads beyond their control. It will be used for all kinds of purposes that erode central authority. The greatest pressure will come from the new middle class, tens of millions of better-educated, relatively affluent Chinese who want access to expanded information resources.

The availability of new telephones, fax machines, copiers, and personal computers strengthens this prospect. Direct-broadcasting satellites beam down news and information programs from the outside world to more than 500,000 small earth stations every day, despite official efforts to ban their use.[47] Beijing authorities have kept a fairly tight rein on data networks, most of which were directly controlled by the government. But expanding Internet connections, both legal and illegal, can circumvent these restrictions.[48] The most intriguing aspect of China's Meganet buildup is its potential for weakening the government's grip on information, which has sustained communist rule for fifty years.

The other Asian giant coping with Meganet problems is India. As with China, the scale of India's effort is outsized. Most of India's 900 million inhabitants live in more than 600,000 villages, two-thirds of which have no phones.[49] Despite an improving economy and a rising middle class, per capita income hovers around $400 per year.

Both China and India are moving in the same direction—toward Meganet modernization—but they are taking different paths. China is committed to command economy measures, with tight, centralized controls over its networks. India has opted for more open, competitive free market approaches, moving away from ineffective government monopoly management. The eventual results in these two countries will determine their relative positions as political and economic powers in Asia.

For the present, China is ahead of India in Meganet expansion. China's ability to channel resources into the project and to control their use gives it an initial advantage. But experience elsewhere suggests that in the long run India will come up with a more effective system—despite the fact that India's present network has fewer than one phone per 100 persons and is in bad shape. During the long monsoon season, which takes a heavy toll on wire circuits, the network's antiquated equipment reduces phone conversations to a cacophony of gurgles and crackles. The waiting list for even this poor service includes tens of millions of people.

The pressure to upgrade India's networks increased during the early 1990s, triggered by complaints from business leaders and the general public. The resultant changes were part of a larger reform plan designed to reduce top-heavy government management of the economy. In May 1994, officials unveiled a grandiose master plan that promised to make on-demand phone service available to city dwellers by 1997. The plan also mandated a phone in each of the country's villages by the same target date. These were wildly optimistic goals, and they were not met.[50] Nevertheless, India's telecom reform plan was a serious statement of purpose, as well as the basis for significant changes in the way the network was to be expanded. Among other innovations, it supported the idea of private-sector competition against the national phone monopoly, including a role for foreign companies.

The first round of bids to choose private competitors for local phone services took place in 1995. Foreign firms were allowed to take up shares totaling as much as 49 percent in joint ventures organized by Indian companies. Companies from the United States, Europe, Japan, Singapore, and Australia jumped in, all eager to compete in the biggest remaining open telecom market in the world. Their initial enthusiasm was tempered by the dampening reactions of die-hard nationalists, labor unions, and others opposed to letting foreigners compete.[51]

When the second round of bidding took place, many of the original foreign investors, including AT&T, dropped out. Their reluctance to stay the course was fueled in part by well-founded rumors of kickbacks and other illegal activities associated with the bidding process.[52] Nevertheless, capital was raised, licenses were issued, and construction of the first competitive local networks was under way in 1997. Full competition was hampered by a central government decision to retain its monopoly over long-distance phone services.

The new facilities promise to give India an advanced wire-based network, reaching into rural areas, by early in the twenty-first century. In the meantime, networks based on two wireless technologies—cellular phones and satellites—have been expanding rapidly throughout the country. Cellular services have boomed since they were introduced in a few large cities during the early 1990s. In 1995, the government issued licenses for new cellular networks in eighteen Indian states.[53] Satellite communications services connecting Indian cities were also growing, specifically tailored for business uses. India's national stock exchange used 1,000 small earth stations to link its operations.[54]

In summary, India and China have strikingly different approaches in developing Meganet resources to meet their needs in the new century. China has been counting on centralized control of the process, focused on economic priorities. India will rely increasingly on a mix of public and private resources, reacting to economic needs but also to pressures from an expanding middle class for telephones and other Meganet services. The result will have a strong bearing on the competition between the two countries for political and economic leadership in Asia's future.

In the meantime, the region's other emerging economies have been positioning themselves to compete with their two giant neighbors. The outsized example is Singapore, an island republic half the size of Rhode Island. Singapore is run by a government that keeps tight control over most aspects of the lives of its 3 million citizens. The emphasis is on persuasion rather than force. Singapore's government has launched publicity campaigns urging love of country and the production of more children, to turn up at wedding receptions on time, and to flush the toilet after use.[55] These exhortations are part a national rags-to-riches story that has transformed Singapore from a backwater British colony to the most prosperous of Asia's emerging economies.

The island's economic success has been the result of a national commitment to make Singapore, in the local phrase, an "intelligent island" with an economy geared to information age needs. In the absence of natural resources, the government's strategy relies on the brain power of its largely Chinese population. This resource is supported by an array of advanced Meganet facilities, including the world's first completely digitized phone system. This network supports a strong industrial base. Singapore is, for instance, the largest producer of computer hard drives in the world. But its major industry, upon which Singapore has staked its economic future, is the production, storage, and distribution of information for its own economy and for the hundreds of foreign companies that have made Singapore their Asian base of operations.

The key player in this transformation has been Singapore Telecom, the national phone monopoly. Singapore Telecom operates a communications infrastructure that is, per capita, the most sophisticated on the planet. And it has been enormously profitable. Measured by market capitalization, Singapore Telecom is the largest company anywhere in Asia outside of Japan.[56] Its operations are carefully overseen by the government, which, in the mid-1990s, owned 89 percent of its stock. This close linkage is changing, however, in line with the global trend way from government monopolies. In 1994, the government authorized the first in a series of sell-offs of the company's shares, primarily to Singaporean citizens and institutions.[57] At the same time, the rules were changed to introduce some private competition. In 1997, MobileOne, a consortium of British and local companies, launched a second cellular phone and paging service.[58]

Singapore stands out among Asia's strengthening links to the advanced global Meganet. Other smaller countries have moved more slowly to upgrade their systems, held back by financial or political constraints. During the late 1990s, most of them were beginning to shake up their telephone monopolies by introducing competition. Korea, Thailand, Indonesia, Malaysia, Taiwan, and the Philippines each adopted variations of this pattern. Even Vietnam, still enmeshed in communist-style economic planning, cautiously opened the door to allow foreign entry into its telecom markets.[59]

As in Singapore and most other Asian countries, Vietnam's shift to competition happened first in mobile telephone service, the quickest and cheapest means of expanding phone resources. Cellular phone use is doubling annually throughout Asia. Within a few years, Asia may well replace North America as the region with the heaviest cellular usage.[60]

The most spectacular Meganet project in Southeast Asia is a $2-billion "multimedia supercorridor" outside of Kuala Lumpur, Malaysia's largest city. Announced in 1996, the corridor is a 500-square-mile zone within which Malaysia's government planned to build what it would call an information technology city (IT City). The project was designed to attract investment from the world's leading technology firms, with the hope of vaulting Malaysia into the top ranks of high-tech Asian economies. To lure major corporations, Malaysia's government offered a "multimedia bill of guarantees" providing a ten-year tax holiday, freedom from restrictive regulations, and an advanced telecommunications structure within the new complex.[61]

Through cellular phones and other technologies, Asia is plugging into the global Meganet with important economic effects. Electronics is the new growth industry, building on the region's experience as an offshore manufacturing base for U.S. and Japanese companies since the 1960s. Increasingly, local firms are exporting electronic equipment within the region. They are also beginning to make their mark in software development, looking for niches to challenge Microsoft and other large Western software producers. This would not happen without the new Meganet facilities.[62]

The quick pace of developments in Asia contrast sharply with Meganet's prospects in the Middle East. From Morocco to the Persian Gulf, the region's communications development has been marked by startling differences. The oil-rich countries have installed state-of-the-art networks while other states continue to stumble along with patchwork systems. Both Egypt and Saudi Arabia announced plans for partial privatization of their networks during the mid-1990s, but there has been no significant movement in that direction in either country.[63] The most active steps toward privatization in the region were taken in 1997 by Jordan, which offered to sell a 20 percent stake in its network to a consortium of international telecommunications firms.[64]

The third large region opening up for Meganet expansion, after Asia and Latin America, is the former Soviet Union. Stretching across nine time zones from the Pacific Ocean to the Baltic Sea, it has broken up into twenty autonomous republics, each seeking to create a new national identity in the post–cold war world.

Among the legacies these new countries inherited from seventy years of communist rule was a ramshackle communications system. The Soviet Union's per capita distribution of phones was the lowest among industrialized countries—less than ten per 100 citizens. The phone system was purposely kept small so that it could be controlled by communist authorities. By the 1980s, the Soviet telecom deficit was a heavy drag on the economy. Mikhail Gorbachev, the last Soviet leader, tried to amend this with a crash program to modernize the phone system.[65] He added millions of phones, but the effort was too little and too late. An obsolete telecom network was part of the dead weight that brought down the entire Soviet structure in 1990.

The post-Soviet republics have been struggling to overcome this infrastructure deficit. The effort is most striking in the biggest country, Russia, constituting most of the land mass and more than 50 percent of the population of the old Soviet empire. Nearly a decade after the breakup of the Soviet Union, Russia was still a nation in political transition. New laws granted unaccustomed liberties, including the right to own property. The new private sector was responsible for more than 70 percent of the country's gross domestic product. About 40 million Russians owned shares traded on the new stock markets. Overall, there have been the fragile beginnings of a civil society, one that could play a constructive role in building the global Meganet and other information age resources.[66] In 1993, Russia had only 1,000 phone-line connections with the outside world. By 1997, this number had expanded to 45,000.[67]

Most parts of the Russian economy have been in recession during the 1990s, but the communications sector has been flourishing. Its strength was a pent-up demand for telecom goods and services. In the mid-1990s, more than 10 million consumers were on waiting lists for ordinary phone service. New Russian businesses wanted other facilities—fax, cellular, and computer lines. The lure of an expanding, potentially profitable Russian component of Meganet also caught the attention of foreign investors.

The technological backwardness of the old system presented a staggering problem. Less than 10 percent of its switches were electronic; the rest were museum-piece mechanical devices. Maintenance had been patchy at best. Moreover, the system was run by the Ministry of Communications, incapable of managing an expanding advanced network but unwilling to give up its traditional monopoly rights.

After an epic bureaucratic fight, the government passed a telecommunications reform law in February 1995. The legislation authorized commercial joint ventures and investment in local and regional networks. This gave some needed assurance to potential investors, but it was offset by the law's reaffirmation of strong government controls over telecommunications. The 1995 reform law left the level of competition far short of that which has energized Meganet expansion in other countries. Nevertheless, an important competitive venture got under way in Russia's second largest city, St. Petersburg: the Petersburg Long Distance Co. (PLD), which began operations in March 1993 with a range of services competing against the local monopoly. The firm adopted a Western management style from the beginning, introducing such exotic (for Russia) innovations as strict cost controls, friendly customer service, and technical efficiency. PLD's success made it the first Russian company in the 1990s to be listed on an American stock exchange.

PLD's mentor and guide is Cable & Wireless, the British telecom group that took a minority stake in the enterprise. PLD began by building a cellular phone network as the quickest way to get more phones into the hands of customers. The results delighted the phone-deprived citizens of St. Petersburg and demonstrated that a Russian network could actually deliver services efficiently. PLD has been a bright but small spot in Russia's effort to upgrade its communications systems. Other networks have been struggling to make their partially privatized systems work. Cash flow is a problem. Many Russians have an aversion to paying their phone bills. In 1994, their arrears added up to 28 percent of the industry's total revenues.[68] This has complicated the industry's attempts to raise local capital and to attract foreign investors.

The biggest barrier has remained the heavy hand of government regulation. Old habits die hard, and Moscow bureaucrats still have an effective veto over most of the industry's operations. The government moved to reduce its role in 1995 when it proposed to give up part of its control over *Syvazinvest*, the holding company for its 51 percent stake in eighty-five local and regional phone companies. It invited U.S. and European phone companies to bid on what would have been a $1.4 billion infusion of foreign capital.[69] The deal collapsed several months later due to fears of foreign bidders that the political opposition, including a resurgent communist movement, would reinstate stricter government controls over the new private networks.[70] These concerns have slowed down but not stopped foreign investment in Russian communications systems.

The prospects are reasonably good that the Russian phone system can eventually be brought up to world Meganet standards. In the late 1990s, the system enjoyed a 25 percent compound annual growth rate. Ordinary customers have a chance to get a telephone as plans to add 15 million new lines begin to materialize. Russian businesses have also begun to enjoy the benefits of new fax, videoconferencing, and computer networking services. This is particularly true for the banking sector. The number of banks in the country expanded from four to 2,800 during the early 1990s. This increase was spurred by the introduction of high-technology electronic networking to replace outdated money transfer practices.[71]

Similar advances have been occurring more slowly in the other former Soviet republics. Communications needs in areas beyond the old Russian lands were virtually ignored during the communist era. The result has been to hamper economic development in the non-Russian republics and, particularly, to discourage foreign investment. When a major U.S. oil company was negotiating a multibillion-dollar exploration deal in one of the new states, it gave the government a long list of its telecommunications requirements. The government responded by offering six telephone lines.

Telecommunications reforms have fared better in the former communist countries in Eastern Europe. All of them have moved toward privatized systems and competition.[72] This changeover was facilitated by the fact that telecommunication projects accounted for a large part of the $27 billion poured into the region by foreign banks and companies between 1990 and 1995, with the expectation that this investment would double during the succeeding five years.[73]

In other developing areas of the world, Meganet development has proceeded at a very slow pace. This is particularly true of most countries in Africa.

Africa is the final frontier for Meganet expansion. The continent's fifty countries collectively possess fewer phones than the Tokyo region. A dozen of the poorest countries—Liberia, Somalia, and Sudan among them—are gaining population faster than telephones, and the region has only one phone for every 200 persons. The ITU has estimated that it would cost $28 billion to improve this ratio by one-half. Even if that were to happen, Africa would still have the lowest telephone rate of any continent.[74] Moreover, the money needed to upgrade Africa's phone networks has been in short supply. During the early 1990s, Africa received less than 5 percent of the funds invested by Western institutions in developing economies. This ratio has improved somewhat in recent years, but two-thirds of the new funds were being channeled to one country—South Africa.[75]

Africa's telecommunications woes reflect larger problems that have made it a graveyard of economic development hopes in recent decades. The litany of troubles runs from tribal wars, official corruption, illiteracy, and disease to economic dependency on commodities such as coffee and cocoa, the prices of which can swing wildly in global markets. Another barrier is that most African countries are still run by authoritarian regimes that have little or no interest in putting telephones into the hands of potential enemies.

The classic case of mismanagement is Nigeria. The largest and one of the richest African countries, Nigeria enjoyed an oil boom during the 1970s and 1980s. The money was there to build a modern phone system, but it didn't get built. U.S. and European communications companies colluded with Nigerian officials to divert funds or to use them for equipment that was ill-suited for local conditions.[76] The situation has not improved in recent years. In 1995, the World Bank canceled a $195 million loan to expand the Nigerian phone network, charging mismanagement of the system.[77]

The bright spot in African communications is South Africa. With the ending of white minority rule in 1994, the country faced stark differences in the levels of phone service available to the different segments of its divided society. Whites enjoyed European-standard services while access for blacks was at the low levels of other African countries. The country's new president, Nelson Mandela, assigned a high priority to correcting this imbalance. His plans included attracting foreign investment. In 1995, Telekom, the state telecommunications company, announced a program to seek minority equity partners from the private sector.[78] A consortium of U.S., British, and South African companies was formed to install 1 million phone lines throughout the country.[79]

Another important step toward upgrading the network was taken in 1997 with the completion of plans to sell off a minority share of Telekom, the state-owned network, to foreign investors.

As in other African countries, the most daunting problem for South Africa has been expanding phone service to rural areas. The old methods of wiring up houses one at a time were too slow and costly. Thus, South Africa relied on an innovative shortcut to speed up the process: the installation of community pay phones in rural areas, served by digital wireless networks. A company partly owned by Britain's Cable & Wireless has installed thousands of brightly painted phone booths in a landscape of tin roofs and grazing goats. Access to the pay phones is by prepaid credit cards.[80]

Similar wireless systems could cut back communications deficits in other African countries. More than thirty countries in the region have cellular networks. For those who can afford them, cellular phones are often the only way to get a reliable connection. Cellular growth began in Africa's large cities. But as in South Africa, it is beginning to spread to the countryside. In Ghana, a private firm, Capital Telecom, is building a network to serve 50,000 rural homes by the end of 1997.

The phones will be busy. The average monthly usage of each cellular phone in Africa is four to six times higher than that in the United States or Europe. Despite the clear advantages that wireless telephony offers, its expansion in Africa is threatened. Most cellular systems are private-sector enterprises, bypassing government monopolies. The loss of government revenues has thus led some politicians to try to curb cellular use. In one 1996 incident, a private company had installed a cellular network in Zimbabwe, but the government issued an order making it illegal for anyone to use it.[81]

Despite such setbacks, wireless telephony is a promising technology for Africa. Increasingly, African networks will also use communications satellites. Small, cheap earth stations can readily supply a range of services to the most remote village. Elaborate plans for developing such regional capabilities have been thwarted for years as African governments quarreled over formulas for financing and operating the systems. Recently, U.S. and European satellite companies have moved in to offer services for what could eventually be a very large market. Another promising development is an AT&T project to invest more than $1 billion in an undersea fiber-optic cable system that will encircle the entire continent, supplying high-capacity links to more than thirty mainland countries.[82]

In summary, Meganet's biggest challenges lie in wiring up the emerging economies and their 4 billion citizens. There is a special sense of urgency for doing this. The West took the better part of a century to build its electronic communications structure. The result was a system of networks that still depends largely on wires hanging from poles or buried in the ground or resting under the ocean. It was a system for its time, and it is gradually being updated as a result of new technical and economic pressures.

The developing countries don't have the luxury of repeating this century-long process. The process must be speeded up to achieve a tolerable level of parity with the West in the next ten to twenty years. A turnaround will not be easy, but there is reason for a degree of optimism. Large pockets of communications poverty will undoubtedly remain, but the yawning gap in North-South resources can be at least partially closed. The means for bringing this about will vary from country to country. But all countries will share two requirements. The first is to take full advantage of technological leapfrogging. This involves adapting new communications techniques to local needs in ways that skip generations of intermediate technologies.

Mobile phones may be the technology of choice. In Cambodia, for instance, two out of three telephones these days are small, handheld wireless instruments—a technology that did not exist there a decade ago. Internet connections are another option. The World Wide Web has opened up a wealth of information resources in developing countries, often for the price of a local phone call. There is increasing evidence that these low-cost alternatives tend to take off faster in poor countries than in richer ones. They are not merely convenient add-ons. They are sometimes the only answers to felt and urgent needs.

Still, neither mobile phones nor any other new device can supply all the answers to Meganet problems in developing economies, which will still need big, expensive infrastructure equipment, such as advanced switching systems and fiber-optic trunk lines, to fully build out their communications systems. But even here, advanced technology will help hold down costs by supplying unprecedented capacity per circuit.

The second (and related) requirement is a new set of political attitudes. National policies will have to be revamped to match the social and economic benefits opened by advanced Meganet resources. The communications policies of many countries in Asia, Africa, and Latin America are still fixated on centralized control over telecommunications. Political motives include protecting the profits of entrenched PTT organizations.

The evidence against continuing this approach in the emerging economies is now overwhelming. The countries that are on the fast track to social and economic development these days are those that willingly free their communications from old-style monopoly controls.

THE OPEN-ENDED FUTURE

Arnold Toynbee, the British historian, once suggested that the twentieth century was the first in which mankind could seriously consider the welfare of the entire race. Meganet is a critical element in this historic change. Its evolution as a universal communications resource can be a powerful force in breaking us out of our geographic and tribal isolations.

The task of assembling the advanced global Meganet is in full motion. Moreover, it is as certain as anything in this uncertain world that the network's expansion will continue at a rapid rate well into the twenty-first century.

There are many reasons for this. The overriding one is the coming together of political, economic, and technological forces favoring Meganet's growth. This change builds on a more elemental human need: the desire to be in touch. Over thousands of years, we have communicated through a complex series of codes, including language, writing, and the arts.

In modern times, electronic resources have been added, beginning with the telegraph and the telephone. New communications technologies have forced radical changes in political and economic affairs. The rapid expansion of Meganet resources is the result of a new convergence of this triad of technology, economics, and politics.

Measuring this change is difficult. Earlier prophets of the impact of electronic communications on our lives generally got it wrong. A few examples suffice:

- The telegraph binds together by a vital cord all the nations of the earth. It is impossible that old prejudices and hostilities should longer exist, while such an instrument has been created for an exchange of thought between all the nations of the earth. (Charles Briggs and Augustus Maverick, 1858.)

- It seems to us that we are getting perilously near the ideal of the modern Utopian whose life is to consist of sitting in armchairs and pressing a button. It is not a desirable prospect: We shall have no wants, no money, no ambition, no youth, no desires, no individuality, no names and nothing wise about us. (*Electrician*, a British publication, commenting on telephones, 1890.)
- It is inconceivable that we should allow so great a possibility for service and for news and entertainment and education as radio . . . to be drowned in advertising chatter or used for commercial purposes. (Herbert Hoover, 1922.)
- Whereas a calculator like the Eniac is equipped with 18,000 vacuum tubes and weighs 30 tons, computers in the future may have only 1,000 tubes and perhaps weigh only one and a half tons. (*Popular Mechanics*, 1949.)
- Never before has the individual been so empowered. . . . We wrestled the power of LSD away from the CIA, and now the power of computers away from IBM. (Dr. Timothy Leary, 1994.)

Such predictions are usually based on misguided expectations about a new technology. Among others, the British novelist H. G. Wells fell victim to this in 1937 when he proposed a World Brain project. The project's purpose was to organize the totality of human knowledge into one easily accessible format. "There is no practical obstacle," he wrote, "to the creation of an efficient index to *all* human knowledge, ideas and achievements, to the creation, that is, of a complete planetary memory for all mankind." The means by which he proposed to create his World Brain was microfilm, a technology that has since been displaced by digital resources.[1]

The odds of correctly forecasting Meganet's future are not much better. We are in the middle of a shift in the way we communicate, looking both ways as we go from the age of steel to the age of silicon. And as Marshall McLuhan once noted, we see the future through a rearview mirror.

The future is a receding reality, rushing away from us these days at an ever-increasing pace. The time for adjusting to the introduction of new electronic technologies is steadily diminishing. Mathematician John von Neumann, a computer pioneer, pointed out that modern technology increases the rate of change not so much by shortening the time involved as by expanding the areas—political, economic, social—that are affected. In Meganet-related technologies, new inventions no longer develop in a steady, linear fashion with time between enough for their implications to be sorted out and phased into active use. Now we are dealing with a wide range of converging technologies, forcing us to make quicker choices and allowing considerably less margin for error.

There will be many unexpected surprises as Meganet expands, forcing us to revise our ideas about its role in our lives. The current example of this is the Internet. Until recently, the Internet was familiar only to a comparative handful of computer buffs. Most politicians and communications industry moguls ignored it. The network grew, largely because it was left to its own devices. But it filled an important need, providing an elegantly simple way to connect otherwise incompatible computers. Using existing technology, it turned telephone networks into an information highway.

Today, the Internet is the fastest growing interactive network in the world. It links more than 50 million users, with prospects for doubling this user base in the next few years. The main cause of this spurt is an Internet add-on, the World Wide Web. The Web puts vast data resources within easy reach of ordinary men and women. Moreover, the Internet is currently undergoing another transformation as its technical capabilities expand beyond print data networking to include voice and video services.

The Internet's growth is not a fad or a fluke but the result of a digital free market. As such, it is a paradigm for the Meganet, an efficient way to access vast information resources that will shape the next century as much as the telephone shaped this century.

Meanwhile, Meganet is being assembled without any clear sense of the overall effect of its many parts, including the Internet. The network's main function is hard to quantify—the global movement of weightless electronic bits and bytes at the speed of light, to use computer guru Nicholas Negroponte's phrase. This does not excuse us from trying to identify where we are now and where we want to go in Meganet's evolution. The stakes are too high to be riding on Pollyanna hopes that everything will turn out okay. A century ago, historian Jacob Burkhardt warned that the denial of complexity is the beginning of tyranny: There are decisions to be made about the Meganet that call for hard thought and timely action.

Because of the lead time needed to build telecommunications resources, plans for expanding the network by 25 percent in the next few years are already firm. When these plans are carried out, an additional 1 billion people will be linked to the network. This means that for the first time a majority of the world's population will have access at least to ordinary telephone service.

We have reached this point through the convergence of technological, economic, and political forces. Of the three factors in this triad, technology has been the driving force. Economic and political decisions have usually been made in reaction to the rising pressures of technological change. Recent decades have seen research break-throughs that have dramatically altered the prospects for a global information utility. Three technologies led the way: communications satellites, fiber-optic cable, and semiconductor chips. Their capabilities have forced a radical rethinking of both the form and pace of Meganet development.

We have probably reached a plateau in terms of the technologies needed to complete the network. Perhaps not. It is risky to hazard such a guess considering the history of errors in judgment about new technologies. In the late 1970s, IBM thought that the potential market for small personal computers was about 250,000 machines. Today, there are more than 100 million PCs in operation around the world. The fact is that a fully functioning global Meganet can be built with current technology. Clearly, there will be improvements that will increase the network's efficiency, but the basic tools for completing an advanced network are already available.

Many of the technological improvements yet to come will take place in software rather than in hardware. Old machines will not be discarded. Instead, they will take on added capabilities as they are colonized by new software codes overlaying the older codes. The main problem is assuring compatibility of these new codes with older software. For example, the software operating Windows 95 includes millions of lines of code carrying the ghost of Windows past—and of the DOS operating system before it.

New types of software will prevail over the old, only to be replaced by more advanced types. This churn is the reason why the software industry is among the largest and fastest growing in the world, with an expansion rate approaching 15 percent annually. Software development continues to attract big investment money despite disappointments with hyped promises that have put the industry's stock prices on a roller coaster in recent years. The now classic example is Netscape Communications, whose initial stock offering in 1995 set off a buying frenzy. At one point, the firm was valued at $6.7 billion before it earned a single dime.

This gold rush–type atmosphere is as much a part of the software sector as the so-called computer geeks who sit in front of computer monitors trying to work out new codes. Many of these programming efforts will fail. Others will succeed, adding new members to the charmed circle of software millionaires, not to mention the somewhat smaller circle of Gatesian billionaires.

This success appeals to the American faith in the power of technology. It reinforces a view of society as progressing toward an earthly ideal and not, as in older civilizations, an acceptance of unchangeable conditions. Yet there is a dark side to this trust in technologies. The late French sociologist Jacques Ellul cataloged the paradoxes that technology presents. He noted that all technical progress exacts a price. It raises more problems than it solves, tempting us to see the consequent problems as technical in nature—and prodding us to seek technical solutions to them. The negative effects of technological innovation are inseparable from the positive. It is naive to say that technology is neutral, that it may be used for good or bad ends. The good and the bad effects are, in fact, simultaneous and inseparable. These cautions are useful to keep in mind as we move more deeply into the Meganet environment.[2]

A somewhat similar set of cautions applies to Meganet's economics. Technology may be the spur to Meganet growth, but economics gives it reality. Twenty-five years after Harvard professor Daniel Bell theorized about an information-based postindustrial society, it is happening. Among its effects is the transformation of electronics into the world's leading industry, with a rising annual growth rate fueled by Meganet needs.

The electronics sector's primary products are invisible binary digits. As communications researcher Gregory Staple has pointed out, the sector is driven by three sets of producers: bit makers (content companies), bit shifters (telecom operators), and bit processors (manufacturers).[3] Together, they are the newly important players in economic development, not only because of their own ubiquitous presence but also because of the impact their products and services have on every other part of the global economy.

They are the prime movers of a new cycle of what economist Joseph Schumpeter called "creative destruction," the ability of an economy to transform itself to meet the needs of rapid technological change. Cycles of creative destruction are spinning the global economy toward a digitized Meganet world.

This transformation is forcing a reexamination of the received wisdom about the workings of modern economies. In particular, it raises questions about the corporate model that has dominated Western economies for the past century. This model, emphasizing vertically integrated operations and top-down management, is now being reshaped in the new electronic environment. This change affects all industries but none more than those in the communications and information sectors.

The change is taking a heavy toll on corporate practices, even among companies that were, by business school rules, models of success. The most visible example is IBM, pillar of the electronics establishment and the source of many of the technological innovations that have come back to humble it in recent years. The company's button-down managerial style began to show cracks during the early 1980s, and within a decade things were crumbling at Big Blue, which sustained an $8.1-billion loss in one year. The company has since reorganized itself to cope with Meganet realities. Its new mantra (replacing "Think") is "netcentric communications," stressing the integration of all its operations into the Meganet mold. The bottom line is that the company chalked up $5.4 billion in net earnings in 1996.

Other firms have also done a better job of anticipating the impact of new Meganet-related products and services. 3M, an electronics power, restructured itself in the early 1990s in order to substantially increase the ratio of new products. Its executives decided that 30 percent of its annual production must come from products that did not exist four years earlier. Motorola is another firm that has been successful in adjusting to rapid change. Tom Galvin, the company's president, pointed out: "We try to be first in innovation—that gives us the significant edge. In the next era you will have to look for the next 32 surprises because things will accelerate. We like to think we are preparing ourselves to recognize the next possible surprise."[4]

The most dramatic example of a corporate response to information age realities was the 1995 AT&T decision to split its three major operations into separate companies. The idea of vertical integration of many activities, managed top-down from a corporate summit, was abandoned. A few years earlier, the move would have been denounced as corporate strategy gone berserk. Today, it is seen as a smart adjustment to a new business environment.

These changes will have a major impact on Meganet's core operations—the planning, building, and operation of a global telecommunications network. Meganet is a sprawling enterprise with no organizational center. The network itself is a mosaic of local operations spread across 180 countries. Most of it is not a business in the normal sense. Meganet's resources are still largely owned or tightly controlled by governments that are not beholden to bottom-line economics. But this is changing. Two decades ago, government monopolies totally controlled the network outside the United States. This pattern of ownership and control is being reshuffled into three more or less distinct groups directly concerned with building and managing the Meganet infrastructure.

The first and still largest group is the conglomeration of government-dominated national networks, which are run either by bureaucratic PTTs or newly privatized organizations. Their grip over local networks is gradually being loosened in ways that permit some competition, usually at the fringes of their core telephone business. This erosion of the old telecommunications monopolies is a critical element in the economics of global Meganet expansion.

The second group includes the big private telecom companies, such as AT&T and British Telecom. They have the technical, financial, and management resources to operate on a worldwide scale, either on their own or in alliance with local groups. They are Meganet's master builders, taking on the big projects that integrate many smaller systems into a global grid. An example is the submarine cable networks that link continents. They were once built and managed by government telecom monopolies. Today's fiber-optic cables are being assembled largely by private companies.

The third group can be described generally as the newcomers—organizations that are challenging telecommunications practices that have prevailed for the better part of a century. This new model emerged twenty-five years ago, when MCI successfully took on the AT&T monopoly. Today, other agile newcomers are setting up networks that bypass the old-line companies, selling their services directly in an expanding consumer market. The change is being hurried along by flexible new technologies, particularly in wireless communications.

Wireless telephony has become the weapon of choice around the world for introducing competition to telecom systems. Cable television is poised to become another direct competitor to the old-line phone networkers. The satellite industry has taken on new life as a provider of information and entertainment resources to ordinary consumers.

The newcomers are especially strong in the United States. They have won piecemeal entry into traditionally closed telecom areas during a cycle of regulatory reforms that began more than two decades ago. The cycle culminated in the Telecommunications Act of 1996, which removed most of the remaining barriers that had limited telecom companies, old and new, from competing among themselves in a full range of voice, video, and data services.[5]

This American experience is being replicated elsewhere. Most telecommunications services in the fifteen member nations of the European Union will be opened to full competition in 1998, largely as the result of pressure from economic planners at the EU's Brussels headquarters. The other major pressure, candidly acknowledged by the Europeans, is the need to match U.S. capabilities. Outdated national laws and practices are being adjusted to this new reality. The result is a new mix of telecom providers on the Meganet. This is forcing adjustments as powerful interests, old and new, jockey for position. It may take a decade or more to sort things out.

A central issue in this transition is how to finance Meganet expansion. Until very recently, this was not a problem. Overseas, the monopoly PTTs were relatively small but fiscally sound operations, usually returning a profit to the governments that owned them. In the United States, AT&T and other carriers were guaranteed comfortable rates of return, which were set by regulatory agencies and allowed companies to cover most of the costs of capital expansion.

These cozy arrangements are increasingly obsolete in the new competitive environment at home and abroad. As Meganet resources expand, the fiscal pie is being divided and subdivided among a larger group of competitive players. This is happening at a time when the industry faces increasingly heavy costs for upgrading Meganet facilities.

In recent years, funds for telecommunications expansion have poured out of Wall Street and other money centers. Some of this money has gone to high-flying startup ventures betting on a new technology or an innovative business plan. Most of the funds, however, have gone to established firms that have either a regulated rate of return or some other form of fiscal insurance. These are the companies that issue conservative stocks and bonds, investments that appeal to "widows and orphans" and that keep money markets relatively stable, year in and year out.

Will the money needed to fund Meganet expansion, at home and abroad, be available? Laurence Heyworth of Robert Fleming Securities has pointed out that new infrastructure costs will add up to about $800 billion in the next few years, just within the industrialized West. (Emerging markets are another matter and are discussed later in this chapter.) Most of it will be covered by the industry's current cash flow. The rest will have to be raised in the markets, a formidable task given other demands on what is an expanding but still finite capital pool.[6]

A large share of this new Meganet funding will continue to go to the phone companies that still dominate the telecom sector. A new wild card is coming into play, however, as some of the old hands are discarded. In country after country overseas, PTT monopolies are being dissolved at varying paces. In the United States, phone companies are restructuring themselves for a changing market. Above all, they are dealing with a new set of marketing prospects opened up by digital technologies. This change is called *one-stop shopping*, and it is sweeping away the old image of a phone company as simply a provider of voice connections. Replacing the old image are telecom organizations that package a range of services—voice, video, data—that are affordable and easy to use. In recent years, U.S. phone companies have been increasingly successful in assembling such packages for corporations and other large organizations. Now they are extending these services into 100 million U.S. households. As this occurs, the big phone companies find themselves in competition with cable-TV systems, satellite networkers, and others who are bypassing the traditional phone network.

A precursor of this consumerization of one-stop shopping surfaced during the mid-1980s. U.S. consumers found that they could choose among several providers of long-distance phone service. AT&T, MCI, Sprint, and other long-distance carriers battled for customers, and phone rates tumbled. More recently, consumers have been given a new set of long-distance options. These are the "dial-around" services, firms that lease circuits from the big telecom companies at wholesale and then market retail phone service at discount rates. Thanks to recent regulatory changes, customers can access the dial-around service easily by punching in a five-digit access code before placing a long-distance call. Typically, discount rates are 20–25 percent below regular long-distance charges, an incentive that is attracting a growing clientele.

The Dial & Save service, run by the Telco Communications Group in Chantilly, Virginia, is no immediate threat to AT&T or MCI, but it is one of a half-dozen U.S. discount services that together earned an estimated $700 million in 1996. This is just 1 percent of the $70 billion long-distance market, but it is enough for the big phone companies to begin taking notice.[7]

Dial & Save's discount service foreshadows a larger market shift likely to take place soon in the United States and, eventually, abroad. At present, most discount companies supply only long-distance service. However, the business climate is right for them to add other services, such as video and data. The result will be to speed up the mass consumerization of the multimedia packages that the big phone companies now offer to corporations and other large institutions. This prospect was strengthened by the 1996 telecommunications law. The legislation encourages competition among the three major suppliers of communications circuits—phone companies, cable-TV operators, and satellite networkers—for one-stop shopping. It is only a small step in the new regulatory environment to expand competition to include smaller providers, such as the discount networkers.

The big telephone companies will be around for a long time. They control the major electronics pathways. They will exploit this advantage in competing with pesky newcomers to whom, by law, they must lease their circuits. The phone companies are already moving rapidly into mass-consumer packaging of multimedia services. In 1996, MCI began marketing MCI One, a one-stop service that includes regular and cellular phone service, a pager, an e-mail address, and Internet access. Everything works on one phone number and is paid for on a single monthly bill.[8]

The old-line telephone companies will continue to dominate, but they will no longer call all the shots. The cable-TV and satellite industries will be serious competitors along with the bypassers. All these groups will be in the business of assembling packages of services, tailoring them to suit the many levels of the mass market.

A plausible scenario of how this will work is offered by Columbia University telecommunications researcher Eli Noam: "A pluralistic multi-network system emerges. This process is accelerated by the emergence of 'systems integrators,' who offer customized networks by assembling packages of various types of services, equipment, etc. Today systems integration already exists for large customers. But tomorrow's systems integrators will put together networks for group use."[9] Professor Noam cited the Internet as an early experiment in the formation of thousands of such interest groups, from New Age disciples to baseball card collectors. Meganet can amplify the trend. Networks will cease to be organized geographically under the control of governments or big corporations. Territoriality, Noam pointed out, suited these institutions because it allowed them to control "their" network. As networking becomes more flexible, these territorial limits are becoming irrelevant. Political boundaries are made anachronistic as like-minded interest groups overflow national borders electronically. Their concerns are increasingly continental and global, and the new customized network facilities will reflect these changing alignments.

Meganet will gradually transform itself from a network of networks into a system of systems. Each system or subnetwork will link groups with shared personal and professional interests in a vastly expanded version of the current Internet model. As this happens, Meganet will begin to reach its full potential as an information utility, serving the multiple needs of billions of users around the globe.

This pattern is forming first in the United States, but it will eventually spread through the entire global Meganet. Western Europe is moving in this direction. There is good reason to believe that similar patterns will soon appear in the big emerging markets of Asia and Latin America as technical facilities improve and as regulatory barriers to competition lower.

Technology and economics are pushing events in this direction. But the pace of development will be determined by the third factor in Meganet's triangle of convergences: politics.

Meganet is grounded in politics. For all the movement toward an open, competitive system, most Meganet facilities are still owned or closely regulated by governments. In most cases, these controls are relatively benign, intended primarily to protect a traditional source of revenues.

Other governments have a different motive, namely, to maintain repressive controls over what their citizens say and hear. The largest remaining example in China. Like other totalitarian regimes, Chinese leaders are trying to square the circle between tight control and their need for advanced telecommunications. Cuba's government gave an ideological twist to this dilemma several years ago by setting up an Institute for Cybernetic Socialism. Meanwhile, most other governments are ceding their power to control telecommunications facilities. It is a slow process, given the mix of political forces that are contending to either advance or hamper the change. Among the contenders are employees of monopoly PTTs, the civil servants who are usually organized well enough to resist changes to their protected status. Arrayed against them are equally powerful business interests who are pressing governments to promote more efficient, competitive telecom resources.

As demonstrated throughout the discussion in this book, the political tide favors a new competitive status in telecommunications. Almost 100 countries are currently moving toward dismantling their PTT monopolies. The major telecom countries, responsible for more than 80 percent of all global traffic, are deep into the process. Most of the rest will follow suit in the next decade.

The political implications of deregulation extend well beyond the details of rearranging the telephone system, important as they are. They involve a new role for government in an information-oriented society. This trend was first identified thirty years ago by Harvard political scientist Karl Deutsch in a groundbreaking study, *The Nerves of Government*. Information is power, he wrote, and—equally important—it is a multiplier of power. He foresaw the massive power inherent in advanced communications resources. It is a power that cannot be contained within traditional patterns of political authority.[10]

In democratic societies, Deutsch argued, information resources are more important than the police and the military. Governments must deal effectively with the rising flood of information needed to survive and thrive in a postindustrial environment. Advanced information technologies can do this by providing what he called "intelligence amplification," using the new machines not simply to store and distribute data but to increase personal and communal understanding. Their greatest value is as satellites of conscience, monitoring and identifying social needs in much the same way that a remote-sensing satellite in space monitors earth's environmental conditions.

Karl Deutsch wrote a generation ago, before the widespread use of computers, satellites, and other high-tech devices of the information age. His vision of democracy in a Meganet age is now being tested in day-to-day practice. Along with the rest of society, governments are being wired to meet new information needs. In the process, bureaucracies are being reshaped. A decade ago, a U.S. government study group, headed by industrialist Peter Grace, estimated that three-fourths of the federal workforce was engaged in processing information. The ratio is undoubtedly higher now. It is part of a shift from old-fashioned bureaucracy to what Rand researcher David Ronfeldt has called cyberocracy, which he defines as an information-based elite that may "slowly but radically affect who rules, how, and why."[11]

Meanwhile, the topsy-turvy growth of government information capabilities has both positive benefits and inherent dangers. The benefits are the increasing ease with which information resources are made available, particularly in the United States. A vast amount of official data is on the World Wide Web, from daily White House statements to hot-line information for Social Security recipients. The U.S. Government Printing Office, the largest publisher on earth, is getting out of the print business. A survey several years ago found that only 35 percent of its publications were available in print; the rest can be accessed electronically.[12]

The underside of this transformation is the enormous concentration of information in government computers. The ultimate result could be a sort of benign authoritarianism in which a governing elite is in effective control of the facts and figures needed to keep order.

This prospect has been caricatured, not wholly in jest, by Columbia University law professor Alan Westin. He envisioned a national data bank centered in Philadelphia run by an elite Establishment. The facility is attacked by democratic dissidents, the Fold, Staple, Spindle, and Mutilate movement. The dissidents are defeated, and the Establishment decides to program every event in every citizen's life to prevent further disruption. The dissidents win eventually, but not without some sobering insights from Professor Westin as to the relevance of information to the democratic process.

Other observers are not as optimistic. Bertram Gross of Hunter College has suggested that the concentration of government and corporate information power could lead to an era of "friendly fascism" in the United States.[13] Lewis Mumford, perhaps the most perceptive critic of twentieth-century U.S. society, saw us moving toward an authoritarian megamachine future because of the lack of adequate social restraints on communications machines and other advanced technologies. His analogy was that of a locomotive with neither brakes nor an engineer, inexorably gathering speed and heading for a crash.[14]

Mumford and like critics are wrong, primarily because they underestimate the complex web of checks and balances in U.S. society.

Nevertheless, their warnings alert us to the need for resiliency in dealing with the opportunities opened by the new technologies, including Meganet.[15]

For Americans, the touted information age is no longer a theory. Meganet's impact is a daily reality, affecting all of us in our work and in our personal lives. Old-line institutions and certainties are weakening in the new electronic environment. A new kind of economic underclass is developing in a society where the highest economic rewards are accruing largely to a slim segment of the population at the top. Squeezed between is a middle class that despite general prosperity worries about jobs and the futures of its children.

Meganet is only one part of the tectonic shifts taking place in U.S. society. Its impact is pervasive, affecting almost every other change. We bump into it every time we log on to a computer, as tens of millions of Americans do every day, or listen to an electronic phone message. It is also reflected in the new attention being paid to what are collectively called information highway issues. A consensus is beginning to form on the need for coherent policies to deal with the implications of Meganet and the wider societal changes connected with it.

An informed national consensus is necessary, but its working-out has proved difficult. The primary example of this in recent years was the debate leading up to passage of the Telecommunications Act of 1996. The debate was not, to put it mildly, a reasoned discourse on organizing for a bright and shining Meganet future. It was, too often, a selfish scramble among politicians and corporate executives, each invoking information age clichés while they jockeyed for advantage to protect narrow interests. The legislation is full of tax breaks, subsidies, and other gifts favoring individual corporations at the expense of a competitive, open-ended communications structure. The public interest was an orphan in the proceedings.

Realism dictates that it probably could not have happened any other way. The underlying emotion in all the wheeling and dealing that led up to the final law was fear. None of the corporate players or their congressional allies had a clear idea of the future Meganet pattern. Their visceral impulse was not to be left out in the competitive scramble that marks the new Meganet era.

Nevertheless, the 1996 legislation was, in balance, a useful step. It recognized the basic technological and economic facts of Meganet life. It removed many of the regulatory restraints that were holding up the completion of a national information utility: the U.S. portion of the global Meganet.

Above all, the new law advances the prospects that this utility can be made available to everyone. The operative phrase is *universal ser-*

vice, a valued national tradition that has undergirded U.S. communications in modern times. Its origins are in the Communications Act of 1934, which mandated universal access to telephone and radio broadcasting services, the major electronic technologies of the time. By and large, the goal was achieved. In the case of telephone service, Congress gave one company, AT&T, an effective monopoly and the economic incentives to provide universal access.

Today's situation is vastly more complicated. AT&T's monopoly has gone by the board. Thousands of companies now compete to provide a much broader range of communications services. Since 1994, the FCC, working with state regulatory commissions, has been trying to develop rules for a new universal service regime. They are considering, among other proposals, a universal service fund to subsidize communications and information resources in underserved parts of the country and to low-income groups.[16]

The amount of detail in any universal service project is daunting. Essentially, however, all the plans are about extending First Amendment guarantees into an advanced Meganet environment. Eli Noam has suggested that the stakes warrant updating the First Amendment for an electronic era. Whether or not this suggestion is politically practical, it points to a fundamental issue in postindustrial America.[17]

The universal service issue turns on an important constitutional principle. With Meganet, we are dealing with what may be called a multimedia First Amendment—information rights in a technological system in which all kinds of information services can be squeezed into a two-way communications pipe (e.g., fiber-optic cable). This calls for a comprehensive review of First Amendment guarantees, well beyond the limited question of information access as we have understood it during the past two centuries.

The U.S. effort to come to grips with universal service issues in this new electronic environment has global implications. Sooner or later, other countries will face the same issues. The European Union has already begun a regional discussion on full citizen access to Meganet's high-capacity, multimedia resources, paying particular attention to the effect this access will have on the region's social and cultural development. The subject is being raised, in fits and starts, in other countries, too.

The United States has a powerful stake in the outcome of these discussions. Historically, U.S. policies have rested on the principle of free flow of information, at home and abroad. The First Amendment has reinforced this principle at home, but its protection does not extend past U.S. borders. Few other nations, including some of our democratic partners, have as strong a tradition of protecting the information rights of their citizens. U.S. attempts to build such protections into international law and practice have often been rebuffed.[18]

Such attempts have often been regarded as part of a crafty U.S. strategy to impose American culture on the rest of the world. Resistance to this perceived threat brought a new phrase into international diplomacy—*cultural imperialism*. Fear of U.S. cultural domination was rooted in the ubiquitous influence of U.S. media around the world. Hollywood films dominate the world's movie screens. MTV, the music video channel, is seen in more than 100 countries. CNN reaches every continent. Tokyo's Disneyland draws a larger annual audience than its Florida counterpart.[19]

During the 1970s, more than 100 countries banded together in the United Nations to propose a "new world information order," pointedly aimed at restricting U.S. media access to their territories. This initiative failed. But other projects to limit U.S. media continued to surface. The fifteen members of the European Union tried for ten years to limit showings of non-European (i.e., American) television programs in their countries. They abandoned the effort in 1996, primarily because their broadcasting industries opposed the limit, which affected some of their most popular programs.[20]

Canada has been the most persistent in trying to limit U.S. media influence. Canadian laws restrict wholly owned foreign companies from competing with domestic companies in cultural industries. In one outsized example, Canada's government proposed to stop broadcasts of the U.S.-based Country Music Television cable channel in 1996 when a similar Canadian service was launched. U.S. trade officials protested vigorously, and the issue was settled by merging the two operations into a single network. Other media disputes between the two countries have not be settled as amicably.[21]

Information highway initiatives during the first Clinton administration called attention to these foreign restrictions on information flow. This was due, in part, to the newly enhanced role of communications services as the fastest growing U.S. export sector. As we have seen, Washington mounted a successful effort to include communications services under new World Trade Organization rules agreed to in 1993. It also stepped up its pressure on individual countries to cut back on restrictions of U.S. communications exports.

These actions have not only helped the U.S. economy but also enhanced prospects for speeding up Meganet development worldwide. The greatest challenge to completing the network progress is closing the North-South gap, the two-tiered world of information haves and have-nots. The northern industrial countries still possess three-quarters of all information resources; the emerging economies, with more than three times the population, have the rest. This ratio is changing, but too slowly. As we have seen, the big emerging markets are making significant progress in building communications structures. In part this is happening because foreign investors, led by U.S. firms, are ready to invest in these projects. Telecommunications is a money-maker. Klas Ringskog, a World Bank adviser, has estimated that $3 in telecom infrastructure funding generates $1 in annual revenue—a very favorable rate of return.[22]

But the telecom investment pattern is uneven, concentrated in about thirty of the top emerging economies. This leaves almost 100 countries with poor prospects for outside investment. The disparity is highlighted by comparing the investment prospects of China and Russia. China has emerged as a major target for the world's money markets and has received twenty-five times more foreign direct investment than Russia during the late 1990s.[23]

There is no one-size-fits-all solution to improving the North-South communications imbalance. The pressure to privatize monopoly PTTs in developing areas and to open them up to competition is an important factor. So is the greater willingness to adopt "leapfrogging" techniques that use new technologies (satellites, wireless phones, etc.) to skip generations of intermediate technologies such as wires strung from telephone poles. Country by country, these strategies are building confidence that an advanced Meganet can be built within the next generation. As James Bond of World Bank has pointed out, the result will be to realign the global economy and to shift the world's geopolitical fault lines.[24]

In light of such a massive transformation, predicting the impact of a truly global Meganet is a risky business. Old habits and attitudes will be overturned as we create a resource that will, for the first time in human history, link all humankind.

A new map of the world is being drawn. It is an information map, comparable to a weather map in that it indicates environmental conditions rather than linear directions. The map now shows a dense mass of organized information over North America, with smaller masses over Europe, Japan, and a few other countries. Elsewhere the density of information shades off into thinness. Meganet can change this pattern in ways that will affect our own lives, and those of future generations, in ways we can only dimly see.

APPENDIX:
A MEGANET
GLOSSARY

Addressability. The function in a cable television system that allows a subscriber to contact, through keypad input, the system's central office in order to receive special programs (e.g., pay-per-view entertainment).

Amplitude modulation (AM). In broadcasting, a method of modulating electrical impulses in which the amplitude (power) is varied and the frequency remains constant. AM is used in the radio broadcast band (540–1,605 kilohertz), in the picture portion of television transmissions, and in shortwave broadcasting.

Analog. In telecommunications transmissions, the representation of numerical or alphanumerical values by physical variables (e.g., voltage, current). See **Digital.**

Anonymous File Transfer Protocol (FTP). Anonymous FTP allows an Internet user to retrieve documents, files, programs, and other archived material at any point on the Net without having to establish a password. It allows the user to bypass local security checks and to access publicly accessible files on the remote system.

Artificial intelligence. A computer's capability to perform functions normally associated with human intelligence (i.e., reasoning and learning). Early attempts to replicate human thought have been overtaken by more limited but practical applications such as neural networking.

Aspect ratio. The ratio of a television screen's width to its height. Current television sets have a 4:3 aspect ratio. High-definition television sets will have aspect ratios that will provide a wider screen.

Baby Bells. The original seven regional telephone companies created as a result of the 1984 divestiture of AT&T's local telephone holdings. The Baby Bells, known more formally as the Regional Bell Operating Companies, will be major suppliers of phone company information and entertainment services to homes as a result of deregulation provisions in the Telecommunications Act of 1996.

Bandwidth. The range within a band of wavelengths, frequencies, or energies.

Basic services. An FCC designation for transmission capacity offered by a common carrier (e.g., a phone company) to move information between two or more points. See **Value-added services.**

Baud. A measure of signaling speed in a digital communications circuit. The speed in baud is the number of signal elements per second.

BCNU. Internet shorthand for "Be seein' you."

Betamax. The videocassette standard supported by Sony in the 1980s, which was superseded by Matsushita's VHS standard. Although Betamax faded as a standard for home VCRs, it continues to be used for other applications within the media industries.

Birds of a Feather (BOF). On the Internet, a BOF is an informal discussion group, usually formed ad hoc to discuss a specific issue.

Bit. A contraction of "binary digit," a bit is the smallest unit of information that a computer recognizes. A bit is represented by the presence or absence of an electronic impulse, usually symbolized by a zero or a figure one.

Bits per second (bps). The digital information rate expressed as the number of binary information units transmitted per second.

Broadband. A signal that requires a large bandwidth to be transmitted, alternately applied to equipment that must be capable of receiving or transmitting accurately a signal with a large bandwidth.

Byte. A group of adjacent binary digits (often shorter than a word) that a computer processes as a unit. Usually, one byte is eight bits long.

Cable antenna television (CATV). The original name for cable television systems that provided coaxial cable retransmission of over-the-air television. The name was dropped after the introduction of national satellite-delivered channels in the 1970s.

Cable-telco debate. The political and economic contest between telephone companies and the cable-TV industry to gain the upper hand in supplying multimedia information and entertainment services to U.S. households.

Cellular telephone. A telephone that uses radio links to complete the connection from a customer's phone to a cellular base station. The base station, in turn, is interconnected to the public switched telephone network (PSTN).

Chapter. One independent, self-contained segment of a computer program or interactive video program.

Chip. A silicon-based device on which microscopic electronic circuitry is printed photographically to create passive and active devices, circuit paths, and device connections within the solid structure.

Circuit switching. One of two common methods of switching. In telecommunications, circuit switching refers to dialing a connection of one device, like a telephone, to another. The other common switching method is packet switching, which is used by computers and other devices to switch digital information.

Coaxial cable. Insulated cable used to transmit telephone and television signals in a high-frequency mode. Composed of a center conductor, a conductive shield, and optional protective covering, this type of cable has excellent broadband frequency characteristics, noise immunity, and physical durability. "Coax" has been the standard channel carrier for cable-TV.

Codec. Acronym for coder/decoder, a device that encodes outgoing signals and decodes incoming signals. The coder and decoder functions are integrated within a single device and are most often used in analog-to-digital and digital-to-analog conversion applications.

Common carrier. The provision of transmission capability over a telecommunications network. A common carrier company offers public communications services. It is subject to regulation by federal and state regulatory bodies that establish operating rules and tariffs in order to make the services available at a fair price and on a nondiscriminatory basis. Telephone companies are common carriers.

Communications Act of 1934. The basic national legislation that regulated the use of electronic communications for more than sixty years. The act mandated a national telephone system—the first such legislation to recognize the importance of telecommunications for social and economic growth. It was superseded in 1996 by new congressional legislation that incorporates regulatory changes made necessary by the introduction of advanced telecommunications and media technologies.

Compact disc. An optical storage medium, used for music and for computer data, among other services.

Compact disc audio (CD-A). A popular compact disc format for high-fidelity digital music. Each disc offers up to seventy-five minutes of programmable sound with no degradation of quality during playback.

Compact disc interactive (CD-I). A disc storage medium for interactive audio, video, and data information. Pioneered by Sony and Philips, CD-I was originally developed for business training uses. It is currently being introduced into the home market, with marketing efforts focused on consumer information and entertainment applications.

Compact disc–read-only memory (CD-ROM). A prerecorded, nonerasable disk that stores up to 600 megabytes of digital data. On the market since the late 1980s, early applications have focused on reference materials, databases, and audio and video files.

Compression. The reduction of certain parameters of a signal while preserving the basic information content. The result is to improve overall transmission efficiency and to reduce cost. In media operations, the most extensive use of compression techniques is in cable-TV coaxial cable, where compression can double or triple the number of available channels.

Compunications. A description, proposed by Harvard professor Anthony Oettinger, of the convergence of computer and telecommunications technology, which results in an integrated information network.

Computer network. A set of communications channels used to link computers and/or terminals together so that they can share a workload or access a particular computer where facilities and services are provided in the network.

Convergence. The coming-together of computer, cable, telephony, and satellite capabilities to electronically deliver information in video, voice, or data forms. The end result of these converging technologies will likely be the provision of universal access to a vast range of interactive, on-demand multimedia products and services.

Customer premises equipment (CPE). Any advanced telecommunications network equipment located on the premises of the customer (e.g., a PBX telephone device). The phrase is also used by telephone companies to refer to customer-provided (as opposed to company-provided) equipment in offices and homes.

Cyberspace. A computer-generated artificial environment designed to maximize the user's freedom of movement and imagination. The term was coined by William Gibson in his fantasy novel Neuromancer. Gibson described cyberspace as "a consensual hallucination experienced daily by billions." In general terms, cyberspace is that borderless area where electronic data and communications are exchanged. The Internet, for instance, can be said to "exist" in cyberspace.

Data. Alphabetical or numerical representations of facts or concepts, in a manner suitable for communication, interpretation, or processing by human or automatic means.

Data communications. The transfer, reception, and validation of data between a source and a receiver via one or more data links, using appropriate code conversions or protocols.

Dedicated circuit. A circuit designated for exclusive use by two users. Also known as a dedicated line.

Demodulation. Making communications signals compatible with computer terminal signals.

Digital. A method of signal representation by a set of discrete numerical values (ones and zeros), as opposed to a continuously fluctuating current or voltage. Compare **Analog.**

Digital audio broadcasting (DAB). Digital transmission of sound signals by cable, terrestrial microwave, or communications satellites. DAB will eventually replace AM and FM technology in radio broadcasting.

Digital audio tape (DAT). A tape format for storing digital audio signals. Each tape can store more than 2.5 gigabytes of data. DAT is often used as a computer storage backup system.

Digital video interactive (DVI). A technology for compressing and decompressing video and audio to create multimedia applications. DVI can store up to seventy-two minutes of full-motion video on a compact disc. Using DVI, a viewer can interact with the image being shown. As an example, a viewer may "walk" through a computer-generated building, seeing details of the interior from any angle.

Direct broadcasting satellite (DBS). A communications satellite whose signal both radiates over a large area and is capable of being picked up by small earth stations. DBS technology has been used in recent years to deliver information and entertainment services to homes and other locations.

Direct-read-after-draw (DRAW). An optical disc technology that allows a user to record material that cannot be erased. A high-powered laser "burns" pits into a heat-sensitive layer beneath the surface of a recordable disc. The information is then read by a lower-power laser.

Disk. A flat, circular, rotating platter that can store and replay various types of information, both analog and digital. "Disk" is often used when describing magnetic storage media. "Disc" usually refers to optical storage media.

Distributed network. A network in which processing or intelligence is spread among many interconnected computers.

Divestiture Agreement. The plan, finalized in 1984, in which AT&T and the federal government set the terms for AT&T's relinquishment of control over its local phone companies in exchange for permission to enter the information services market. The resultant document is also called the Modified Final Judgment.

Domain Name System (DNS). On the Internet, the DNS is a general purpose, distributed, and replicated data query service. Host names on the Internet are called "domain names," because they are the style of names used to look up anything in the DNS. Some of the more common domains are .com (commercial), .edu (educational) and .gov (government). Countries also have a domain designation, e.g., .us (United States) and .au (Australia).

Dynabook. A concept advanced by MIT researcher Alan Kay to describe an all-purpose handheld computer that would store vast amounts of data, as well as have the capability to access other data sources.

Dynamic random access memory (DRAM). A type of computer memory in which information can be stored and retrieved in miscellaneous order, but which must be "maintained" or refreshed by a periodic electrical charge if the memory is not read out or used immediately.

Electronic data interchange (EDI). Networks that eliminate intermediate steps in processes that rely on transmission of paper-based instructions and documents by performing them electronically, computer to computer. EDI networking is growing rapidly in the United States.

Electronic funds transfer (EFT). A capability, based on a network of computers, that allows electronic transactions as a replacement for cash transactions. EFT allows, for instance, paychecks to be automatically deposited from an employer's bank to the employee's bank. In recent years, EFT has expanded to include the daily transfer of billions of dollars between financial institutions around the world.

Electronic mail (e-mail). The forwarding, storage, and retrieval of messages by electronic transmission systems, usually using digital techniques.

Electronic manuscript production. In book production, computerized tracking of the preparation of the book on a day-by-day basis, including keeping current tallies on costs, man-hours, and production scheduling.

Electronic news gathering (ENG). In broadcasting, coverage of events outside the studio through the use of satellite dish–equipped trucks, providing live or taped coverage.

Electronic publishing. Replaces traditional means of delivering and storing text information by using computerized delivery. The information is held in a storage device for delivery to computer screens rather than printed on paper.

E-mail address. The domain-based address that is used to send electronic mail to a specified destination.

Encoding. The process of transforming an analog signal into a digital signal, or a digital signal into another digital format.

Enhanced definition television (EDTV). A variation on high-definition television, providing a better picture than current TV sets but offering less resolution than high-definition technology. See **High-definition television.**

Enhanced services. A telecommunications category established by the Federal Communications Commission to describe services that result in additional, different, or restructured transmitted information or that involve user interaction with stored information, whether voice or data. See **Basic services.**

Erasable rewritable optical disc (EROD). A read/write storage medium that uses a laser and reflected light to store and retrieve data on an optical disc. The discs can store more than one gigabyte of data and are generally used to replace a hard drive.

Erlang. A dimensionless unit of measure used in telecommunications traffic engineering. One erlang equals one call hour, 60 call minutes, or 3,600 call seconds. It is used to calculate the required number of circuits (called trunks) between telephone switches. Named after Danish telephone engineer A. K. Erlang.

Facsimile (fax). A form of electronic mail, or remote copying. Also, the document resulting from a fax transmission.

FAQ. Frequently Asked Questions. An Internet acronym designed to guide new users through the intricacies of the system.

Federal Communications Commission (FCC). The federal independent regulatory agency that licenses and sets standards for telecommunications and electronic media. FCC deregulatory policies in recent decades have had a major impact on U.S. media patterns by expanding the range of delivery services available.

Femtosecond. A millionth of a billionth of a second. The capabilities of fiber-optic systems now under development will be measured in femtoseconds (i.e., millions of times the capacity of present systems).

Fiber optics. The technology of guiding and transmitting light for use as a communications medium. Modulated light-wave signals, generated by a laser or a light-emitting diode, are propagated along a silicon-based waveguide and then demodulated back into electrical signals by a light-sensitive receiver. The bandwidth capacity of fiber-optic wire is substantially greater than that of coaxial cable or copper wire.

File Transfer Protocol (FTP). A protocol that allows a user on one host to access, and transfer files to and from, another host over the Internet or other network. FTP is also used as the name of the program the user selects to execute the protocol.

First Amendment. The Bill of Rights provision that is the ideological base, and protector, of information freedoms in the United States.

Flame. On the Internet, a strong opinion or criticism, often inflammatory, in an e-mail message. Such a message can lead to "flame wars," in which users fire electronic volleys against the flamers.

Flash-memory chip. A recent major advance in chip technology. Flash-memory chips retain information when a computer is turned off, unlike earlier chips. The result is to eliminate the need for disk-drive storage systems, permitting much smaller, lighter computers.

Freenet. Community-based bulletin board system that often includes e-mail, information services, interactive communications, and conferencing. Freenets are usually funded and operated by individuals and volunteers.

Frequency modulation (FM). In broadcasting, a method of modulation in which the frequency is varied and the amplitude (power) remains constant. In addition to its radio uses, FM is used in the sound portion of TV transmissions. See **Amplitude modulation (AM)**.

Gateway terminal. In satellite networks, an earth terminal that serves as an interconnection point with terrestrial networks.

Generator. Any device that facilitates a computer task such as text, graphics, or program design.

Gigabit. A measure of the quantity of binary digits. A gigabit equals 1 billion bits per second. A gigabyte is one billion bytes.

Gopher. A distributed information service that makes available hierarchical collections of information available across the Internet. A Gopher client can access information from any accessible Gopher server, providing the user with a single "Gopher space" of information. Gopher derives its name from the fact that it was begun by a group at the University of Minnesota, which has adopted the Golden Gopher as its mascot.

Graphical User Interface (GUI). In computers, a user-friendly method of initiating programs and selecting options, normally including the use of a mouse and special graphics (icons) to indicate selections and enter commands. The Apple Macintosh was the first major use of GUI techniques, followed by Microsoft's Windows. GUI is pronounced "gooey."

Groupware. Software that facilitates communications among members of work groups, often used with personal computers attaches to local area networks (LANs). It is used, for example, for electronic meetings and shared-document systems.

GUI. See **Graphical User Interface**.

Headend. A cable TV system's control center where program signals from satellites and other sources are transferred to the system's network.

High-definition television (HDTV). A group of technical systems, each of which can encode, transmit, and display greatly enhanced levels of information compared to conventional TV, making possible a sharper video picture, improved color fidelity, and the use of stereophonic sound. HDTV is scheduled for large-scale adoption in the United States, Europe, and Japan by the end of the decade.

Host. A computer that allows users to communicate with other host computers on a network.

Hypermedia. A way of storing information so that it can be referenced and used in a nonlinear manner, one point of information being accessed directly from another without the need to go to an intervening index or table of contents.

Hypertext. Computer software that allows users to link information together through a variety of paths or connections. Users can randomly organize the information in a manner that conforms to their own needs. Hypercard programs ("stacks") are made up of "cards" that when activated allow users to move to another part of the material they are working with. Hypercard programs are written in "hypertalk," a simple, object-oriented programming language.

Icon. In computer operations, a symbolic, pictorial representation of any function or task.

Image technology. A general category of computer applications that convert documents, illustrations, photographs, and other images into data that can be stored, distributed, accessed, and processed by computers and special-purpose workstations.

IMHO. Internet acronym for "In my humble opinion."

Information utility. The concept of a national and, eventually, global electronic network that will supply a full range of media and other information resources to all locations (comparable to water and electricity utility networks).

Integrated services digital network (ISDN). A long-term plan for the transition of the world's telecommunications systems from analog to digital technology, permitting the integrated transmission of any combination of voice, video, graphics, and data over a common electronic "information pipe." ISDN is a software standard that will eliminate current technical incompatibilities between telecommunications systems and allow uninterrupted transfer of traffic between them.

Interactive media. Media resources that involve the user in providing the content and duration of a message, permitting individualized program material. Also used to describe media production operations that take maximum advantage of random access, computer-controlled videotape and videodisc players.

Interactive video. A combination of video and computer technology in which programs run in tandem under the control of the user. The user's choices and decisions directly affect the ways in which the program unfolds.

Interface. The point or boundary at which hardware or software systems interact (e.g., the connection between a computer and a terminal).

International Telecommunications Union (ITU). A United Nations agency that sets the technical and administrative standards for the global telecommunications network. ITU has been a leader in promoting ISDN standardization. Its headquarters are in Geneva, Switzerland.

internet. Using the lowercase *i*, internet usually refers to a collection of networks interconnected with routers, the devices that forward traffic between networks.

Internet. The largest internetworking system in the world. It is a multilevel hierarchy, composed of backbone networks (e.g., NSFNET), midlevel networks, and stub networks.

Internet Society (ISOC). A non-profit, professional membership organization with headquarters in Reston, Virginia. ISOC facilitates and supports the technical evolution of the Internet and promotes the development of new applications of the system. Its work in developing technical standards is supported by funds from a U.S. government group, the Corporation for National Research Initiatives. In recent years, similar organizations have been established abroad.

Interoperability. The ability of software and hardware on multiple machines from multiple vendors to communicate meaningfully.

Intranet. A closed-circuit version of the Internet, increasingly used by corporations and other large institutions for their internal communications.

KA band. The new frontier of the radio frequency spectrum. Located in the 20–30 gigahertz frequency bands, KA is, for the present, the upper limit of spectrum use for media and other normal communications needs. The KA frequencies are capable of handling enormous amounts of information. The other high-capacity bands currently in use are C band and KU band, both used extensively for satellite and terrestrial microwave transmissions.

Laser. Technically, *l*ight *a*mplification by *s*timulated *e*mission of *r*adiation. Lasers amplify and generate energy in the optical, or light region of the spectrum above the radio frequencies. In a typical media application, lasers are used to read the micropits on a videodisc, which contain video or sound signals.

Light-emitting diode (LED). A semiconductor device that changes electrical energy into light energy.

Light guide. An extremely clear, thin glass fiber that is to light what copper wire is to electricity. It is synonymous with optical fiber.

Media Lab. A unit of the Massachusetts Institute of Technology that has done much of the pioneering research on applying advanced technologies to media uses.

Megabit. One million binary digits or bits.

Microprocessor. An electronic circuit, usually on a single microchip, that performs arithmetic, logic, and control operations, customarily with the assistance of a small internal memory, also on the chip.

Microsoft Network (MSN). A consumer-oriented database established in 1995 by the Microsoft Corp. to compete with American Online, Prodigy, and similar services.

Minitel. A national information-retrieval network in France that supplies thousands of data services to millions of homes. High-tech versions of Minitel, such as Prodigy and CompuServe, are being developed commercially in the United States.

Modem. Contraction of modulator/demodulator. A device that converts a computer signal from digital technology to analog technology so that data can be sent great distances without losing its ability to be understood and interpreted.

Multichannel microwave distribution system (MMDS). Television delivery system that uses line-of-sight microwave circuits to transmit programs similar to those supplied on cable-TV. MMDSs have limited channel capacity, however, compared to cable systems. MMDS is often referred to as "wireless cable."

Multimedia. Information delivery systems that combine different content formats (e.g., text, video, sound) and storage facilities (e.g., videotape, audiotape, magnetic disks, optical discs).

Multiplexing. A technique that allows handling of multiple messages over a single channel. It is accomplished either by varying the speed at which the messages are sent (time division multiplexing) or by splitting the frequency band (frequency division multiplexing).

Multi-User Dungeon. Role-playing adventure games or simulations played on the Internet. The games can feature, among other possibilities, fantasy combat, booby traps, and magic, with players interacting in real time.

National Information Infrastructure. A phrase coined by Michael Dertouzis, chief of the computer research lab at MIT, to describe the eventual development of an integrated multimedia telecommunications system. See **Information utility.**

National Science Foundation. A U.S. government–funded agency whose purpose is to fund the advancement of science. It has been instrumental in promoting the use of the Internet for scientific and academic purposes. See **NSFNET.**

Newbies. The term for inexperienced Internet users, sometimes used derisively to distinguish them from longtime Net buffs.

NSFNET. A "network of networks" that is part of the Internet and is funded by the National Science Foundation. It is hierarchical in nature. At the highest level, it is a high-speed backbone network, spanning the United States. Attached to that are midlevel networks and attached to the midlevels are campus and local networks. NSFNET has international connections with networks throughout the world.

Optical memory. Technology that deals with information storage devices that use light (generally laser-based) to record, read, or decode data.

Packet. The unit of data sent across a network.

Packet switching. The transfer of data by means of addressed blocks ("packets") of information in which a telecommunications channel is occupied only for the time of transmission of the packet. This allows more efficient use of channels, which ordinarily have periods of low use.

Peripheral equipment. Equipment that works in conjunction with a communications system or a computer but that is not integral to them (e.g., printers, scanners, storage drives).

Personal electronic media. Networks serving the specialized information needs of their users, usually through e-mail exchanges. Eventually such personal networking will incorporate video capabilities.

Photon. The fundamental unit of light and other forms of electromagnetic energy. Photons are to optical fibers what electrons are to copper wires; like electrons, they have a wave motion.

Protocol. A set of rules that defines procedures for the transfer of information in a communications system.

PTT. The common acronym for government-owned or -controlled postal and telecommunications agencies abroad. The acronym refers to *p*osts, *t*elegraph, and *t*elephone services.

Public switched telephone network (PSTN). The worldwide switched telephone network provided by local exchange carriers (LECs) and interexchange carriers (IEXs) in the United States and internationally through a mixture of government-owned posts, telephone, and telegraph agencies (PTTs) and commercial vendors.

Quicktime. A computer file format that enables Macintosh computers to compress and play digitized video without additional hardware.

Random-access memory (RAM). A computer memory, the contents of which can be altered at any time. It is the most commonly used method of defining computer capability (e.g., 32MB RAM).

RBOC. In the United States, the seven *R*egional *B*ell *O*perating *C*ompanies that were created from the telephone companies divested by AT&T in 1984. The number of RBOCs had been reduced to four in 1996 as a result of mergers.

Read-only memory (ROM). A computer chip that stores data and instructions in a form that cannot be altered. It is thus distinguished from random-access memory, the contents of which can be changed.

Reseller. In the public switched telephone network (PSTN), a carrier that is not facilities-based, i.e., it doesn't own telecommunications network facilities. They aggregate, repackage, or resell the transmission services of facilities-based carriers.

Roaming. In cellular mobile telephony, the ability to use a cellular telephone in many cellular service areas, or in areas that are not within the service area of the company from which the customer obtains cellular service.

Satellite. An orbiting space station primarily used to relay signals from one point on the earth's surface to one or many other points. A geosynchronous or "stationary" satellite orbits the earth exactly in synchronization with the earth's rotation, so that it appears fixed in the same location relative to the earth.

Semiconductor. A material (e.g., silicon, germanium, gallium arsenide) with properties between those of conductors and insulators. Semiconductors are used to manufacturer solid-state devices such as diodes, transistors, integrated circuits, injection lasers, and light-emitting diodes.

Semionics. The discipline that deals with the development and use of symbols. Symbol and symbol manipulations are an integral part of the emerging new media. A familiar example are the icons used in Macintosh and Windows software.

SONET. The acronym for *Synchronous Optical Network*, a standard for signals used in optical fiber networks. It provides a basic data transfer format that can be used for all types of digital information—voice, video, data, facsimile, and graphics.

Spectrum. A specified range of electromagnetic frequencies or, in come cases, the whole range of frequencies considered to constitute electromagnetic signals.

Snail mail. A pejorative term, used primarily by computer buffs to describe the U.S. Postal Service.

Software. The detailed instruction or programs that tell the computer what to do byte by byte. Also: the digital information flowing through computer and telecommunications circuits.

Squarial. A small earth terminal that is square or rectangular in shape and designed to be attached to the roofs or sides of houses and other, smaller structures.

Telecomputer. A combined television receiver and computer, which may be the central information and entertainment unit of homes in the new multimedia environment.

Teletext. One-way broadcast transmissions that piggyback digital data onto the regular television broadcasting signal by inserting their messages into unused lines of the vertical blanking interval.

Television receive only (TVRO) terminal. A small earth station that receives video signals from a space satellite.

Telex. A switched telegraph service that makes use of "start-stop" character-by-character transmissions. It has been replaced by computer-to-computer and facsimile communications in the United States but is still commonly found in other countries.

Transparent. In telecommunications, a circuit or device is transparent to a signal when that signal is transmitted with little or no distortion to its original form.

Transponder. A component in a satellite that receives and transmits television or data signals.

Ultra-high frequency (UHF). The radio spectrum from 300 megahertz to gigahertz. It is the frequency band that includes TV channels 14–83, as well as cellular radio frequencies.

Value-added network (VAN). Data processing done as part of a transmission service package.

Very high frequency (VHF). The radio spectrum from 30 to 300 megahertz, which includes TV channels 2–13, the FM broadcast band, and various specialized services.

Very small aperture terminal (VSAT). A range of small earth station designs that are capable, due to advanced semiconductor technology, of receiving signals from space satellites. A newer generation of VSATs can also transmit signals to the satellites.

Videotext. The transmission of information by television channels, FM frequencies, or telephone circuits to a TV or computer monitor. There are many variations of videotext services, the most advanced of which is full two-way transmission, in which a television receiver is equipped to function as a computer terminal.

Virtual private network (VPN). A voice or data "network" that is actually a prearranged subset of a carrier's network. VPN connections are available for customers' exclusive or private use. Carriers typically charge customers a lower price for voice and data traffic carried on a VPN than for similar traffic carried on the public switched telephone network.

Virtual reality. Software that produces multidimensional visual images. The computerized images can create "realities," which are manipulated in many different formats by a user wearing computerized gloves or helmet.

Virus. A program that replicates itself on computer systems by incorporating itself into other programs that are shared among computer systems.

Wireless cable. See **Multichannel microwave distribution system.**

World Wide Web (WWW). A hypertext-based, distributed information system on which Internet users may create, edit, or browse hypertext documents. The Web was created by researchers at CERN, the nuclear research facility near Geneva, Switzerland.

Write once, read many (WORM). An optical storage medium that becomes readable only after data are written into the disk. It can store large amounts of information and has a long shelf life. Some WORM disks are analog and some are digital.

WYSIWYG. Internet term for "what you see is what you get."

NOTES

Chapter 1

1. "Seventy nations agree to lay longest undersea cable," *Financial Times* (London), 16 January 1997, p. 2.

2. The chart was developed by the editors in the June 1996 issue of *World Paper*, a Boston publication.

3. "A match made in heaven," *Economist* (London), 6 April 1996, p. 64.

4. Claude Shannon and Warren Weaver, "A mathematical theory of communications," *Bell System Technical Journal*, 22, No. 3, July 1948.

5. "The end of the line," *Economist* (London), 15 June 1995, p. 61.

6. "Motorola joins 1 gigabit consortium," *Financial Times* (London), 25 October 1995, p. 6.

7. "Speed gets a whole new meaning," *Business Week*, 29 April 1996, p. 90.

8. U.S. Congress, Office of Technology Assessment, *Global communications: Opportunities for trade and aid*, Publication No. OTA-ITC-642, Washington DC, September 1995, p. 123.

9. Peter Cowhey, "Building the global information highway: Toll booths, construction contracts, and rules of the road," in William J. Drake (ed.), *The new information infrastructure: Strategies for U.S. Policy.* New York: Twentieth Century Fund, 1995, pp. 175–204.

10. The shift to an information-based economy was first documented by economist Fritz Machlup in *The production and distribution of knowledge in the United States.* Princeton NJ: Princeton University Press, 1962.

11. "Major trends in the service sector," *CSI Reports*, The Coalition of Service Industries, Washington DC, June 1996, p. 2.

12. U.S. Department of Commerce, *The U.S. global trade outlook, 1995–2000*, Washington DC, March 1995, p. 182.

13. Herbert Dordick, Helen G. Bradley, and Burt Nanus, *The emerging network marketplace.* Norwood NJ: Ablex Publishing, 1981.

14. "Call me," *Economist* (London), 8 June 1996, p. 71.

15. "Sorry, we don't take cash," *Business Week*, 12 December 1994, p. 42.

16. "Prospects for Internet banking," *Telecommunications*, June 1996, p. 22.

17. Interview in "The Revenge of the Nerds," Public Broadcasting System documentary, July 1996.

18. "Secession of the successful," *New York Times Magazine*, 20 January 1991, p. 16.

19. Gregory C. Staple, "Telegeography and the explosion of place," remarks at the Columbia Institute for Tele-Information, Columbia University, 29 October 1993.

20. "Shining Path wages flame war," *Financial Times* (London), 13 May 1996, p. 13.

21. For a useful discussion of this issue, see: Colin R. Blackman, "Universal service: Obligation or opportunity?" *Telecommunications Policy*, 19, No. 3, April 1995, pp. 171–176.

Chapter 2

1. For an overall survey of electronic commerce, see: U.S. Congress, Office of Technology Assessment, *Electronic enterprises*, Publication No. OTA-TCT-600, Washington DC, May 1994.

2. For a survey of First Amendment implications of electronic technologies, see: Ithiel de Sola Pool, *Technologies of freedom*. Cambridge MA: Harvard University Press, 1983.

3. "Historical premonitions of the information superhighway," *Wired*, August 1994, p. 64.

4. Fritz Machlup, *The production and distribution of knowledge in the United States*. Princeton NJ: Princeton University Press, 1962.

5. Daniel Bell, *The coming of post-industrial society*. New York: Basic Books, 1973.

6. U.S. Department of Commerce, Office of Telecommunications, *The information economy*. Nine volumes. Special Publication No. 77-12. Washington DC, 1977.

7. Stephen S. Cohen and John Zysman, *Manufacturing matters: The myth of the post-industrial economy*. New York: Basic Books, 1987.

8. "Growth industry," *Washington Post*, Washington Business supplement, 7 August 1996, p. 15.

9. William Baumol, *Production and American leadership*. Cambridge MA: MIT Press, 1989, p. 158.

10. Ithiel de Sola Pool, *The social impact of the telephone*. Cambridge MA: MIT Press, 1977.

11. Jeffrey B. Abramson, F. Christopher Arterton, and Gary R. Orren, *The electronic commonwealth: The impact of new media technologies on democratic politics*. New York: Basic Books, 1988.

12. "Data highway ignoring poor, study charges," *New York Times*, 24 May 1994, p. D-1.

13. Ibid.

14. *Communications Industry Forecast*, Veronis, Suhler, and Associates, New York, August 1995, p. 15.

15. "Please hold for the new technology," *Business Week*, 8 April 1996, p. 82.

16. "The race is on to simplify," *Business Week*, 24 June 1996, pp. 72–110.

17. "Microsoft advances PC-TV," *Interactive Week*, 12 January 1997, p. 12.

18. *Communications Industry Forecast*, p. 310.

19. "TV revolution 'will fuel sales,'" *Financial Times* (London), 4 February 1997, p. 4.

20. "Financing across the spectrum," *Infrastructure Financing*, January 1996, p. 1.

21. "Putting people into social computing," *Interactive Week*, 27 November 1995, p. 73.

22. "Peter Drucker, salvationist," *Economist* (London), 1 October 1994, p. 83.

23. "Too many computers spoil the broth," *Economist* (London), 24 August 1991, p. 30.

24. "Taking care of business without leaving the house," *Business Week*, 17 April 1995, p. 106.

25. "The new workplace," *Business Week*, 29 April 1996, pp. 106–117.

26. "The virtual corporation," *Business Week*, 8 February 1993, p. 101.

27. "Rethinking computers, companies," *Washington Post*, 11 April 1992, p. F-1.

28. "Technology causes wave of anxiety," *Washington Post*, 23 January 1995, p. 17.

29. Shoshana Zuboff, *In the age of the smart machine: The future of work and power*. New York: Basic Books, 1988.

30. For a useful summary of the early years of the Clinton administration initiatives, see: Jonathan Blake and Lee J. Tiedrich, "The national information infrastructure initiative and the emergence of the electronic superhighway," *Federal Communications Law Journal*, 46, No. 3, June 1994, pp. 394–437.

31. "A confident America," *Financial Times* (London), 8 March 1993, p. 14.

32. Edward Luttwak, "The coming global war for economic power," *International Economy*, September/October 1993, p. 18.

33. For an overall analysis of this thesis, see: "The Information Edge," *Foreign Affairs*, 75, No. 2, March/April 1996, pp. 20–54.

34. Cornelia Small, "A Kaleidoscopic View of the 21st Century." Report by Scudder, Stevens, and Clark, New York, November 1993, p. 3.

35. "Commerce study highlights service sector's positive impact on U.S. economy." Report by the Coalition of Service Industries, Washington DC, April 1996, p. 7.

36. *Global telecommunications*. Equity Research Series. Salomon Brothers, New York, 25 October 1994, p. 2.

37. European Union, *Europe and the global information society: Recommendations to the European Council*. European Union, Brussels, May 1994.

38. Japanese Ministry of International Trade and Industry, *The plan for an information economy*. Jacudi Publishers, Tokyo, 1972.

39. *Information resources policy: Arenas, players, and stakes*. Annual Report of the Program on Information Resources Policy, 1975–1976, Harvard University, 1976, p. 4.

Chapter 3

1. *Global telecommunications*. Equity Research Series. Salomon Brothers, New York. 25 October 1994, p. 3.

2. The best description of the situation at the time is a U.S. Congressional staff study, *Option papers*, House Subcommittee on Communications, Committee on Interstate and Foreign Commerce, 95th Congress, 1st Sess. Committee Print 95-13, May 1971.

3. For a useful summary of the results of the AT&T divestiture, see: Robert W. Crandall, *After the breakup: U.S. telecommunications in a more competitive era*. The Brookings Institution, Washington DC, 1991.

4. "The money it takes: What the US majors are spending on interactive America," *Intermedia* (London), 23, No. 2., April/May 1995, pp. 17–20.

5. Eli Noam, *The impending doom of common carriage*. Communications and Society Program. The Aspen Institute, Washington DC, January 1993.

6. "Phone Frenzy," *Business Week*, 20 February 1995, pp. 92–97.

7. "Cable firms motor towards telephony," *Interactive Week*, 27 November 1995, p. 51. See also: "Deluged," *Economist* (London), 22 June 1995, pp. 77–78.

8. The estimates are from *Infrastructure Finance*, January 1996, p. 1.

9. "Twinkle, twinkle, Echostar," *Business Week*, 22 July 1996, p. 78.

10. "By any means necessary: Utility companies go after the telecom market," *Local Competition Report*, Telecom Publishing Group, Washington DC, 4 April 1996, p. 1.

11. "Wall Street tips its hat to caps," *Business Week*, 11 December 1995, p. 109.

12. "AT&T to begin offering access to the Internet," *Washington Post*, 28 February 1996, p. C-3.

13. "Let your PC do the walking," *Business Week*, 6 November 1995, p. 140.

14. "It's the net best thing to being there," *Washington Post*, 23 January 1996, p. C-1.

15. "The telephone's second chance," *Economist* (London), 13 July 1996, p. 88.

16. For a useful summary of this development, see: "Local operators are standing by," *New York Times*, 14 July 1996, p. D-1.

17. "The American Telephone & Telegraph Company Divestiture: Background, provisions, and restructuring," Congressional Research Service, Library of Congress, Washington DC, 20 June 1994.

18. Remarks by Robert E. Allen, AT&T chairman, at the Economic Club, Chicago, 15 October 1992.

19. "AT&T mobilizes with record telecoms deal," *Financial Times* (London), 7 August 1993, p. 17.

20. "Mild-mannered no more!" *Washington Post*, 18 December 1994, p. H-1.

21. "Lines are drawn in battle of the telecoms groups," *Financial Times*, 19 February 1996, p. 16.

22. For a useful survey of AT&T's early entry into local phone operations, see: "AT&T eagerly plots a strategy to gobble local phone business," *Wall Street Journal*, 21 August 1995, p. 1. See also: "Ready, set, devour," *Business Week*, 8 July 1996, pp. 118–120.

23. "AT&T introduces local services offerings for businesses in California, nationwide," *TR Daily*, 27 January 1997, p. 2.

24. "AT&T's access arsenal," *Interactive Week*, 29 January 1996, p. 1.

25. "Info highway juggernaut," *Business Week*, 3 March 1996, p. 44.

26. "AT&T's big guns reverberate across cyberspace," *Financial Times* (London), 1 March 1996, p. 21.

27. "Fatal attraction," *Economist* (London), 23 March 1996, p. 73.

28. "Going against the grain," *New York Times*, 21 September 1995, p. 1.

29. "The bloodletting at AT&T is just beginning," *Business Week*, 15 January 1996, p. 30.

30. "AT&T's problems may get its chairman thrown to the wolves," *Washington Post*, 1 October 1996, p. C-3.

31. "AT&T faces hard calls," *Business Week*, 2 September 1996, p. 40.

32. *Global Telecommunications Review*, Issue 5, Lehman Brothers, New York, 14 March 1995.

33. Gregory Staple (ed.), *Telegeography 1994: Global telecommunications traffic statistics and commentary*. London: International Institute of Communications, 1994, p. 91.

34. "Who'll be the first global phone company?" *Business Week*, 27 March 1995, pp. 176–180.

35. "McLeod Inc.—Ultimate in telephone one-stop shopping." *Telecommunications Services Report*, Salomon Brothers, New York, 5 August 1996.

36. For a useful survey of the development of one-stop shopping arrangements abroad, see: "The challenge of convergence," in Staple (ed.), *Telegeography 1994*, pp. 11–37.

37. "AT&T and Unisource in Europe alliance," *Financial Times* (London), 15 May 1996, p. 15.

38. Quoted in "Global trade meets James Bond," *Asian Business*, September 1994, p. 17.

39. "MCI is swarming over the horizon," *Business Week*, 16 February 1996, p. 68.

40. "MCI makes big plans for local service," *Interactive Week*, 26 August 1996, p. 8.

41. "In search of a strategy," *Economist* (London), 3 February 1996, p. 56.

42. "Sprint, unsung network performer," *Interactive Week*, 26 August 1996, p. 43.

43. "For whom the Baby Bells toll," *Business Week*, 6 May 1996, p. 32. See also: "SBC-Pactel: A credible hulk?" *Business Week*, 15 April 1996, p. 45.

44. "Can the Bells shape up for the challenge?" *Interactive Week*, 24 June 1996, pp. 48–50.

45. "The global free-for-all," *Business Week*, 26 September 1994, pp. 36–44.

46. "Dreams that circle the globe," *Financial Times* (London), 19 July 1993, p. 36.

47. "United States DBS: A tour guide to tomorrow's media," *Via Satellite*, April 1995, pp. 20–36.

48. "Casting big nets for Latin American channel surfers," *New York Times*, 5 June 1996, p. D-7.

49. For a survey of the financial stakes involved, see: "Far Out," *Barron's*, 19 June 1995.

50. For a summary of Teledesic and other U.S. mobile satellite operators, see: "Going global," *Via Satellite*, February 1996, pp. 50–60.

51. "PanAmSat announces satellite-based Internet service," *TR Daily*, 27 January 1997, p. 3.

Chapter 4

1. Lee McKnight and W. Russell Neuman, "Technology policy and national information infrastructure," in William J. Drake (ed.), *The new information infrastructure: Strategies for U.S. policy*. New York: Twentieth Century Fund, 1995, pp. 137–154.

2. Simon Nora and Alain Minc, *The computerization of society*. Cambridge MA: MIT Press, 1981.

3. Cited in Wilson P. Dizard, "Europe calling Europe," in Alan W. Cafruny and Glenda G. Rosenthal (eds.), *The state of the European Community: The Maastrict debates and beyond.* Boulder: Lynne Rienner Publishers, 1993, p. 321.

4. "BT set to launch Internet service," *Financial Times* (London), 27 February 1996, p. 5.

5. "A serious switch to the continent," *Financial Times* (London), 22 February 1995, p. 15.

6. For background, see: Dizard, "Europe calling Europe," pp. 321–336.

7. Commission of the European Communities, *On the development of the common market for telecommunications services and equipment*. Report No. COM 87-260. Brussels, 1987.

8. "Data networks disappoint," *Communications Week International*, 16 July 1990, p. 1.

9. Quoted in *European Trends*, No. 2, Economist Intelligence Unit, 1989, p. 49.

10. "Mobiles overtake fixed phones," *Financial Times* (London), 30 August 1994, p. 6.

11. *Cellular service overview*. European Research Series, Goldman, Sachs, New York, October 1995, p. 2.

12. "European telecom mergers up after deregulation," *Financial Times* (London), 13 August 1996, p. 6.

13. "Europe's markets are getting re-wired, too," *Business Week*, 8 April 1996, p. 87.

14. "Competition down the line," *Financial Times* (London), 11 January 1995, p. 11.

15. Commission of the European Union, *Europe and the global information society*. Brussels, June 1994.

16. For a useful summary of the Bangemann report, see: Hans Schoof and Adam Watson Brown, "Information highways and media policies in the European Union," *Telecommunications Policy*, 19, No. 3, April 1995, pp. 325–338.

17. "Europe lagging behind in technology race, says report," *Financial Times* (London), 4 February 1997, p. 20.

18. "Clunk-click every trip," *Economist* (London), 19 September 1995, p. 63.

19. "France outlines plan to reform telecom sector," *Financial Times* (London), 10 January 1996, p. 3.

20. "Optic link arrives via the sewers," *Financial Times* (London), 22 May 1996, p. 5.

21. "Users: French I-way lacks road map," *Communications Week International*, 14 November 1994, p. 40.

22. "Expectations mixed in new law," *Financial Times* (London), 5 June 1996, p. 2.

23. "DBKom telecoms partners plan to spend up to DM4bn," *Financial Times* (London), 23 July 1996, p. 15.

24. "Deutsche Telekom in joint pact to build Chinese phone system," *Wall Street Journal*, 30 September 1996, p. 13-A.

25. "Italy to press ahead with telecoms sell-off," *Financial Times* (London), 8 August 1996, p. 10.

26. "Olivetti to compete with Telecom Italia," *Financial Times* (London), 14 March 1996, p. 18.

27. "Telecomm Eireann deal pleases all," *Financial Times* (London), 28 June 1996, p. 23.

28. "A Latin strategy for Spain's telephone company," *New York Times*, 2 April 1994, p. 32.

29. "Telefonica's overseas arm flexes its muscles," *Financial Times* (London), 10 October 1995, p. 22.

30. "Controversy highlights difficulties," *Financial Times* (London), 14 October 1994, p. 16.

31. *Japan's information society: Its themes and visions.* Tokyo: Japanese Government Printing Bureau, 1969.

32. For a useful survey of Japan's information strategy, see: Jonathan M. Jaffe, "The informatization of Japan: Creating an information society or just good salesmanship?" *Pacific Telecommunications Review*, June 1996, pp. 1–13.

33. Edward A. Feigenbaum and Pamela McCorduck, *The fifth generation: Artificial intelligence and Japan's computer challenge to the world.* Reading MA: Addison-Wesley, 1983.

34. "GE is world's biggest group," *Financial Times* (London), 24 January 1997, p. 19.

35. "NTT delays break market," *Financial Times* (London). Special supplement on Asia-Pacific telecommunications, 9 April 1996, p. 3.

36. "Hanging on the line," *Economist* (London), 24 February 1996, p. 67.

37. "Breaking up is hard to do," *Far Eastern Economic Review*, 15 February 1996, p. 52.

38. For a general survey of Japanese communications policies, see: Michael Latzer, "Japanese information infrastructure initiatives," *Telecommunications Policy*, 19, No. 7, October 1995, pp. 515–529.

39. Telecommunications Council, Ministry of Posts and Telecommunications, "Communications in Japan, 1996 (white paper)." Tokyo, June 1996. An English-language version is printed in *New Breeze*, the quarterly magazine of the New ITU Association of Japan, July 1996, pp. 17–29.

40. "Cable comes to Fuchu," *Forbes*, 6 November 1995, p. 44.

41. "Japan's Internet tangle," *Economist* (London), 15 July 1996, p. 50.

42. "Study says Japan's executives are behind in technology," *New York Times*, 15 May 1995, p. D-7.

43. "An unMITIgated success," *Economist* (London), 31 August 1996, p. 51.

44. "NTT and C&W in mobile cable deal," *Financial Times* (London), 5 October 1995, p. 17.

45. "NTT shuns global alliance," *Financial Times* (London), 7 January 1997, p. 1.

46. "Murdoch and Son break the cozy mold," *Financial Times* (London), 4 July 1996, p. 16.

47. "Canada paves way for telecoms battle," *Financial Times* (London), p. 3.

48. "Old rivalries move north," *Business Week*, 18 July 1994, p. 36.

49. For a survey of the Asian lead in telecommunications expansion, see: Ben A. Petrazzini and Peter Lovelock, "The 'Asian-ness' of telecom reform," *Intermedia* (London), June 1996, pp. 18–22.

50. The origins of Intelsat, and the critical role the United States played in creating the organization, are described in James F. Galloway, *The politics and technology of satellite communications*. Lexington MA: Lexington Books, 1972.

51. "U.S. separate systems," *Via Satellite*, March 1996, pp. 38–53.

52. "World space markets: The next ten years," *Satellite Communications*, September 1994, p. 18.

53. "Editor's note," *Via Satellite*, August 1996, p. 6.

54. "International satellites," *Satellite News*, 9 September 1994, p. 2.

55. For a discussion of the complexities of restructuring Intelsat, see: Leonard Waverman, *Global speak*. Washington DC: American Enterprise Institute, 1996.

56. "U.S. proposes Intelsat privatization," *Via Satellite*, August 1995, p. 10.

Chapter 5

1. "WTO sees rapid rise in global growth," *Financial Times* (London), 13 November 1995, p. 6.

2. "The global economy," *Economist* (London). Special supplement, 1 October 1994, p. 1.

3. "The deal of the century," *Institutional Investor*, September 1993, p. 53.

4. For a useful survey of the development of chip technology, see: T. R. Reid, *The chip: How two Americans invented the microchip and launched a revolution*. New York: Simon and Schuster, 1984.

5. Ibid., p. 63.

6. G. Daniel Hutcheson and Jerry D. Hutcheson, "Technology and economics in the semiconductor industry," *Scientific American*, January 1996, pp. 54–63.

7. "Highway information," *New York Times*, 6 November 1995, p. D-5.

8. "Electronics' driving force," *Financial Times* (London), 25 May 1995, p. 8.

9. "IBM, Mercedes in deal to develop car systems," *Financial Times* (London), 8 August 1996, p. 13.

10. "The technology paradox," *Business Week*, 6 March 1995, p. 77.

11. "Siemens and Motorola link up to build U.S. chip plant," *Financial Times* (London), 26 October 1995, p. 16.

12. "Suiting up for America's high-tech future," *New York Times*, 3 December 1995, p. F-14.

13. "Intel unbound," *Business Week*, 9 October 1995, p. 43.

14. "Semiconductor trade: A wafer-thin case," *Economist* (London), 27 July 1996, p. 53.

15. "Siemens and Motorola link up," p. 16.

16. "High cost of computer chips fuels Silicon crime wave," *Washington Post*, 8 July 1995, p. C-1.

17. "The end of the line," *Economist* (London), 15 July 1995, p. 61.

18. "Correlation is now causation," *Economist* (London), 4 May 1996, p. 85.

19. "NYNEX reconstruction," *Communications Week*, 14 December 1987, p. 22.

20. "Surge in telecom investment in Asia forecast," *Financial Times* (London), 9 September 1994, p. 9.

21. "Fast forward—A survey of consumer electronics," *Economist* (London), 13 April 1991, p. 18.

22. "Zenith sold to S. Korean competitor," *Washington Post*, 18 July 1995, p. D-1.

23. "U.S. telecommunications role shrinks," *Washington Post*, 8 July 1990, p. C-3.

24. "The chips are down," *Far Eastern Economic Review*, 27 June 1996, pp. 54–56.

25. U.S. Department of Commerce, International Trade Administration, *U.S. global trade outlook, 1995–2000.* Washington DC, March 1995, pp. 11–21.

26. "International telecommunications map," *Financial Times* (London), 1 December 1995, p. 6.

27. "Prospects lie in IT's rapid rate of change," *Financial Times* (London), 2 March 1996, p. 8.

28. "International telecommunications map," p. 6.

29. "Going against the grain," *New York Times*, 21 September 1995, p. 1.

30. "Mitsubishi/Lucent agree on HDTV chip development," *Communications Industry Report*, August 1996, p. 18.

31. "Let the high-wire act begin," *New York Times*, 5 November 1995, p. F-1.

32. "Alcatel to double China investment," *Financial Times* (London), 10 February 1995, p. 7.

33. "The site-seers guide to some way-out Internet futures," *Washington Post*, 3 July 1996, p. 1.

34. "Did Motorola make the wrong call?" *Business Week*, 29 July 1996, p. 66.

35. "Roving Wallenbergs stay true to home," *Financial Times* (London), 7 September 1994, p. 20.

36. "Samsung to buy 40 per cent of U.S. computer maker," *Financial Times* (London), 1 March 1995, p. 1.

37. "Koreans invest $10Bn in China," *Financial Times* (London), 29 May 1996, p. 23.

38. "China's little guys churn out PCs, taking market share from U.S. firms," *Wall Street Journal*, 28 August 1996, p. B-3.

39. "Estimated value of expected U.S. satellite launches," *Space Business News*, 31 January 1995, p. 8.

40. "A little local interference," *Economist* (London), 3 February 1996, p. 53.

41. "Far out," *Barron's*, 19 June 1995, p. 9.

42. "Tiny satellites aim to please the bean counters," *New York Times*, 13 September 1995, p. D-3.

43. Richard Jay Solomon, "Telecommunications technology in the twenty-first century," in William Drake (ed.), *The new information infrastructure: Strategies for U.S. policy*. New York: Twentieth Century Fund, 1995, pp. 93–111.

44. "Going global via private satellite networks," *Via Satellite*, November 1995, p. 79.

45. "Delivery via the satellite route," *Financial Times* (London), 18 July 1996, p. 8.

46. "Business television in the digital era," *Via Satellite*, December 1995, pp. 36–44.

Chapter 6

1. Norbert Wiener, *The human use of human beings, cybernetics, and society*. Boston: Houghton Mifflin, 1950.

2. "The Web keeps spreading," *Business Week*, 8 January 1996, p. 92.

3. "IT companies march to a fast beat," *Communications Week*, 1 July 1996, p. 57.

4. "Software's chronic crisis," *Scientific American*, September 1994, p. 87.

5. "When the bloat comes in," *Economist* (London), 2 October 1993, p. 91.

6. "Software's chronic crisis," p. 88.

7. For a useful overview of the software sector, see: "The world gone soft," *Economist* (London), 25 May 1996. Special supplement.

8. U.S. International Trade Commmission, *Global competitiveness of the U.S. computer software and services industries*. U.S. International Trade Commmission staff research study No. 21, Washington DC, June 1995, p. v.

9. Ibid, p. vi. See also: "It's feast, not famine at the software table," *New York Times*, 23 March 1995, p. F-3.

10. Quoted in "Going for the gold," *Washington Post*, 4 August 1996, p. H-1.

11. "U.S. corporations expanding abroad at a quicker pace," *New York Times*, 25 July 1994, p. 1.

12. "Everybody's favorite monsters," *Economist* (London), 27 March 1993. Special supplement on multinational corporations, p. 1.

13. "High-tech edge gives U.S. firms global lead in computer networks," *Wall Street Journal*, 9 September 1994, p. 1.

14. "Strategies built upon knowledge base," *Financial Times* (London), 30 October 1994. Special supplement on the world economy and finance, p. 12.

15. "Why EDS won't be sorry to be single again," *Business Week*, 15 April 1996, p. 45. See also: "Under Alberthal, EDS is out of the limelight, but triples revenue," *Wall Street Journal*, 12 February 1996, p. 1.

16. "EDS: Getting to know all about you," *Financial Times* (London), 18 April 1995, p. 21.

17. "3M: Whole earth corp.," *Forbes ASAP*, 4 December 1995, p. 56.

18. "The world turned upside down," *Economist* (London), 18 October 1993, p. 90.

19. "We are the wired: Some views on fiberoptic ties that bind," *New York Times*, 24 October 1995, p. E-16.

20. "EDI: What benefit is it?" *Financial Times* (London), 27 March 1995, p. 13.

21. "Going global via private satellite networks," *Via Satellite*, November 1995, p. 70.

22. For an analysis of the Ford project, see: "The world that changed the machine," *Economist* (London), 30 March 1996, p. 67.

23. "QR keeps jeans moving," *Stores*, February 1991, p. 23.

24. "The rag trade hits the information highway," *Business Week*, 13 May 1995, p. 94-A.

25. "Russia counts cost of change as U.S. set to issue new $100 bill," *Financial Times* (London), 16 January 1996, p. 21.

26. Walter B. Wriston, *The twilight of sovereignty: How the information revolution is transforming our world*. New York: Scribner, 1992. See also: "The future of money: An interview with Walter Wriston," *Wired*, October 1996, p. 140.

27. "More power to capital markets," *Financial Times* special supplement, 24 September 1993, p. 2.

28. "U.S. financial firms seize dominant role in the world markets," *Wall Street Journal*, 5 January 1996, p. 1.

29. For a useful survey of banking's new international role, see: United National Conference on Trade and Development, Program on Transnational Corporations, *The tradeability of banking services: Impact and implications*. Current Studies A, No. 27. Geneva, 1994.

30. "Borderless finance: Fuel for growth," *Business Week*, 20 May 1995. Special issue on twenty-first-century capitalism, p. 54.

31. "When money talks, government listens," *New York Times*, 24 July 1994, p. E-3.

32. "Wall Street takes a high-tech turn," *Interactive Week*, 13 February 1995, p. 50.

33. "On Wall Street, the writing is on the wall," *Washington Post*, 6 August 1994, p. F-1.

34. "Insert money, press start," *Economist* (London), 12 February 1996, p. 72.

35. "Swift spreads its net," *Financial Times* (London), 10 June 1996, p. 4.

36. "Blood on the marble floors," *Business Week*, 27 February 1995, p. 98.

37. "Global finance sector maintains its IT edge," *Financial Times* (London), 4 September 1996. Special supplement on information technology in financial services, p. 3.

38. "The future of money," *Business Week*, 12 June 1995, p. 47.

39. "That wild, wild cyberspace frontier," *Rand Research Review*, 19, No. 2, Fall 1995, p. 1.

40. For a useful discussion of the initial effects of this change, see: Kalpak Gude, "The integration of banking and telecommunications," *Federal Communications Law Journal*, 46, No. 3, June 1994, pp. 521–547. See also: "E-money—that's what I want," *Wired*, December 1994, pp. 174–179.

41. "Here come the super-ATMs," *Fortune*, 14 October 1996, p. 232. See also, "California banks vie for supermarket share," *Financial Times* (London), 9 January 1997, p. 14.

42. "TeleBank's specialty: Services for savers by phone," *Washington Post*, Washington Business supplement, 3 March 1996, p. 10.

43. "The ways we pay," *Business Week*, 8 April 1996, p. 8.

44. "Bonfire of the retail bankers," *Financial Times* (London), 11 December 1995, p. 10.

45. "10 banks to develop own on-line network," *Washington Post*, 12 May 1996, p. D-3.

46. "Surf's up for new-wave bankers," *Economist* (London), 7 October 1995, pp. 77–78.

47. "Cybercash seeks that which it sells," *Interactive Week*, 12 August 1996, p. 57.

48. For an overview on technology in consumer banking, see: F. Jean Wells and Glenn J. McLaughlin, *Electronic money: Technology and retail payment innovations*. Report No. 95-828. Congressional Research Service, Library of Congress, Washington DC, August 1995.

49. "On-line banking has bankers fretting PCs may replace branches," *Wall Street Journal*, 23 October 1995, p. 1.

50. "Technobanking takes off," *Business Week*, 20 May 1995. Special issue on twenty-first-century capitalism, p. 52.

51. "Going for Olympic gold cards," *Economist* (London), 30 March 1996, p. 67.

52. "New York in smart move to cashless society," *Financial Times* (London), 11 April 1996, p. 10.

53. "Smartcards looking for a way onto the Net," *Interactive Week*, 12 August 1996, p. 28.

54. "Microsoft launches Windows NT 4.0," *Financial Times* (London), 1 August 1996, p. 12.

55. "IBM unveils a lower-cost alternative to desktop PCs," *Washington Post*, 6 September 1996, p. D-1.

56. "The Web keeps spreading," p. 92.

57. "The software revolution," *Business Week*, 4 December 1995, pp. 78–90.

58. "Microsoft says it's going after the Internet market," *New York Times*, 8 December 1995, p. D-1.

59. "Microsoft trying to dominate the Internet," *New York Times*, 16 July 1996, p. C-10.

60. "3 firms seek improved World Wide Web software," *Washington Post*, 5 December 1995, p. C-1.

61. "European Communities build knowledge-based industries," *Transborder Data and Communications Report*, January 1988, pp. 14–15.

62. "Europe's software war," *Economist* (London), 10 October 1992, p. 81. See also: "Will Europe roar down the infobahn?" *Business Week*, 6 March 1995, p. 48.

63. "Europe 'falling behind in IT use,'" *Financial Times* (London), 27 January 1997, p. 18.

64. "Fast forward: Can late-comer Japan compete with the big boys?" *Far Eastern Economic Review*, 22 February 1996, p. 53.

65. "Cyber-mogul," *Business Week*, 12 August 1996, p. 56.

66. "Indians, foreigners build Silicon Valley in Bangalore," *Washington Post*, 1 August 1993, p. 29.

67. "By design: India's software houses lure foreign money," *Far Eastern Economic Review*, 10 August 1995, p. 64.

68. "Can Taiwan's hotshots succeed in software, too?" *Business Week*, 17 April 1995, p. 92E.

69. "Software pirates still muddy waters," *Financial Times* (London), 15 July 1996, p. 11.

70. "Microsoft's long march," *Business Week*, 24 June 1996, p. 52.

71. Anne Branscomb, *Who owns information?* New York: Basic Books, 1994, p. 184.

Chapter 7

1. Daniel R. Headrick, *The invisible weapon: Telecommunications and international politics, 1851–1945*. New York: Oxford University Press, 1991.

2. Sandra Berman, "Horizons of the state: Information policy and power," *Journal of Communications*, 45, No. 4, Autumn 1995, pp. 4–21.

3. The figures are from U.S. Department of Commerce, International Trade Administration, *U.S. global trade outlook, 1995–2000*. Washington DC, March 1995, p. 181.

4. Fred N. Cate, "The First Amendment and the National Information Infrastructure," *Wake Forest Law Review*, 30, No. 1, Spring 1995, pp. 1–50.

5. Bell's predictions, contained in a letter to the stockholders of the new Electric Telephone Company, are documented in Ithiel de Sola Pool (ed.), *The social impact of the telephone*. Cambridge MA: MIT Press, 1977, p. 156.

6. This theme is explored in Leo Marx, *The machine in the garden*. New York: Oxford University Press, 1964. See also: James W. Carey and John J. Quirk, "The mythos of the electronic revolution," *American Scholar*, Summer 1970, pp. 402–420.

7. Claude S. Fischer, *America calling: A social history of the telephone to 1940*. Berkeley CA: University of California Press, 1992, p. 46.

8. For a description of early U.S. diplomatic efforts in telecommunications, see: Wilson Dizard Jr., "International communications," *Encyclopedia of U.S. foreign relations*. New York: Oxford University Press, 1997.

9. Headrick, *The invisible weapon*, pp. 174–177.

10. The U.S. role in creating Intelsat is described in James F. Galloway, *The politics and technology of satellite communications*. Lexington MA: Lexington Books, 1972.

11. "A beleagured Whitehead and a battered OTP," *Broadcasting*, 17 September 1973, p. 16–18.

12. The AT&T divestiture and its aftermath are described in Robert W. Crandall, *After the breakup: U.S. telecommunications in a more competitive era.* Washington DC: The Brookings Institution, 1991.

13. Walter S. Baer, "Telecommunications infrastructure competition: The costs of delay," *Telecommunications Policy*, 19, No. 5, November 1995, pp. 351–363.

14. See: *The Media and the Campaign '92*, a series of reports by the Freedom Forum Media Studies Center at Columbia University in January 1992. See also: "Presidential races being changed by the latest technology," *Wall Street Journal*, 8 August 1995, p. 1; "Virtually kissing babies," *Business Week*, 25 March 1996, pp. 69–71.

15. "Feds on the Web," *Washington Post*, 20 May 1995, Washington Business supplement, p. 15.

16. Jonathan D. Blake and Lee J. Tiedrich, "The national information infrastructure initiative and the emergence of the electronic superhighway," *Federal Communications Law Journal*, 46, No. 3, June 1994, pp. 397–431.

17. "Will America log on to the Internewt?" *Business Week*, 5 December 1994, p. 38.

18. "Competition calling," *Economist* (London), 1 July 1995, p. 59. Also: "The states swing into I-way construction," *Business Week*, 22 September 1994, p. 73.

19. "Move over, Mickey," *Economist* (London), 9 March 1996, pp. 28–29.

20. "A chairman apart," *Broadcasting and Cable*, 21 March 1994, p. 12.

21. For background on the issues involved, see: Henry Geller, *1995–2005: Regulatory reform for principle electronic media.* The Annenberg Washington Program in Communications Policy, Washington DC, November 1994.

22. "Pressler top corporate fundraiser," *Broadcasting and Cable*, 21 August 1995, p. 39.

23. "Roll out the telepork barrel," *Business Week*, 21 August 1995, p. 26.

24. Charles Loveridge (ed.), *The Telecommunications Act of 1996: Let the games begin!* International Communications Studies Program, Center for Strategic and International Studies, Washington DC, February 1996.

25. "Telecom law faces challenge in court," *Wall Street Journal*, 29 August 1996, p. A-3.

26. *The communications devolution: Federal, state, and local relations in telecommunications competition and regulation.* Communications and Society Program, The Aspen Institute, Washington DC, 1996.

27. "Too close for comfort," *Washington Post*, 7 January 1996, p. H-1.

28. For background, see: *Strategic alliances and telecommunications policy*, Communications and Society Program, The Aspen Institute, Washington DC, 1995. Also: "Should Ma Bell be put back together again?" *Washington Post*, 24 April 1996, p. F-1.

29. "The media mess," *Economist* (London), 29 February 1992, p. 54.

30. U.S. Department of Commerce, *U.S. global trade outlook, 1995–2000*, p. 174.

31. Laura D'Andrea Tyson, *Who's bashing whom? Trade conflict in high techology.* New York: Longman, 1992.

32. "U.S. super-salesmanship discounts human rights," *Financial Times* (London), 7 September 1994, p. 4.

33. "U.S. and EU aim to end IT tariffs by 2000," *Financial Times* (London), 1 December 1995, p. 18.

34. "APEC to take new look at IT tariffs," *Financial Times* (London), 24 August 1996, p. 6.

35. David Kelly, *Services industries still growing in a slowing economy.* Report for the Coalition of Service Industries, April 1996, p. 5.

36. "World Trade Organization still on the test bed," *Financial Times* (London), 6 October 1995. Special supplement on the world economy and finances, p. 10.

37. "68 nations agree to widen markets in communications," *New York Times,* 16 February 1997, p. 1.

38. "Theft of U.S. corporate secrets costs business $2Bn a month," *Financial Times* (London), 22 March 1996, p. 20.

39. "Economic espionage rising, FBI director tells Congress," *Washington Post,* 29 February 1996, p. D-11.

40. "The art of the steal," *Washington Post,* 19 February 1995, p. D-3.

41. "Sun's codemaking comrades," *Wired,* November 1995, p. 49.

42. "Computer industry could lose $60 billion, legislators say," *Computer Industry Report,* August 1996, p. 19.

43. Michael P. Ryan, "Enforcing the U.S.-China intellectual property agreement." World Business Policy Brief, Center for International Business Education and Research, Georgetown University, September 1995.

44. For a useful roundup on technical rules developments, see: "International Standards," *Financial Times* (London), 13 October 1995. Special supplement.

45. *America's hidden vulnerabilities: Crisis management in a society of networks.* Washington DC: Center for Strategic and International Studies, 1984.

46. Walter Laqueur, "Postmodern terrorism," *Foreign Affairs,* September/October 1996, p. 35.

47. "Argentine, 22, charged with hacking computer networks," *Washington Post,* 30 March 1996, p. A-4.

48. *War in the pits.* Report No. 61. Institute for National Strategic Studies, National Defense University, Washington DC, February 1996, p. 1.

49. John Arquilla and David Ronfeldt, "Cyberwar and Netwar: New modes, old concepts of conflict," *Rand Research Review,* Rand Corporation, Fall 1995, p. 8.

50. "Information warfare takes a front seat," *Military & Aerospace Electronics,* June 1996, p. 19. See also: "The softwar revolution: A survey of defense technology," *Economist* (London), 10 June 1995. Special supplement.

51. "Cyber Wars," *Economist* (London), 15 January 1996, p. 77.

52. "CIA gears up to thwart 'information attacks,'" *Washington Post,* 26 June 1996, p. A-19.

53. "The Pentagon's new nightmare: An electronic Pearl Harbor," *Washington Post,* 16 July 1993, p. C-3. See also: "Cyber-deterrence," *Wired,* September 1994, p. 116.

54. Joseph Nye and William Owens, "America's information edge," *Foreign Affairs*, March/April 1996, pp. 20–36.

55. Walter Wriston, "The decline of the central bankers," *New York Times*, 20 September 1992, p. F-11.

56. Jeffrey B. Abramson, F. Christopher Atherton, and Gary R. Orren, *The electronic commonwealth: The impact of the new media technologies and democratic politics*. New York: Basic Books, 1988.

Chapter 8

1. "Internet seismic, Negroponte says," *Communications Industries Report*, November 1995, p. 8.

2. Bill Gates, *The road ahead*. New York: Viking, 1995.

3. "Super-highway in need of a route," *Financial Times* (London), 6 September 1994, p. 12.

4. "The information future: Out of control," *New York Times Magazine*, 1 May 1994, p. 57.

5. Clifford Stoll, *Silicon snake oil: Second thoughts on the information highway*. New York: Doubleday, 1995.

6. "World, wide, web: 3 English words," *New York Times*, 14 April 1996, p. E-1.

7. "Net profits," *Economist* (London), 9 July 1994, p. 83.

8. "The accidental highway," *Economist* (London), 1 July 1995. Special supplement.

9. "A cyberspace front in the multi-cultural war," *New York Times*, 6 September 1995, p. D-1.

10. "Globalink Web translator, the Internet's lingua franca." *Washington Post*, Washington Business supplement, 2 September 1996, p. 15.

11. "The new I-way hog: IBM," *Business Week*, 16 September 1996, p. 98.

12. "The creators," *Wired*, December 1994, p. 152.

13. "While the Internet has mushroomed," *Business Week*, 26 August 1996, p. 64.

14. "Counting up growth," *Television Business International* (London), September 1995, p. 83.

15. "New frontier for Web servers: Intranet," *Interactive Week*, 11 March 1996, p. 50.

16. "The Internet's golden switch makers," *Economist* (London), 2 December 1995, p. 69.

17. "Internet users 'likely to reach 500 million by 2000,'" *Financial Times* (London), 15 May 1996, p. 4.

18. "Sex, lies, and the Internet," *Financial Times* (London), 12 February 1996, p. 15.

19. "Usage of Internet surges in U.S., Canada, survey finds," *Washington Post*, 14 August 1996, p. F-1.

20. "Who can I turn to?" *Wired*, May 1996, p. 117.

21. "Caught in the Web," *Financial Times* (London), 25 November 1994, p. 8.

22. "Revenues of $10Bn forecast," *Financial Times* (London), 15 June 1995, p. 4.

23. "Welcome to the world wide lab," *Business Week*, 30 October 1995, p. 66.

24. "School districts to spend $4 billion on technology," *Communications Industry Report*, November 1995, p. 8.

25. "The interminablenet," *Economist* (London), 3 February 1996, p. 70.

26. "Pope puts faith in the Net," *Financial Times* (London), 19 February 1996, p. 13.

27. "Telecoms angst and the awe of the Internet," *Forbes*, 4 December 1995, p. 113.

28. "The dark side of Internet commerce," *Business Week*, 29 April 1996, p. DS-1.

29. "From byways to highways," Goldman Sachs White Paper, New York, February 1995, p. 3.

30. "Internet growth will slow down in the short term," *New Media*, 18 December 1995, p. 37.

31. "Special report," *Business Week*, 8 March 1996, p. 84.

32. "Serving as an agent of change," *Washington Post*, Washington Business supplement, 12 February 1996, p. 5.

33. "Hourly access prices: Netcom's lowest," *Interactive Age*, 5 June 1996, p. 6.

34. "For Netcom, its fans say being down is not out," *New York Times*, 15 April 1996, p. D-15.

35. "Surfing the stars," *Via Satellite*, December 1995, p. 30.

36. For an overview of the network's economic prospects, see: Lee McKnight, *Internet economics*. Cambridge MA: MIT Press, 1996.

37. "Welcome to paranoia.com," *Economist* (London), 16 September 1995, p. 78.

38. "GM opens door on Internet showroom," *Financial Times* (London), 6 February 1996, p. 17.

39. "The marketers are on-lining up for you," *Washington Post*, 27 September 1995, p. F-1.

40. "Web site costs soar," *Interactive Week*, 16 January 1996, p. 1.

41. "Microsoft dealers to sell over Internet," *New York Times*, 6 May 1996, p. D-4.

42. "The big sell: Software online," *Interactive Week*, 22 April 1996, p. 31.

43. "Is there gold in the Internet?" *Economist* (London), 10 April 1994, p. 73.

44. "Wall Street Journal bets Internet readers will pay a fee," *New York Times*, 29 April 1996, p. D-24. For a discussion of the Internet's role as a provider of mass-media materials, see: Merrill Morris and Christine Ogden, "The Internet as mass medium," *Journal of Communication*, 46, No. 1, Winter 1996, pp. 39–50. The challenge of Internet incursions into traditional mass-media businesses is also discussed in Steven Levy, "How the propeller heads stole the electronic future," *New York Times Magazine*, 24 September 1995, pp. 58–59.

45. "In the capital of cyberspace, but far from capital politics," *New York Times*, 24 April 1996, p. D-1.

46. ". . . and the slow transition to the Internet," *Washington Post*, 7 May 1996, p. 21.

47. "Trying to find gold on the Internet," *New York Times*, 3 March 1995, p. C-15.

48. "The changing price of ATM convenience," *Washington Post*, 13 April 1996, p. C-1.

49. "Surf's up for the new-wave bankers," *Economist* (London), 7 October 1995, p. 77. See also: "Players with paperless money," *Washington Post*, Washington Business supplement, 16 September 1996, p. 1.

50. "More banks are offering services via the Internet," *Washington Post*, 6 August 1996, p. D-4.

51. "Mutual funds set up shop on the Web," *Interactive Week*, 10 June 1995, p. 52.

52. "With the World Wide Web, who needs Wall Street?" *Business Week*, 24 April 1996, p. 120.

53. "A hacker's paradise," *Financial Times* (London), 16 April 1996, p. 16.

54. "On-line payment scheme arrives," *Communications Week*, 26 February 1996, p. 1.

55. "Here comes the Intranet," *Business Week*, 26 February 1996, p. 76.

56. Steven G. Steinberg, "Seek and ye shall find, maybe," *Wired*, May 1995, p. 108.

57. "Searching the Web for gigabucks," *New Scientist* (London), 6 April 1996, p. 37.

58. "Yahoo! has big debut, but will it hold up?" *Interactive Week*, 22 April 1996, p. 9.

59. "Searching the Web for gigabucks," p. 38.

60. "Microsoft opens battle of the browsers," *Washington Post*, 11 August 1996, p. D-1.

61. "Searching the Web for gigabucks," p. 39.

62. "Government and communications policy: The impact of the Internet in Asia," *On the Internet* (U.S. Internet Society), July/August 1996, p. 37.

63. "Touchstone," *Wired*, May 1996, p. 127.

64. "Yahoo! shares investors, posts profits," *Interactive Week*, 4 December 1995, p. 12.

65. "Struggle to net customers," *Financial Times* (London), 28 November 1995, p. 16.

66. "France Telecom signs pact with Microsoft to develop Internet," *Wall Street Journal*, 17 April 1996, p. 9.

67. "Host to the London Internet exchange," *Financial Times*, 6 March 1996. Special supplement on information technology, p. 7.

68. "Drowning, not surfing," *Financial Times* (London), 22 January 1996, p. 7.

69. "Fujitsu puts first Japanese translation package online," *Financial Times* (London), 28 April 1996, p. 9.

70. "Not too modern, please," *Economist* (London), 16 March 1996, p. 42.

71. "China to have 120,000 users by end 1996," Reuters Executive news service, 28 June 1996.

72. "Chinese tiptoe into Internet, wary of watchdogs," *New York Times*, 5 February 1996, p. A-3.

73. "A great wall of China slowly gives way," *Washington Post*, 8 April 1996, p. 1.

74. "China blocks user access to 100-plus sites on the Web," *Washington Post*, 10 September 1996, p. C-4.

75. "Russia's newest space venture: Cyberspace," *New York Times*, 9 May 1994, p. 1.

76. "Internet or internot," *On the Internet* (U.S. Internet Society), May/June 1995, p. 29.

77. "Africa's tentative approach to the Net," *Financial Times* (London), 20 November 1995, p. 11.

78. "The intruder in the kingdom," *Business Week*, 27 August 1995, p. 40.

79. For a useful survey of the prospects of digitized video, see: "The new Hollywood: Silicon stars," *Wired*, December 1995, pp. 142–150. Audio prospects are described in "Hello, world! Audible chats on the Internet," *Wall Street Journal*, 2 October 1995, p. 1.

80. Robert Reich, *The work of nations*. New York: Alfred A. Knopf, 1991, p. 303.

81. Terry Curtis, "The information society: a computer-generated caste system," in Vincent Mosco and Janet Wasco (eds.), *The political economy of information*. Madison: University of Wisconsin Press, 1988, pp. 95–107.

82. "Http://www.nuts," *Economist* (London) 3 August 1996, p. 27.

83. "Internet provider to launch censorship," *Financial Times* (London), 6 May 1996, p. 6.

84. "Trial and error in cyberspace," *National Journal*, 27 April 1996, p. 961. See also: Edwin Diamond and Stephen Bates, "Law and order comes to cyberspace," *Technology Review*, October 1995, pp. 21–32.

85. "Limo service for cruising the Net," *Business Week*, 24 June 1996, p. 96.

86. "A radio renaissance worldwide," *Financial Times* (London), 8 July 1996, p. 13.

87. "Web's first all-sports radio station debuts," *Cowles/SIMBA Media Daily*, 27 August 1996.

88. "View from the cybercouch," *Financial Times* (London), 16 June 1996, p. 13.

89. "Calling all surfers, *Business Week*, 5 August 1996, p. 27.

90. "Free long-distance phone calls!" *New York Times*, 5 June 1996, p. D-1.

91. For a discussion of these issues, see: Robert W. McChesney, "The Internet and U.S. communications policy-making in historical and critical perspective," *Journal of Communication*, 46, No. 1, Winter 1996, pp. 98–124.

92. For examples, see: Danny Goodman, "Education and the Internet," *Syllabus*, December 1995, p. 10.

93. "FCC to propose setting aside part of radio spectrum for Internet use," *Washington Post*, 25 April 1996, p. D-11.

Chapter 9

1. "Does the highway go south?" *Intermedia* (London), October 1994, p. 10.

2. These estimates are based on projections made by the International Telecommunications Union, the United Nations telecommunications agency. They are summarized in "The last frontier," *Business Week*, 18 September 1995, p. 98.

3. "Have and have-nots revisited," *New York Times*, 9 October 1995, p. 4.

4. Robert J. Saunders, Jeremy J. Warford, and Bjorn Wellenius, *Telecommunications and economic development*, 2d ed. Baltimore: Johns Hopkins University Press, 1994. See also: Heather E. Hudson, *When telephones reach the village: The role of telecommunications in rural development*. Norwood NJ: Ablex Publishing, 1984. For a useful survey of the factors influencing Third World development, see: "An historical analysis relating causes to effects," in *Global communications: Opportunities for trade and aid*. Publication No. OTC-ITC-642, Office of Technology Asssessment, U.S. Congress, September 1995.

5. *The Missing Link*. Report of the Independent Commission for Worldwide Telecommunications Development, International Telecommunications Union, Geneva, December 1985.

6. "Dialing for European phone dollars," *Washington Post*, 8 August 1992, p. H-1.

7. The figures are World Bank estimates. See: "War of the worlds," *Economist* (London), 1 October 1994. Special supplement on the global economy, p. 1.

8. "The deal of the century," *Institutional Investor*, September 1993, p. 53.

9. "Reforms keep U.S. at top of the league," *Financial Times* (London), 28 May 1996, p. 5.

10. Cynthia Baur, "The foundations of telegraphy and telephony in Latin America," *Journal of Communication*, 44, No. 4, Autumn 1994, pp. 9–24.

11. Daniel R. Headrick, *The invisible weapon: Telecommunications and international politics, 1851–1945*. New York: Oxford University Press, 1991, p. 202.

12. "The deals are good but the dial tone isn't," *Business Week*, 6 April 1992, p. 86.

13. "Latin American telecoms: Half-way there," *Economist* (London), 4 February 1995, p. 62.

14. "On your mark, get set—Phone!" *Business Week*, 6 May 1996, p. 54.

15. "Telmex chief plans U.S. move this year," *Financial Times* (London), 13 January 1997, p. 17.

16. Norman Lerner, "The new telecom scene," *Telecommunications*, October 1995, p. 171.

17. For a review of NAFTA telecommunications issues, see: Wilson Dizard and Lesley Turner, *Telecommunications and the U.S.-Canada free trade talks*. Center for Strategic and International Studies, Washington DC, May 1987.

18. C. Fred Bergsten, "Globalizing free trade," *Foreign Affairs*, 75, No. 3, May/June 1996, pp. 105–120.

19. "Business spurs all-American trade deal," *Financial Times* (London), 22 March 1996, p. 5.

20. "Telfonos de Mexico see 4Bn forex loss," *Financial Times* (London), 25 January 1995, p. 5.

21. "Telecommunications and technology in Latin America," *Latin Finance*, September 1995. Special supplement.

22. Gregory Ingram and Christine Kessides, "Infrastructure for development," *Finance and Development*, September 1994, pp. 18–25.

23. "The deals are good," p. 86.

24. "Private networks in Latin America," *Via Satellite*, March 1994, pp. 30–42.

25. "Direct-to-home satellite services in Latin America," *Via Satellite*, March 1986, pp. 14–18.

26. "Telecoms opened up in Brazil," *Financial Times* (London), 15 May 1996, p. 5.

27. "Telecoms consortia on hold for Brazilian bidding," *Financial Times* (London), 28 June 1996, p. 20.

28. "Winners in the east will inherit the earth," *Financial Times* (London), 9 April 1996. Special supplement on Asia-Pacific telecommunications, p. 1.

29. "Message in a miracle," *Economist* (London), 2 October 1993, p. 18.

30. For a useful survey of Asian telecommunications developments, see: Eli M. Noam, Seisuke Komatsuzaki, and Douglas Conn, *Telecommunications in the Pacific Basin: An evolutionary approach*. New York: Oxford University Press, 1994. Also: Shin Cho and Myeongho Lee, "Competition and deregulation in telecommunications markets: An APEC perspective." Korea Information Society Development Institute, Seoul, January 1996.

31. "Europe 'will lose to Asia' as home for investments," *Financial Times* (London), 24 January 1997, p. 4.

32. "Demand on a grand scale," *Financial Times* (London), 9 May 1995. Special supplement on Asia Pacific telecommunications, p. 1.

33. For a discussion of the prospects for an Asian free-trade zone, see: Fred Bergsten, "An Asian push for world-wide free trade," *Economist* (London), 6 January 1996, p. 62.

34. Mark Z. Taylor, "Dominance through technology," *Foreign Affairs*, 74, No. 6, November/December 1995, pp. 144–120. See also: Sylvia Ostry and Farid Harianto, "The changing pattern of Japanese foreign direct investment in the electronics industry in East Asia," *Transnational Corporations*, 4, No. 1, April 1995, pp. 11–44.

35. Lucien Pye, *Communications and political development*, Princeton NJ: Princeton University Press, 1963.

36. Milton Mueller and Zixiang Tan, *China in the information age: Telecommunications and the dilemma of reform*. Center for Strategic and International Studies, Washington DC (Westport CT: Praeger Publishers, 1996).

37. "China's cellular spending spree," *Communications Week International*, 25 November 1996, p. 27.

38. "Subscribers could double by 2000," *Financial Times* (London), 9 April 1996. Special supplement on Asia-Pacific telecommunications, p. 2.

39. "Satellites in China," *Via Satellite*, February 1996, pp. 98–112.

40. "Electronic commerce in the context of China's national information infrastructure." Briefing Paper, International Communications Study Program, Center for Strategic and International Studies, Washington DC, March 1996.

41. Zixiang Tan, "China's information superhighway: What is it and who controls it?" *Telecommunications Policy*, 19, No. 9, December 1995, pp. 721–731.

42. "China Unicom's chairman comes calling," *Wireless Business and Finance*, 12 October 1994, p. 1.

43. "Flow of foreign funds to China jumps 12 per cent," *Financial Times* (London), 6 February 1996, p. 5.

44. For a summary of Chinese telecommunications trade and investment policies, see: Mueller and Tan, *China in the information age*, ch. 7.

45. "Seven chip plants planned in China," *Financial Times* (London), 2 October 1995, p. 5.

46. "Estimated 60,000 mainland Chinese in cyberspace," Reuters Executive news service, 28 March 1996.

47. "Satellites bring information revolution to China," *New York Times*, 11 April 1993, p. 12.

48. For a survey of Chinese information networks, see: Huijie Chen and Hetung Chu, "Seamless networking in China: Progress, problems, and perspectives," *Bulletin of the American Society for Information Science*, June/July 1995, pp. 14–16.

49. "High-tech meets low wattage in India," *Washington Post*, 2 January 1995, p. A-14.

50. For background on Indian telecommunications reforms, see: M. B. Athreya, "India's telecommunications policy: A paradigm shift," *Telecommunications Policy*, 20, No. 1, January/February 1996, pp. 11–22. Also: "Telecommunications policy in India: The political underpinnings of reform," pp. 39–51, in the same issue.

51. "Politics as usual," *Far Eastern Economic Review*, 24 August 1995, p. 44.

52. "Ali Baba and the mobile phones," *Economist* (London), 24 August 1996, p. 29.

53. "Row over basic services mars Indian telecoms licensing," *Financial Times* (London), 14 December 1995, p. 6.

54. "Indian stock market expands VSAT network," *Satellite Communications*, March 1996, p. 16.

55. "Sing Singapore," *Financial Times* (London), 19 August 1993, p. 6.

56. "Expectations for the future are high," *Financial Times* (London), 25 January 1996, p. 48.

57. "Greater urgency injected," *Financial Times* (London), 18 April 1994, p. 4.

58. "Singapore to speed up phone competition," *Financial Times* (London), 13 May 1996, p. 6.

59. "Red tape snags progress," *Financial Times* (London), 9 April 1996. Special supplement on Pacific telecommunications, p. 4.

60. "Cellular: Promises and challenges in Asia-Pacific," *Pacific Telecommunications Review*, March 1996, p. 75.

61. "Mahathir unveils multimedia 'super corridor,'" *Financial Times* (London), 2 August 1996, p. 14.

62. For a survey of emerging Asian software industries, see: "The new kids in town," *Far Eastern Economic Review*, 22 February 1996, pp. 48–52.

63. "Privatization: The magic word on every lip," *Financial Times* (London), 20 May 1996. Special supplement on Egypt, p. 6.

64. "Jordan plans to privatize telecom," *Financial Times* (London), 14 January 1997, p. 5.

65. Wilson P. Dizard and S. Blake Swensrud, *Gorbachev's information revolution: Controlling glasnost in a new electronic era*. Significant Issues Series, Volume 9, No. 8. Center for Strategic and International Studies, Washington DC (Boulder: Westview Press, 1987).

66. "The only man in Russia," *Economist* (London), 15 June 1996, p. 13.

67. "A new rival steps into the game," *Financial Times* (London), 19 September 1996, p. 8.

68. "Russian telecom: Preparing for an investment frenzy," *Russia Online* (Washington DC), October 1995, p. 1.

69. "Getting a line," *Economist* (London), 14 October 1995, p. 79.

70. "Communists blamed as telecom deal collapses," *Financial Times* (London), 27 December 1995, p. 1.

71. "Electronic cash set to speed up banking in Russia," *Financial Times* (London), 13 September 1995, p. 1.

72. For a survey of post-Soviet developments in Eastern Europe, see: Paul J. Welfens, "Telecommunications and transition in Central and Eastern Europe," *Telecommunications Policy*, 19, No. 7, October 1995, pp. 561–577.

73. "Foreign investment in east Europe doubles," *Financial Times* (London), 25 March 1996, p. 3.

74. Ernest J. Wilson III, *The information revolution comes to Africa*. CSIS Africa Notes No. 165. Center for Strategic and International Studies, Washington DC, June 1996.

75. "Global fund managers make tracks for Africa," *Financial Times* (London), 1 February 1996, p. 3.

76. "ITT allegedly spent millions to obtain contracts in Nigeria," *Washington Post*, 17 August 1980, p. 1.

77. "Nigeria misses out on World Bank loan," *Financial Times* (London), 30 March 1995, p. 9.

78. "Sell-off moves start," *Financial Times* (London), 28 March 1996, p. 5.

79. "Coming of age," *Economist* (London), 20 May 1995. Special supplement on South Africa, p. 13.

80. Rex Winsbury, "South Africa pioneers in cellular equity," *Intermedia* (London), January 1995, pp. 38–41.

81. "Reasons to cut off Mr. Mugabe," *Economist* (London), 14 April 1996, p. 64.

82. "AT&T proposes sea cable that would encircle Africa," *New York Times*, 26 April 1994, p. C-3.

Chapter 10

1. For a survey of wrong predications about new technologies, see: Carolyn Marvin, *When old technologies were new*. New York: Oxford University Press, 1988.

2. Jacques Ellul, "The technological order," *Technology and Culture*, 3, Fall 1962, p. 394–405.

3. Gregory Staple, "Bit makers and shifters," Telegeography Inc., Washington DC, 1996.

4. "Ready for the next surprises," *Financial Times* (London), 2 May 1996, p. 2.

5. The opportunities and pitfalls of the new U.S. telecommunications mix are outlined in: Joseph S. Kraemer, *The realities of convergence: A perspective on how to avoid becoming a road kill on the global information highway*. 1994 Thought Leadership Series, EDS Management Consulting Services, Washington DC, 1994.

6. "Will there be enough money to pay for investment?" *Intermedia* (London), March 1996, p. 40.

7. "Five digits for a discount," *Washington Post*, 15 August 1996, p. B-1.

8. "MCI sees the future in 'one-stop' services," *Financial Times* (London), 8 August 1996, p. 15.

9. Eli M. Noam, "Beyond territoriality: Economics and politics in telesociety." CITI Working Paper 690. Columbia Institute for Teleinformation, Columbia University, June 1994, p. 6.

10. Karl Deutsch, *The nerves of government: Models of political communications and control*. New York: Free Press, 1963.

11. David Ronfeldt, *Cyberocracy, cyberspace, and cyberology: Political effects of the information revolution*. Report P-7745. Rand Corporation, Santa Monica CA, 1991, p. 2.

12. Bob Dixon, "Recent developments in network-produced information," in *Cast Calendar*, Center for Advanced Studies in Telecommunications, Ohio State University, June 1991, p. 7.

13. Bertram Gross, *Friendly fascism: The new face of power in America*. Boston MA: South End Press, 1980.

14. Lewis Mumford, *The pentagon of power*. New York: Harcourt Brace, 1970.

15. For a useful summary of the issues involved, see: Walter Baer, *Technology's challenges to the First Amendment*. Report P-7773. Rand Corporation, Santa Monica CA, 1992.

16. "FCC's universal funding hit," *Communications Week*, 20 May 1996, p. 27.

17. Eli Noam, "Principles for the Communications Act of 2034." Paper delivered at the Massachusetts Institute of Technology, October 1991. For other comments on universal service, see: Colin R. Blackman, "Universal service: Obligation or opportunity?" *Telecommunications Policy*, 19, No. 3, April 1995, pp. 171–176.

18. For a historical survey of these attempts, see: Fred H. Cate, "The First Amendment and the international 'free flow' of information," *Virginia Journal of International Law*, 30, No. 2. Winter 1990, pp. 373–420.

19. "Tokyo's magic kingdom outshines its role model," *New York Times*, 7 March 1994, p. D-7.

20. "Back to the land of make-believe," *Economist* (London), 15 June 1996, p. 60.

21. "The country music row finds harmony," *Financial Times* (London), 31 August 1996, p. 4.

22. "Privacy, please," *Economist* (London), 27 July 1996, p. 54.

23. "China is 'most attractive emerging market,'" *Financial Times* (London), 18 September 1996, p. 10.

24. "Emerging economies: Meeting the challenges of the information age," *Intermedia* (London), February 1996, p. 43.

SELECT BIBLIOGRAPHY

Aborn, Murray, *Telescience: Scientific communications in the information age*. Philadelphia: American Academy of Political and Social Science, 1988.

Abramson, Jeffrey B., F. Christopher Atherton, and Gary R. Orren. *The electronic commonwealth: The impact of new media technologies on democratic politics*. New York: Basic Books, 1988.

Alex Brown and Sons. *Planet Web: Browsing for investment dollars in the Internet and online world*. Baltimore MD: Alex Brown and Sons, September 1995.

Anderson, Robert H., Tora K. Bikson, Sally Ann Law, and Bridger M. Mitchell. *Universal access to e-mail: Feasibility and societal implications*. Santa Monica CA: Center for Information Revolution Analysis, Rand Corporation, 1995.

Aronson, Jonathan D., and Peter F. Cowhey. *When countries talk: International trade in telecommunications services*. Cambridge MA: Ballinger Publishing, 1988.

Aspen Institute Program on Communications and Society, *Universal telephone service: Ready for the 21st century?* Washington DC, The Aspen Institute, 1991.

_____. *The information evolution: How new information technologies are spurring complex patterns of change* (1992).

_____. *The knowledge economy: The nature of information in the 21st century* (1994).

_____. *Crossroads on the information highway: Convergence and diversity in communications technology* (1995).

_____. *The future of community and personal identity in the coming electronic culture* (1995).

_____. *The communications devolution: Federal, state, and local relations in telecommunications competition and regulation* (1996).

Bar, Francois. *Configuring the telecommunications infrastructure for the computer age*. Working Paper No. 43. Berkeley Roundtable on the International Economy, Berkeley CA, 1990.

Bell, Daniel. *The coming of post-industrial society*. New York: Basic Books, 1973.

Benedikt, Michael. *Cyberspace: First steps*. Cambridge MA: MIT Press, 1991.

Beniger, James. *The control revolution.* Cambridge MA: Harvard University Press, 1986.

Birkerts, Sven. *The Gutenberg elegies: The fate of reading in the electronic age.* Boston: Faber and Faber, 1994.

Bracken, James K., and Christopher Sterling. *Telecommunications research resources: An annotated guide.* Mahwah NJ: Lawrence Erlbaum Associates, 1995.

Brand, Stewart. *The media lab: Inventing the future at MIT.* New York: Penguin Books, 1988.

Branscomb, Anne W. *Towards a law of global telecommunications networks.* Science and Technology Section, American Bar Association. New York: Longman Publishers, 1986

_____. *Who owns information?* New York: Basic Books, 1994.

Brock, Gerald. *Telecommunications policy for the information age.* Cambridge MA: Harvard University Press, 1994.

Burstein, Daniel, and David Kline. *Road warriors: Dreams and nightmares along the information highway.* New York: Dutton, 1995.

Cable, Vincent, and Catherine Distler. *Global superhighways: The future of international telecommunications policy.* London: Royal Institute of International Affairs, 1995.

Cafruny, Alan W., and Glenda G. Rosenthal, eds. *The state of the European Community: The Maastricht debates and beyond.* Boulder: Lynn Rienner Publishers, 1993.

Canoy, Martin, ed. *The new global economy in the information age.* University Park: Pennsylvania State University Press, 1993.

Cantelon, Philip L. *The history of MCI, 1968–1988.* Dallas TX: Heritage Press, 1993.

Carpentier, Michel, Sylviane Farnoux-Toporkoff, and Garric Christian. *Telecommunications in transition.* New York: John Wiley and Sons, 1992.

Choate, Pat. *Agents of influence: How Japan's lobbyists in the United States manipulate America's political and economic system.* New York: Alfred A. Knopf, 1990.

Clarke, Neville, and Edwin Riddell. *The sky barons: The men who control the global media.* London: Methuen, 1992.

Codding, George A., and Anthony M. Rutkowski. *The International Telecommunications Union in a changing world.* Dedham MA: Artech House, 1982.

Cohen, Stephen S., and John Zysman. *Manufacturing matters: The myth of the post-industrial society.* New York: Basic Books, 1987.

Cole, Barry, ed. *After the breakup: Assessing the new post-AT&T divestiture era.* New York: Columbia University Press, 1991.

Communications Industry Forecast (New York). Veronis, Suhler, and Associates. August 1995.

Crandall, Robert W. *After the breakup: U.S. telecommunications in a more competitive era.* Washington DC: The Brookings Institution, 1991.

Crawford, Morris H. *The common market for telecommunications and information services.* Publication No. P-60-6. Program on Information Resources Policy, Harvard University. July 1990.

Cringley, Robert X. *Accidental empires: How the boys of Silicon Valley make their millions, battle foreign competition, and still can't get a date.* New York: Addison-Wesley, 1992.

Crowley, David, and Paul Heyer. *Communications in history: Technology, culture, and society.* New York: Longman Publishers, 1995.

Demac, Donna, ed. *Tracing new orbits: Cooperation and competition in satellite development.* New York: Columbia University Press, 1988.

Deutsch, Karl. *The nerves of government: Models of political communications and control.* New York: Free Press, 1963.

Dizard, Wilson P. *The coming information age.* 3d ed. New York: Longman Publishers, 1989.

_____. *Old media, new media.* 2d ed. New York: Longman Publishers, 1997.

Dizard, Wilson P., and Blake Swensrud. *Gorbachev's information revolution: Controlling glasnost in a new electronic era.* Significant Issues Series. Volume 9, No. 8. Center for Strategic and International Studies, Washington DC (Boulder: Westview Press, 1987).

Donlan, Thomas G. *Supertech.* Homewood IL: Business One Irwin, 1991.

Dordick, Herbert. *The information society: A retrospective view.* Thousand Oaks CA: Sage Publications, 1993.

Dordick, Herbert S., Helen G. Bradley, and Burt Nanus. *The emerging network marketplace.* Norwood NJ: Ablex Publishing, 1981.

Drake, William J. *The new information infrastructure: Strategies for U.S. policy.* New York: Twentieth Century Fund, 1995.

Dutton, William, Jay Blumler, and Kenneth Kraemer. *Wired cities: Shaping the future of communications.* Boston: G. K. Hall, 1987.

Economist (London). Special reports on telecommunications and information technology, including: "The third age: A survey of the computer industry" (17 September 1994); "The accidental highway: A survey of the Internet" (1 July 1995); "The death of distance" (30 September 1995); and "A world gone soft: A survey of the software industry" (29 May 1996).

Economist Intelligence Unit (London). Research Report. "Global Telecommunications to the year 2000: The impact on corporate studies" (1996).

Edwards, Paul N. *The closed world: Computers and the politics of discontent in cold war America.* Cambridge MA: MIT Press, 1996.

Egan, Bruce L. *Information superhighways: The economics of advanced public communications networks.* Norwood MA: Artech House, 1991.

Eisenstein, Elizabeth. *The printing press as an agent of change.* Two volumes. New York: Cambridge University Press, 1979.

Ellul, Jacques. *The technological bluff.* Grand Rapids MI: William B. Erdmans Publishing, 1990.

Elton, Martin C.J. *Integrated broadband networks: The public policy issues.* Amsterdam: Elsevier Science Publishers, 1991.

Encyclopedia of U.S. Foreign Policy. New York: Oxford University Press, 1997.

Entman, Robert M., and Charles M. Firestone. *Strategic alliances and telecommunications policy.* Program in Communications and Society. The Aspen Institute, Washington DC, 1995.

European Union. *Europe and the global information society: Recommendations to the European Council.* Brussels: European Union, May 1994.

Feigenbaum, Edward A., and Pamela McCorduck. *The fifth generation: Artificial intelligence and Japan's computer challenge to the world.* Reading MA: Addison-Wesley, 1983.

Firestone, Charles M., and Jorge Reina Schement, eds. *Towards an information bill of rights and responsibilities.* Program in Communications and Society. The Aspen Institute, Washington DC, 1995.

Fischer, Claude S. *America calling: A social history of the telephone to 1940.* Berkeley: University of California Press, 1992.

Flamm, Kenneth. *Creating the computer: Government, industry, and high technology.* Washington DC: The Brookings Institution, 1988.

Fortner, Robert S. *International communications.* Belmont CA: Wadsworth Publishers, 1993.

Fransman, Martin. *Japan's computer and communications industry: The evolution of industrial giants and global competitiveness.* New York: Oxford University Press, 1996.

Frederick, Howard. *Global communications and international relations.* Belmont CA: Wadsworth Publishers, 1993.

Frielander, Amy. *Natural monopoly and universal service: Telephones and telegraphs in the U.S. communications infrastructure, 1837–1940.* Reston VA: Corporation for National Research Initiatives, 1995.

Galloway, James F. *The politics and technology of satellite communications.* Lexington MA: Lexington Books, 1972.

Ganley, Gladys. *Unglued empire: The Soviet experience with communications technologies.* Norwood NJ: Ablex Publishers, 1996.

Gates, Bill. *The road ahead.* New York: Viking, 1995.

Gebase, Len, and Steve Trus. *Analyzing electronic commerce.* Special Publication No. 500-218. National Institute of Standards and Technology. Washington DC: U.S. Government Printing Office, 1994.

Gilder, George. *The quantum revolution in economics and technology.* New York: Simon and Schuster, 1989.

Granger, John V. *Technology and international relations.* San Francisco: W. H. Freeman, 1979.

Greenberger, Martin, ed. *Computers, communications, and the public interest.* Baltimore MD: Johns Hopkins University Press, 1976.

Gross, Bertram. *Friendly fascism: The new face of power in America.* Boston MA: South End Press, 1980.

Grossman, Lawrence K. *The electronic republic: Reshaping democracy in the information age.* New York: Viking, 1995.

Hamelink, Cees. *The politics of world communications.* Thousand Oaks CA: Sage Publications, 1994.

Hammer, Donald P. *The information age: Its development and impact.* Metuchen NJ: Scarecrow Press, 1976.

Handy, Charles. *Beyond certainty: The changing world of organizations.* Boston MA: Harvard Business School Press, 1995.

Hanson, Jarice. *Connections: Technologies of communication.* New York: Longman Publishers, 1995.

Harasim, Lindo, ed. *Global networks, computers, and international communications.* Cambridge MA: MIT Press, 1993.

Headrick, Daniel R. *The invisible weapon: Telecommunications and international politics, 1851–1945.* New York: Oxford University Press, 1991.

Hornik, Robert C. *Development communication: Information, agriculture, and nutrition in the Third World.* New York: Longman, 1988.

Howard, Thomas. *Global expansion in the information age.* New York: Van Nostrand Rheinhold, 1996.

Hudson, Heather E. *When telephones reach the village: The role of telecommunications in rural development.* Norwood NJ: Ablex Publishing, 1984.

Innis, Harold A. *Empire and communications.* Toronto: University of Toronto Press, 1972.

International Encyclopedia of Communications. Four volumes. New York: Oxford University Press, 1989.

International Telecommunications Union. *The missing link.* Report of the Independent Commission for Worldwide Telecommunications Development. Geneva: December 1984.

Johnson, Craig. *The International Cable-Telco tango.* International Communications Studies Program, Center for Strategic and International Studies. Washington DC, March 1991.

Johnson, Leland, and Deborah Castleman. *Direct broadcast satellites: A competitive alternative to cable television.* Report R-4047-MF/RL. Rand Corporation, Santa Monica CA, 1991.

Jones, Glenn R. *Jones cable television and information infrastructure dictionary.* 4th ed. Englewood CO: Jones Interactive, 1994.

Jones, Steven, ed. *Cybersociety: Computer-mediated communication and community.* Thousand Oaks CA: Sage Publications, 1995.

Journal of Communications. Special issue on the Internet. Vol. 46, No. 1 (Winter 1996).

Juffer, Kristin. *Japan and the United States: Revving up for the information superhighway.* International Communications Studies Program, Center for Strategic and International Studies. Washington DC, 1994.

Jussawalla, Meheroo, ed. *Telecommunications: A bridge to the 21st century.* New York: Elsevier Science, 1995.

Kahin, Brian, and Janet Abbate, eds. *Standards policy for information infrastructure.* Center for Science and International Affairs, John F. Kennedy School of Government, Harvard University, Cambridge MA, 1996.

Kahin, Brian, and Ernest Wilson III, eds. *National information infrastructure initiatives: Vision and policy design.* Cambridge MA: MIT Press, 1997.

Koelsch, Frank. *The information revolution.* New York: McGraw-Hill, 1995.

Leebaert, Derek, ed. *Technology 2001: The future of computers and communications.* Cambridge MA: MIT Press, 1991.

Lerner, Daniel. *The passing of traditional society.* Glencoe IL: Free Press, 1958.

Libicki, Martin C. *The mesh and the Net: Speculations on armed conflict in a time of free silicon.* Washington DC: National Defense University Press, 1995.

_____. *What is information warfare?* Washington DC: National Defense University Press, 1995.

Luttwak, Edward N. *The endangered dream: How to stop the United States from becoming a Third World country and how to win the geo-economic struggle for industrial supremacy.* New York: Simon and Schuster, 1993.

Machlup, Fritz. *The production and distribution of knowledge in the United States.* Princeton NJ: Princeton University Press, 1962.

MacDonald, Greg. *The emergence of global multi-media conglomerates.* Working Paper No. 70. Multinational Enterprises Program. International Labor Organization, Geneva, Switzerland, 1990.

Malone, Gifford D., ed. *American diplomacy in the information age.* Lanham MD: University Press of America, 1991.

Marvin, Carolyn. *When old technologies were new.* New York: Oxford University Press, 1988.

Marx, Leo. *The machine in the garden.* New York: Oxford University Press, 1964.

McKnight, Lee. *Internet economics.* Cambridge MA: MIT Press, 1996.

McLuhan, Marshall. *The Gutenberg galaxy.* Toronto: University of Toronto Press, 1962.

McLuhan, Marshall, and Bruce R. Powers. *The global village: Transformations in world life and media in the 21st century.* New York: Oxford University Press, 1989.

Miller, Donald L., ed. *The Lewis Mumford reader.* Athens: University of Georgia Press, 1996.

Mody, Bella, Johannes Bauer, and Joseph Straubhaar, eds. *Telecommunications politics: Ownership and control of the information highway in developing countries.* Mahwah NJ: Lawrence Erlbaum Associates, 1995.

Mosco, Vincent. *The pay-per-view society: Computers and communications in the information age.* Norwood NJ: Ablex Publishers, 1989.

Mosco, Vince, and Janet Wasco, eds. *The political economy of information.* Madison: University of Wisconsin Press, 1988.

Moskin, J. Robert. *Toward the year 2000: New forces in publishing.* Gutersloh, Germany: Bertlesmann Foundation Publishers, 1989.

Mowlana, Hamid. *Global communications in transition.* Thousand Oaks CA: Sage Publications, 1996.

Moynihan, Michael. *The coming American renaissance.* New York: Simon and Schuster, 1996.

Mueller, Milton, and Zixiang Tan. *China in the information age: Telecommunications and the dilemma of reform.* Center for Strategic and International Studies, Washington DC (Westport CT: Praeger Publishers, 1996).

National Defense University. *Strategic assessment 1996: Instruments of U.S. power.* Institute for National Strategic Studies, Washington DC, 1996.

National Research Council. *Keeping the U.S. computer and communications industry competitive.* Washington DC: Computer Science and Telecommunications Board, 1995.

_____. *The unpredictable certainty: Information infrastructure through 2000* (1995).

_____. *Realizing the information future: The Internet and beyond* (1995).

Negroponte, Nicholas. *Being digital.* New York: Alfred A. Knopf, 1995.

Neuman, W. Russell. *The future of the mass audience.* New York: Cambridge University Press, 1992.

Neuman, W. Russell, Richard Jay Solomon, and Lee McKnight. *The Gordian knot: Political gridlock on the information highway.* Cambridge MA: MIT Press, 1996.

Noam, Eli. *Telecommunications in Europe.* New York: Oxford University Press, 1992.

Noam, Eli, Seisuke Komatsuzaki, and Douglas Conn. *Telecommunications in the Pacific Basin: An evolutionary approach.* New York: Oxford University Press, 1994.

Noam, Eli, and Gerard Pogorel, eds. *Asymmetric deregulation: The dynamics of telecommunications policy in Europe and the United States.* Norwood NJ: Ablex Publishing, 1994.

Nora, Simon, and Alain Minc. *The computerization of society.* Cambridge MA: MIT Press, 1981.

Organization for Economic Cooperation and Development. *Communications outlook 1995.* Paris: OECD, February 1995.

Pelton, Joseph N. *Global communications satellite policy: Intelsat, politics, and functionalism.* Mt. Airy MD: Lomond Books, 1974.

Penzias, Arno. *Ideas and information: Managing in a high-tech world.* New York: W. W. Norton, 1989.

Perelman, Lewis. *School's out.* New York: William Morrow, 1992.

Petrazzini, Ben A. *The political economy of telecommunications reform in developing countries.* Westport CT: Greenwood Publishing Group, 1995.

Peyton, David. *The national information infrastructure—Overcoming the obstacles.* Washington DC: Information Technology Association of America, September 1994.

Pool, Ithiel de Sola, ed. *The social impact of the telephone.* Cambridge MA: MIT Press, 1977.

_____. *Technologies of freedom.* Cambridge MA: Harvard University Press, 1983.

_____. *Technologies without boundaries: Telecommunications in a global age.* Cambridge: Harvard University Press, 1990.

Postman, Neil. *Technology: The surrender of culture to technology.* New York: Alfred A. Knopf, 1992.

_____. *Amusing ourselves to death.* New York: Penguin Books, 1986.

Pye, Lucian. *Communications and political development.* Princeton NJ: Princeton University Press, 1963.

Reeves, Byron, and Clifford Nass. *The media equation: How people treat computers, televisions, and new media as real people and places.* New York: Cambridge University Press, 1996.

Reid, T. R. *The chip: How two Americans invented the microchip and launched a revolution.* New York: Simon and Schuster, 1984.

Rheingold, Howard. *Virtual reality.* New York: Simon and Schuster, 1991.

Robinson, Kenneth G. *Building a global information society.* Communications and Society Program. The Aspen Institute, Washington DC, 1996.

Runin, Michael R., and Mary T. Huber. *The knowledge industry in the United States, 1960–1988.* Princeton NJ: Princeton University Press, 1986.

Schwartau, Winn. *Information warfare: Chaos on the electronic highway.* San Francisco: PUGT Publishers, 1996.

Scientific American. Special issue. "Computers, Communications, and Networks." September 1991.

Sirois, Charles, and Claude Forget. *The medium and the muse: Culture, communications, and the information highway.* Montreal: Institute for Research on Public Policy, 1995.

Smith, Anthony. *The geopolitics of information: How Western culture dominates the world.* London: Faber and Faber, 1980.

_____. *The age of behemoths: The globalization of mass media firms.* Report for the Twentieth Century Fund. New York: Priority Press, 1991.

Smith, Delbert D. *International telecommunications control.* Leyden, Netherlands: A. W. Sijthoff, 1969.

Smith, Paul A. Jr. *On political war.* Washington DC: National Defense University Press, 1989.

Staple, Gregory, ed. *Telegeography: Global telecommunications traffic statistics and commentary.* Annual publication of the International Institute of Communications, London.

_____. *The TeleGeography 100.* Washington DC: TeleGeography, 1996.

Stevenson, Robert L. *Communication, development, and the Third World: The global politics of information.* New York: Longman Publishers, 1988.

Stoll, Clifford. *Silicon snake oil: Second thoughts on the information highway.* New York: Doubleday, 1995.

Stonier, Tom. *The wealth of information: A profile of the post-industrial society.* London: Thomas Methuen, 1983.

Tedeschi, Anthony M. *Live via satellite: The story of Comsat and the technology that changed world communications.* Washington DC: Acropolis Books, 1988.

Telecommunications Policy. Special issue. "Lessons from the Internet." Vol. 20, No. 3 (April 1996).

Tenner, Edward. *Why things bite back: Technology and the revenge effect.* New York: Alfred A. Knopf, 1996.

Turkle, Sherry. *Life on the screen: Identity in the age of the Internet.* New York: Simon and Schuster, 1995.

Tyson, Laura D'Andrea. *Who's bashing whom? Trade conflict in high-technology industries.* Washington DC: Institute for International Economics, 1992.

U.S. Congress. *Option papers.* Prepared by the staff of the House Subcommittee on Communications, Committee on Interstate and Foreign Commerce. 95th Congress, 1st Sess. Committee Print 95-13, May 1977.

U. S. Congress, Office of Technology Assessment. *Critical connections: Communications for the future.* Publication No. OTA-CIT-407, January 1990.

_____. *The big picture: HDTV and high-resolution systems.* Publication No. OTA-BP-CIT-64, June 1990.

_____. *Wireless technologies and the national information infrastructure.* Washington DC: U.S. Government Printing Office, July 1995.

_____. *Global communications: Opportunities for trade and aid.* Publication No. OTA-ITC-642, September 1995.

U.S. General Accounting Office. *Information superhighway: Issues affecting development.* Report No. GAO/RCED-94-285. Washington DC, October 1994.

U.S. Department of Commerce, National Institute of Standards and Technology. *Networking, telecommunications, and information technology: The requirements of U.S. industry.* Advanced Technology Program. August 1994.

U.S. Department of Commerce, National Telecommunications and Information Administration. *Telecommunications in the Age of Information.* NTIA Special Publication No. 91-26, October 1991.

_____. *NTIA Telecom 2000: Charting the course for the new century.* NTIA Special Publication No. 88-21, October 1988.

U.S. Department of Commerce, Office of Telecommunications. *The information economy.* Nine volumes. Publication No. 77-12, 1977.

Wallace, James, and Jim Erickson. *Hard drive: Bill Gates and the making of the Microsoft empire.* New York: John Wiley and Sons, 1992.

Waverman, Leonard. *Global speak.* Washington DC: American Enterprise Institute, 1996.

Wellenius, Bjorn, Peter A. Stern, Timothy E. McNulty, and Richard D. Stern. *Restructuring and managing the telecommunications sector.* Washington DC: World Bank, 1989.

Wiener, Norbert. *The human use of human beings: Cybernetics and society.* Boston: Houghton Mifflin, 1950.

Wilhelm, Donald. *Global communications and political power.* New Brunswick NJ: Transaction Press, 1990.

Williams, Frederick. *Measuring the information society.* Newbury Park CA: Sage Publications, 1988.

Winograd, Morley, and Dudley Duffa. *Taking control: Politics in the information age.* New York: Henry Holt, 1996.

Wriston, Walter B. *The twilight of sovereignty: How the information revolution is transforming our world.* New York: Scribner, 1992.

Yoneji, Masoda. *The information society as post-industrial society.* Bethesda MD: World Future Society, 1969.

Zacher, Mark W. *Governing global networks: International regimes for transportation and communication.* New York: Cambridge University Press, 1996.

Zuboff, Shoshona. *In the age of the smart machine: The future of work and power.* New York: Basic Books, 1988.

ABOUT THE BOOK AND AUTHOR

São Paulo, Brazil's largest city, has more mobile phones than does Paris. The largest phone system in Cambodia is cellular. In the next twenty years, within one generation, everyone on earth will be able to place a phone call to anyone else anywhere. This Meganet is a patchwork of networks, big and small, local and global, primitive and high-tech, that fit together because they share compatible technologies.

Most of Meganet is hidden in underground cables or in microwave circuits that send signals through the atmosphere at the speed of light. Meganet involves linemen stringing wire through South American jungles and Motorola executives investing $4 billion to link millions of mobile phones.

Why is Meganet emerging now? Two of our largest industries, electronics and communications, are changing quickly, often in an escalating tango of investment, technological breakthroughs, and distribution. The barriers to an advanced, digitized Meganet are economic and political. More than fifty governments are dismantling their communications monopolies by converting them wholly or partly into private enterprises. This new, competitive, and private sector–oriented milieu has become the most important factor favoring the completion of the advanced global Meganet early in the twenty-first century.

Wilson Dizard Jr.'s *Meganet* is a report on the progress and setbacks in expanding Meganet resources to everyone on earth. He examines not only the advantages, such as Internet linkups and global toll-free numbers, but also such downsides as electronic threats to privacy and the question of who will control Meganet. Dizard describes the major players: from AT&T and MCI to emerging innovators in Europe, Asia, and Latin America.

Wilson Dizard Jr. is senior associate at the Center for Strategic and International Studies in Washington, D.C. He is a telecommunications authority with thirty years' experience in international and U.S. communications. He has taught at MIT and Georgetown and is the author of six books, including *The Coming Information Age* and *Old Media, New Media*. His work has been translated into French, Spanish, Russian, Japanese, Portuguese, Thai, and Korean.

INDEX

254